# CHILDREN'S ENCYCLOPEDIA OF
# Earth

CHILDREN'S ENCYCLOPEDIA OF

# Earth

MICHAEL ALLABY

templar publishing

A TEMPLAR BOOK

First published in the UK in 2009 by Templar Publishing,

An imprint of The Templar Company Limited,

The Granary, North Street,

Dorking, Surrey, RH4 1DN

www.templarco.co.uk

Conceived and produced by Weldon Owen Pty Ltd

59-61 Victoria Street, McMahons Point

Sydney, NSW 2060, Australia

**Group Chief Executive Officer** John Owen

**President and Chief Executive Officer** Terry Newell

**Publisher** Sheena Coupe

**Creative Director** Sue Burk

**Vice President, International Sales** Stuart Laurence

**Vice President, Sales and New Business Development** Amy Kaneko

**Vice President, Sales, Asia and Latin America** Dawn Low

**Administrator, International Sales** Kristine Ravn

**Publishing Coordinator** Mike Crowton

**Project Editor** Jessica Cox

**Copyeditor** Barbara Shepherd

**Designers** DiZign Pty Ltd, Juliana Titin

**Additional text** Brian Choo, Dr. Robert Coenraards, Robert Coupe

**Index** Puddingburn Publishing Services

ISBN: 978-1-84011-629-8

Color reproduction by Chroma Graphics (Overseas) Pte Ltd

Printed in China by SNP Leefung Printers Ltd

A WELDON OWEN PRODUCTION

Previous page: Molten lava meets the sea with clouds of steam
on the island of Kilauea, Hawaii, USA.

Right: From a helicoper, the cliffs of one of the 115 islands of
the Seychelles can be seen rising from turquoise-blue waters.

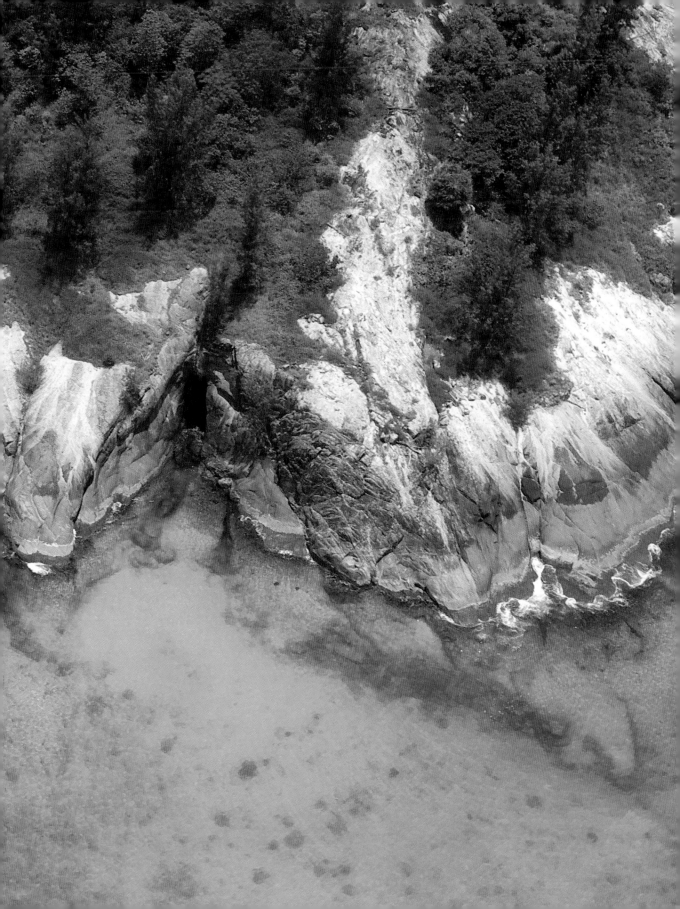

# Contents

# How to use this book

This book is divided into eight chapters. The first chapter locates Earth in the Solar System and the Universe. The second chapter guides us through the history of life on Earth. The third and fourth chapters delve deep beneath Earth's surface to discover what it is made of and witness it in action. The fifth chapter explores the oceans; the sixth travels over the land. The seventh chapter looks above at the weather. The final chapter reviews Earth's resources and energy sources. An extensive fact file and glossary can be found at the end of the book.

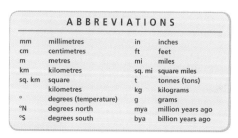

| ABBREVIATIONS | | | |
|---|---|---|---|
| mm | millimetres | in | inches |
| cm | centimetres | ft | feet |
| m | metres | mi | miles |
| km | kilometres | sq. mi | square miles |
| sq. km | square kilometres | t | tonnes (tons) |
| | | kg | kilograms |
| ° | degrees (temperature) | g | grams |
| °N | degrees north | mya | million years ago |
| °S | degrees south | bya | billion years ago |

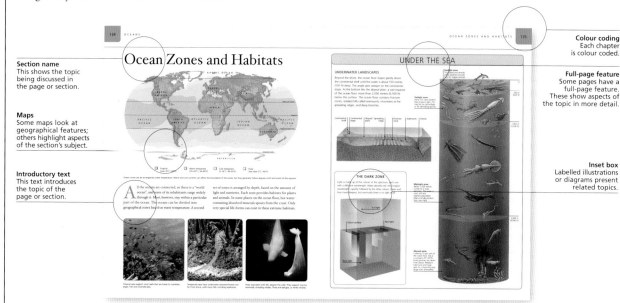

**Section name**
This shows the topic being discussed in the page or section.

**Maps**
Some maps look at geographical features; others highlight aspects of the section's subject.

**Introductory text**
This text introduces the topic of the page or section.

**Colour coding**
Each chapter is colour coded.

**Full-page feature**
Some pages have a full-page feature. These show aspects of the topic in more detail.

**Inset box**
Labelled illustrations or diagrams present related topics.

---

**PACIFIC FACTS**

| | |
|---|---|
| Area | 169.4 million square kilometres (65.4 mil. sq. mi) |
| Average depth | 4,001 metres (13,127 ft) |
| Maximum depth | 10,920 metres (35,826 ft) |

The Pacific Ocean is about 15 times the size of the U.S. It contains about 25,000 islands, most of which are south of the equator.

**WORLD RECORDS**

**WORLD'S SMALLEST COUNTRY**
Vatican City, 0.44 square kilometre (0.17 sq. mi)

**WORLD'S TALLEST STALAGMITE**
Krásnohorská Cave, Slovakia, 32 metres (105 ft)

**FAST FACT**
You cannot travel to Earth's centre The pressure would squeeze you and the heat would cook you before you reached the mantle. The deepest you can go is 2,080 metres (6,824 ft) into Voronya Cave, Georgia.

## GEOLOGICAL TIMELINE ▼

A number of spreads in the Earth's History chapter are accompanied by a geological timeline. This is divided into two parts—larger eras and smaller periods. In each spread, one period of time is highlighted.

## FACT BOXES ▲

Three kinds of fact boxes appear in this book: Ocean Facts in the Oceans chapter; World Records in the Land chapter; and Fast Facts throughout.

| PALEOZOIC: AGE OF ANCIENT LIFE | | | | |
|---|---|---|---|---|
| CAMBRIAN | ORDOVICIAN | SILURIAN | DEVONIAN | CARBONIFEROUS |
| 542 mya | 488 | 444    416 | 359 | 299 |

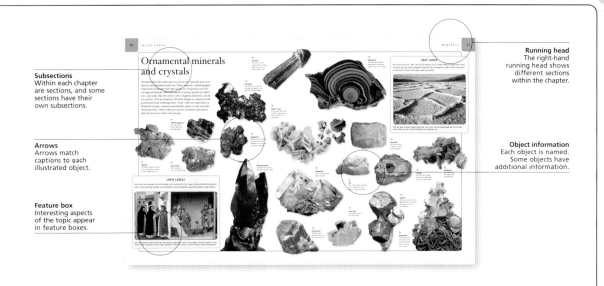

**Subsections**
Within each chapter are sections, and some sections have their own subsections.

**Arrows**
Arrows match captions to each illustrated object.

**Feature box**
Interesting aspects of the topic appear in feature boxes.

**Running head**
The right-hand running head shows different sections within the chapter.

**Object information**
Each object is named. Some objects have additional information.

**Distribution map**
This is explained in detail at the bottom of this page.

**Photo and caption**
Captioned photos show scenes or images relating to the theme of the page.

**Habitat watch**
This is explained in detail at the bottom of this page.

**Main image**
This illustrates the theme of the page and is accompanied by a caption.

**Labelled diagram**
Detailed, labelled diagrams supply more information.

## DISTRIBUTION MAP ▶

Each ecosystem discussed in the Land chapter is located on a world map. The featured ecosystem is coloured yellow. If a second ecosystem is shown, it is coloured blue. Green indicates where the ecosystems overlap.

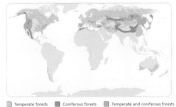

☐ Temperate forests  ☐ Coniferous forests  ☐ Temperate and coniferous forests

## HABITAT WATCH ▶

Most habitats and ecosystems on Earth are fragile—they are sensitive to changes, which may be caused by humans. Habitat Watch boxes highlight habitats, or animals within them, that are particularly vulnerable.

### HABITAT WATCH

Crown-of-thorns starfish, seen here feeding on coral polyps, attack reefs throughout the world. They have caused considerable damage to Australia's Great Barrier Reef. Reefs also suffer from bleaching, caused by the loss of their algae due to pollution.

| | MESOZOIC: AGE OF REPTILES | | | CENOZOIC: AGE OF MAMMALS | |
|---|---|---|---|---|---|
| RMIAN | TRIASSIC | JURASSIC | CRETACEOUS | PALEOGENE | NEOGENE |
| 251 | 200 | 146 | | 65.5 | 23 | 0 |

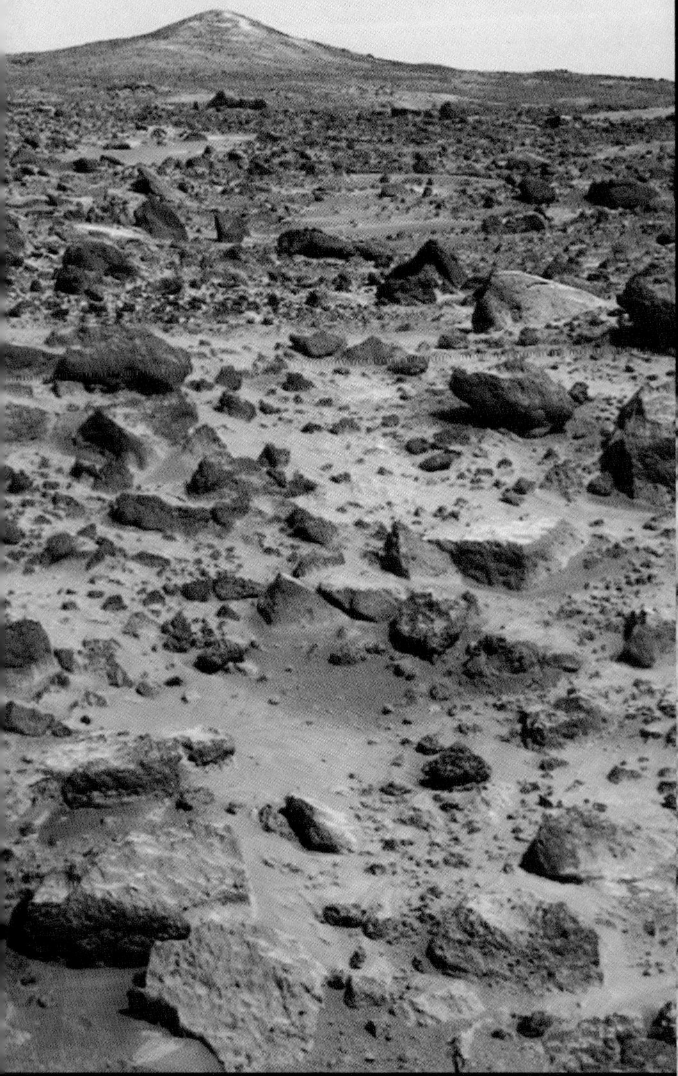

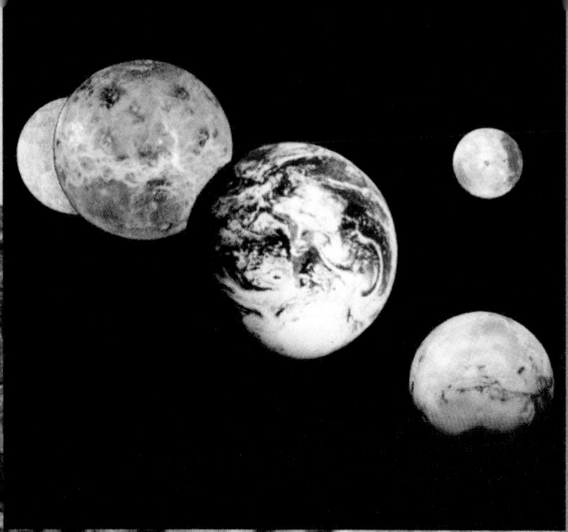

# Our Place in Space

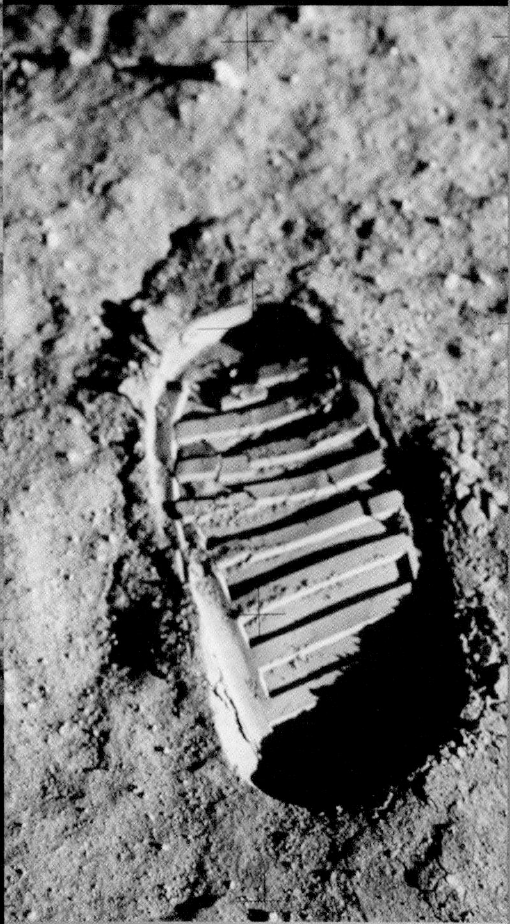

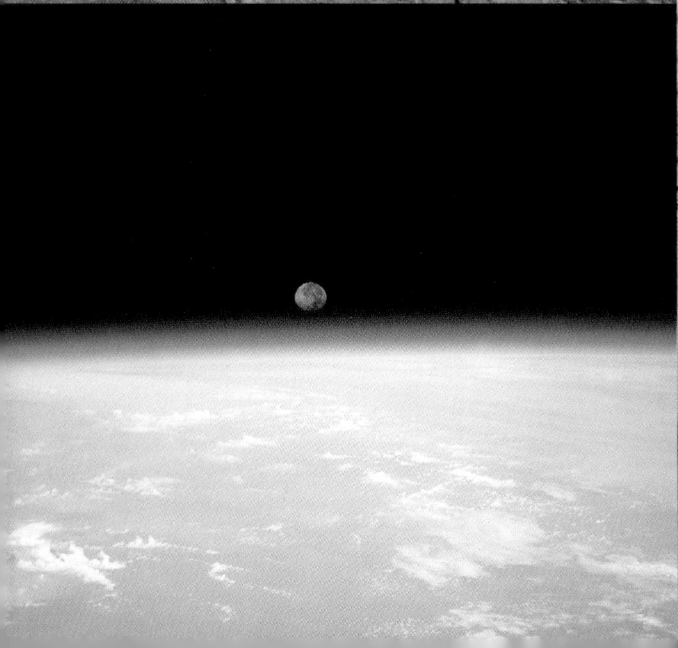

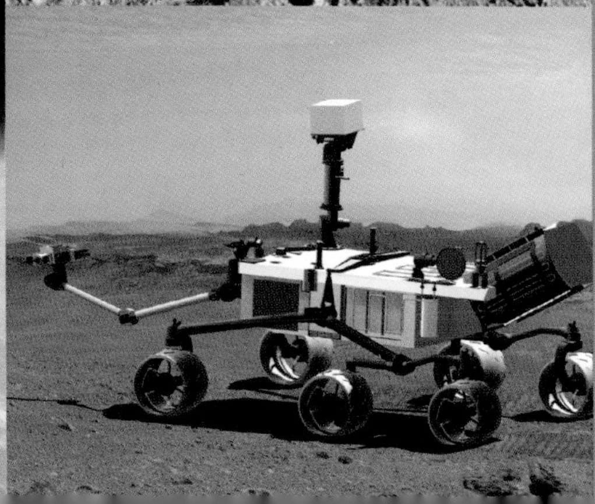

# The Universe

Earth and the other planets, the Sun and the other stars, galaxies, the space around them and the energy that comes from them are all part of what we call the Universe. About 14 billion years ago, all matter and energy, even space itself, was packed into a single point. Then there was a tremendous explosion—the Big Bang—and the basic materials of the Universe, the gases hydrogen and helium, came to be. These gases collected into large bodies called galaxies. As stars within the galaxies exploded, other elements formed, including carbon, the building block of life on Earth.

Earth and the Solar System formed from a cloud of gas and dust 4.6 million years ago. The Orion Nebula may one day collapse to form a solar system much like ours.

## LIFE IN THE UNIVERSE

We have learned a lot about the Universe with the help of satellites and space probes. Since the 1960s they have travelled through the Solar System to explore where no human has ever been. So far, no probe has found evidence of life beyond Earth.

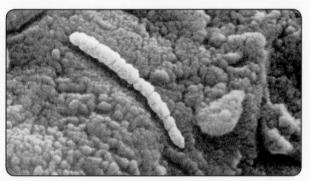

When a meteorite from Mars was viewed under a microscope in 1996, this tube-like structure was found. Some think this may be a tiny Martian fossil.

**HOW WOULD LIFE LOOK?**
The earliest living things on Earth were simple cells. Perhaps other life in the Universe is as simple as this single-celled creature?

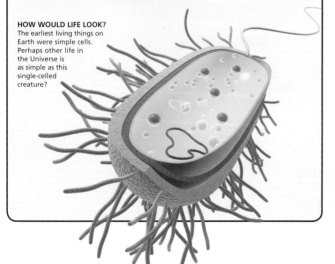

**1 EARTH**
Our home is a small, watery, blue planet that orbits about eight light-minutes from the warmth and light of an ordinary yellow star, the Sun. So far, Earth is the only place in the Universe where we know life exists.

## OUR PLACE IN SPACE

Earth is just one of eight major planets in the Solar System. Our Solar System is part of the Milky Way galaxy, just one galaxy in a cluster of galaxies called the Local Group. These clusters of galaxies gather into superclusters of billions of galaxies.

**THE BLUE MARBLE**
Astronauts who visited the Moon saw the distant Earth as a blue marble floating in the blackness of space, above the grey, lifeless landscape of the Moon.

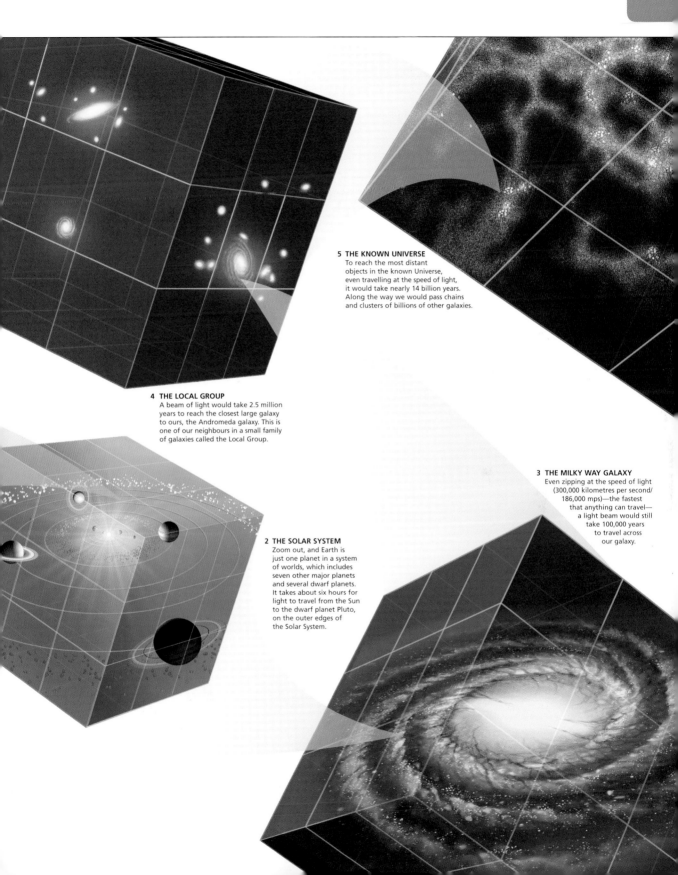

**5 THE KNOWN UNIVERSE**
To reach the most distant
objects in the known Universe,
even travelling at the speed of light,
it would take nearly 14 billion years.
Along the way we would pass chains
and clusters of billions of other galaxies.

**4 THE LOCAL GROUP**
A beam of light would take 2.5 million
years to reach the closest large galaxy
to ours, the Andromeda galaxy. This is
one of our neighbours in a small family
of galaxies called the Local Group.

**3 THE MILKY WAY GALAXY**
Even zipping at the speed of light
(300,000 kilometres per second/
186,000 mps)—the fastest
that anything can travel—
a light beam would still
take 100,000 years
to travel across
our galaxy.

**2 THE SOLAR SYSTEM**
Zoom out, and Earth is
just one planet in a system
of worlds, which includes
seven other major planets
and several dwarf planets.
It takes about six hours for
light to travel from the Sun
to the dwarf planet Pluto,
on the outer edges of
the Solar System.

# The Solar System

The major planets travel around the Sun in ring-like paths called orbits. The inner planets do not take very long to orbit the Sun, but it takes the outer planets many years.

Earth belongs to a cosmic family called the Solar System. The Sun controls this collection of eight major planets, dozens of moons and countless asteroids and comets. The major planets fall into two groups. The inner, rocky planets are Mercury, Venus, Earth and Mars. The outer gas giants are Jupiter, Saturn, Uranus and Neptune. Tiny Pluto was called a planet when it was discovered in 1930, but in 2006 it was reclassified as a dwarf planet. It is just one member of the Kuiper Belt, a vast collection of small, icy worlds at the edge of the Solar System. The other two dwarf planets are Ceres and Eris, but there are many more objects waiting to be classified.

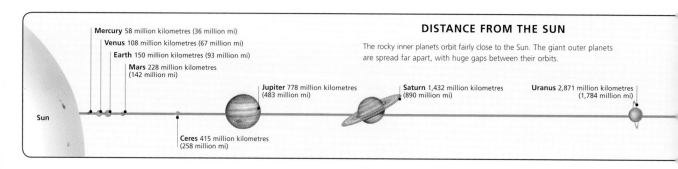

## DISTANCE FROM THE SUN

The rocky inner planets orbit fairly close to the Sun. The giant outer planets are spread far apart, with huge gaps between their orbits.

Sun

**Mercury** 58 million kilometres (36 million mi)

**Venus** 108 million kilometres (67 million mi)

**Earth** 150 million kilometres (93 million mi)

**Mars** 228 million kilometres (142 million mi)

**Ceres** 415 million kilometres (258 million mi)

**Jupiter** 778 million kilometres (483 million mi)

**Saturn** 1,432 million kilometres (890 million mi)

**Uranus** 2,871 million kilometres (1,784 million mi)

Earth
Venus
Mars
Mercury
Earth's Moon
Ceres

**THE INNER PLANETS**
The four planets closest to the Sun make up the inner Solar System. Earth's Moon is just one of many in the Solar System. Ceres is a dwarf planet.

Jupiter
Saturn
Uranus
Neptune
Earth
Pluto  Eris

**THE OUTER PLANETS**
The four planets of the outer Solar System are largely made up of the gases hydrogen and helium. Pluto and Eris are much smaller dwarf planets.

**Asteroid belt** Asteroids are made of rock and metal. Many thousands of them orbit between Mars and Jupiter in the asteroid belt.

**Comet Hale Bopp** A comet is a body of ice and dust that orbits the Sun. As it nears, the ice warms up and the comet forms long gas and dust tails.

# THE PLANETS

The eight major planets in the Solar System are very different in their size and structure. Together, the mass of all the planets would make 447 Earths, which is just 0.13 per cent of the mass of the Sun.

 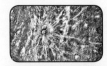
**MERCURY**
Mercury's surface is covered with craters and basins. It has a large central core.

 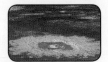
**VENUS**
Venus is covered with white sulphuric clouds, under which lie volcanoes and mountains.

**EARTH**
Earth has a solid core of iron and nickel, a liquid outer core and a lighter mantle and crust.

**MARS**
Mars is a freezing planet with ancient craters and volcanoes. Water is frozen at the poles.

 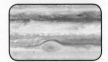
**JUPITER**
Jupiter is a giant ball of gas—mainly hydrogen and helium—and does not have a solid surface.

**SATURN**
Saturn is a gas giant topped with cloud belts and swirling storms of ammonia and ice crystals.

**URANUS**
Uranus has a gassy surface, below which is a slushy mix of water and gases and a rocky core.

**NEPTUNE**
Neptune is coloured blue by the methane in its surface, below which is slush and a rocky core.

**Neptune** 4,498 million kilometres (2,795 million mi)

**Pluto** 5,914 million kilometres (3,675 million mi)

**Eris** 10,122 million kilometres (6,290 million mi)

# Planet Earth

Earth's landforms can be photographed from satellites in space. This view shows part of Europe and Africa, with the boot-shaped Italy extending into the Mediterranean Sea.

Earth is the only place we know of in the entire Universe with the right conditions for life to thrive. Liquid water is vital for all life and Earth is at the right distance from the Sun for water to exist on the surface. If Earth were closer to the Sun, our rivers and oceans would boil and evaporate. If further away from the Sun, Earth would be a frozen world of ice. Beneath the rocky surface, Earth has a hot, molten interior. Liquid rock erupts to the surface from volcanoes and weaknesses in Earth's crust. This activity continuously renews the surface, creating new mountains and raising minerals from deep within the planet.

## OUR ATMOSPHERE

Earth's atmosphere is a layer of gases that surrounds the planet. It is divided into several regions. The troposphere contains most of the water vapour that we see as clouds. Above that is the stratosphere, where the ozone layer protects us from harmful radiation. Beyond the upper boundary of the atmosphere lies the cold darkness of space.

**Exosphere**
More than
500 kilometres (310 mi)

**Thermosphere**
80–500 kilometres
(50–310 mi)

**Mesosphere**
50–80 kilometres
(30–50 mi)

**Stratosphere**
15–50 kilometres (9–30 mi)

**Troposphere**
0–15 kilometres (0–9 mi)

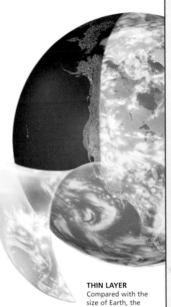

**THIN LAYER**
Compared with the size of Earth, the atmosphere is as thin as a coat of varnish.

## PLANET OF EXTREMES

The surface of Earth offers an incredible variety of environments. Life of some kind can exist in almost all of them.

**Polar regions** The frigid poles receive much less sunlight than the rest of the planet.

**Deserts** Rainfall is so low in these harsh regions that little vegetation can grow.

**Tropics** The regions near the equator are warm all year round, with plentiful rainfall.

**Mountains** Plant life changes higher up a mountain as the temperature drops.

## HIGHEST AND LOWEST IN THE SOLAR SYSTEM

Earth is a very active world. Activity above and below the surface is continuously forming new mountains and trenches. These surface features are slowly worn away by water in rivers, rain, ice and the pounding ocean waves. Our closest neighbour planets, Venus and Mars, do not have liquid water on their surfaces. Their mountains and trenches have not eroded as much and are larger than anything on Earth.

**Olympus Mons** Mars
(26 kilometres / 16 mi)

**Maxwell Montes** Venus
(10.8 kilometres / 6¾ mi)

**Mount Everest** Earth
(8.85 kilometres / 5½ mi)

**Diana Chasma** Venus
(–2.9 kilometres/–1¾ mi)

**Mariana Trench** Earth
(–11 kilometres/–7 mi)

# Earth's formation

About 4.6 billion years ago, a massive, rotating cloud of hot gas and dust condensed to form the Solar System. The planets first appeared around a young star, the Sun, as grains of dust that clumped together, forming larger and larger bodies. Evidence suggests at least two planets formed about 150 million kilometres (93 million mi) from the Sun: the young Earth and a small planet called Theia. The two worlds smashed together and debris from both planets formed the Moon. Earth suffered countless collisions with smaller objects, slowly gaining extra mass. Initially, the planet was completely molten, but as Earth grew it cooled and formed a solid crust. Enough gravity was generated to retain a gaseous atmosphere that includes water vapour.

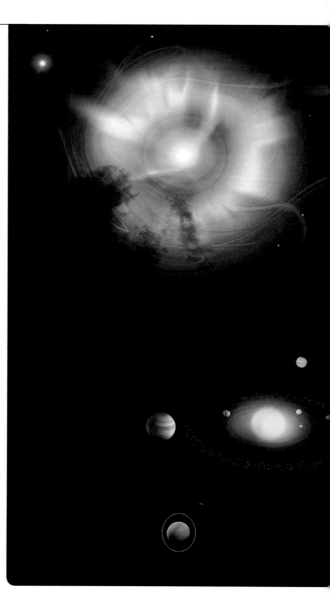

## ROCKS FROM SPACE

Not all material from the early Solar System became the Sun and the planets. Millions of small, rocky bodies called asteroids circle the Sun, mainly between the orbits of Mars and Jupiter. Some are mere pebbles; others are the size of mountains. Objects that burn up in Earth's atmosphere are called meteors. Objects that reach its surface are called meteorites.

From the air, the scar of Meteor Crater in Arizona, USA, is clearly seen. It was caused by a large meteorite about 50,000 years ago.

A SHORT HISTORY OF EARTH

**In the beginning**
Dust and debris from the massive cloud around the young Sun collect together to form the inner planets. Because of gravity these little worlds collide, forming larger and larger objects, eventually becoming planets.

**Heating up**
Earth is struck, and debris from the impact forms the Moon. Many bombardments, plus heat from within Earth, create a superheated, molten planet. Heavy elements sink to the centre while lighter ones rise.

**Cooling off**
Earth cools and forms a solid, rocky crust. The atmosphere forms. Gases ejected from volcanoes and other sources from deep within the planet add to the atmosphere.

**Settling down**
There are fewer impacts from space. Earth's interior divides into a core and mantle. Water vapour in the sky condenses and rain falls on the planet, creating oceans. The stage for life is set.

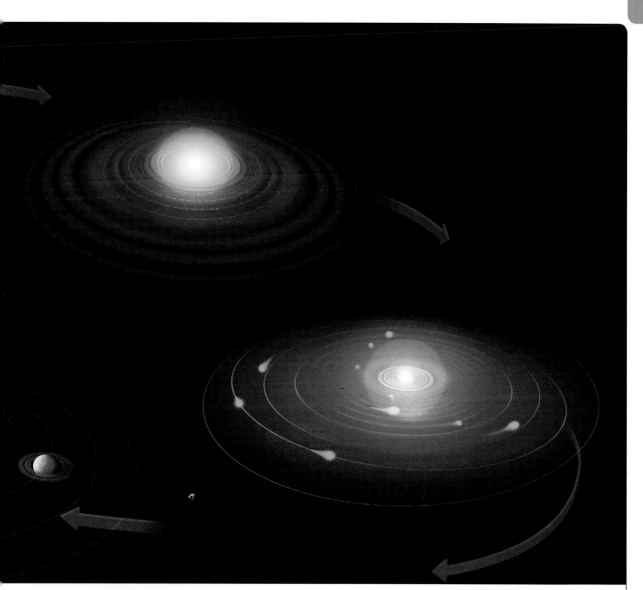

## FORMING THE SOLAR SYSTEM

1 A gigantic cloud of gas and dust collapses. The cloud begins to rotate and develops into a flattened disc.

2 After millions of years, most of the material gathers in the centre, forming what eventually becomes the Sun. Out along the disc, matter clumps together in bands.

3 Collections of dust form rocky bodies several kilometres across, which collide and join with each other to become the inner planets.

4 Eight major planets, including Earth, remain in orbits around the Sun.

Earth underwent a period of intense bombardment early in its history. Each impact added more mass to the young planet.

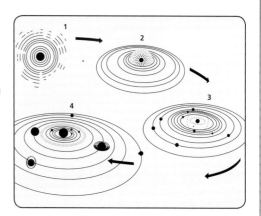

# Earth's Sun

The Sun is the centre of the Solar System. This enormous star gives us all the light and heat we need to grow food and keep warm. But it is not the largest star in the Universe—in fact, it is quite a small one. It seems very big and bright to us because it is only 150 million kilometres (93 million mi) away from Earth. Light from the Sun takes only eight minutes to reach us; light from the next brightest star takes eight years! Scientists believe the Sun was formed about 4.6 billion years ago, perhaps when a nearby star exploded and caused a huge cloud of dust and gas to collapse in on itself. The hot, central part of the cloud became the Sun, while some smaller pieces formed around it and became the planets.

Photosphere

Convective zone

Radiative zone

Core

## SUN FACTS

**ORIGIN OF NAME**
From Old English word *sunne*

**DISCOVERED**
Known since antiquity

**AGE OF THE SUN**
4.6 billion years

**GRAVITY**
28 (Earth = 1)

**VOLUME**
1,304,000 (Earth = 1)

**DIAMETER**
1,392,530 kilometres (865,278 mi)

**CORE TEMPERATURE**
15 million°C (27 million°F)

Sunspots

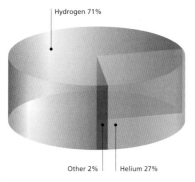

Hydrogen 71%

Other 2%    Helium 27%

**INSIDE THE SUN**
The Sun is made up of gases, mostly hydrogen, and is powered by a process called nuclear fusion. Energy is produced in the superhot core.

Prominence

Jupiter

Jupiter

Earth

## HOW BIG IS THE SUN?

The Sun is 900 times bigger than Jupiter, the largest planet. Jupiter itself is 1,112 times larger than Earth.

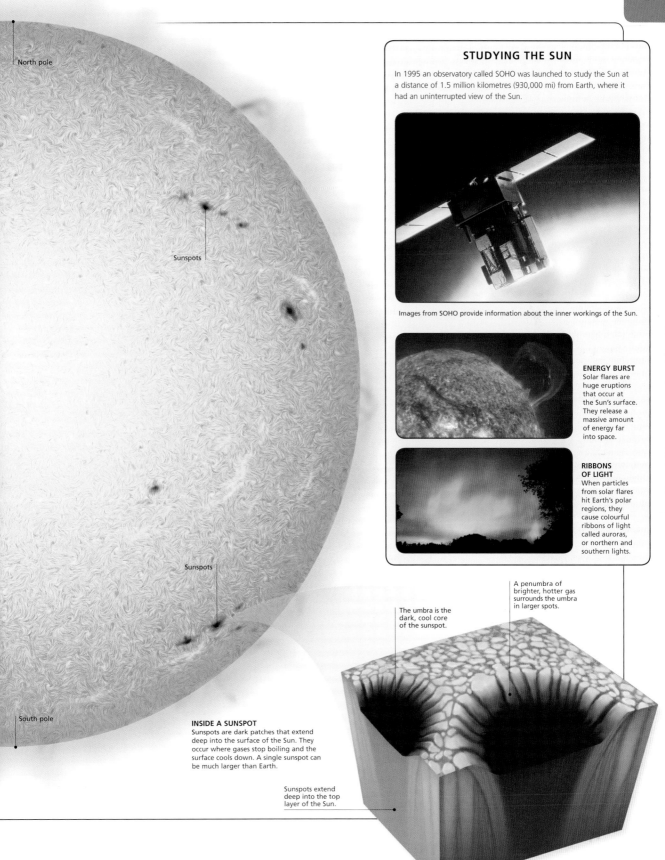

North pole

Sunspots

Sunspots

South pole

## STUDYING THE SUN

In 1995 an observatory called SOHO was launched to study the Sun at a distance of 1.5 million kilometres (930,000 mi) from Earth, where it had an uninterrupted view of the Sun.

Images from SOHO provide information about the inner workings of the Sun.

**ENERGY BURST**
Solar flares are huge eruptions that occur at the Sun's surface. They release a massive amount of energy far into space.

**RIBBONS OF LIGHT**
When particles from solar flares hit Earth's polar regions, they cause colourful ribbons of light called auroras, or northern and southern lights.

The umbra is the dark, cool core of the sunspot.

A penumbra of brighter, hotter gas surrounds the umbra in larger spots.

### INSIDE A SUNSPOT
Sunspots are dark patches that extend deep into the surface of the Sun. They occur where gases stop boiling and the surface cools down. A single sunspot can be much larger than Earth.

Sunspots extend deep into the top layer of the Sun.

# Earth's Moon

The Moon is Earth's only natural satellite. It formed soon after Earth did, from the debris that flew out when another object struck Earth. As the Moon formed, it was constantly bombarded by meteorites, which punched deep craters into its surface and created broad basins. Dark lava flowed from under the surface to fill the basins. Early astronomers thought these dark areas were the dried-up beds of oceans, so they called them maria, which means "seas" in Latin. Astronomer Neil Armstrong became the first human to walk on the Moon in 1969. From then until 1972 the Apollo programme landed another 11 people on the Moon for stays of a few days.

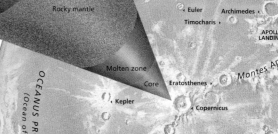

Rocky crust

Montes Jura

SINUS IRIDUM
(Bay of Rainbows)

Plato

MA
(Sea

MARE IMBRIUM
(Sea of Showers)

Cassini

Aristillus

Euler    Archimedes

Timocharis

APOLLO 15
LANDING SITE

Rocky mantle

Montes Apenninus

Eratosthenes

Molten zone

Core

OCEANUS PROCELLARUM
(Ocean of Storms)

Kepler

Copernicus

Letronne

APOLLO 12
LANDING SITE

APOLLO 14
LANDING SITE

Ptolemaeus

MARE
COGNITUM
(Sea of Knowledge)

Gassendi

Alphonsus

Albatec

MARE
HUMORUM
(Sea of Moisture)

MARE
NUBIUM
(Sea of Clouds)

Arzachel

Pitatus

Purbach

Deslandres

Tycho

## MOON FACTS

**ORIGIN OF NAME**
*Mona*, the Anglo-Saxon word for "Moon"

**DISTANCE FROM EARTH**
384,401 kilometres (238,856 mi)

**DIAMETER**
3,476 kilometres (2,160 mi)

**MASS**
1.2% of Earth's mass

**ATMOSPHERE**
None

**LENGTH OF DAY (IN EARTH DAYS)**
Rotation time and solar day: both 29.5

## FORMING A CRATER

The Moon's craters were formed when asteroids, meteorites or comets smashed into its surface at high speed.

The object hits the surface and a wide cavity is formed.

Material from the surface is thrown outward and sometimes forms other craters where it lands.

## PHASES OF THE MOON

As the Moon revolves around us, we see different parts of it lit by the Sun. When the Moon lies between us and the Sun, the side of the Moon facing us is dark—the New Moon. When it is opposite the Sun, the Moon appears fully lit—the Full Moon.

New Moon

Waxing Quarter

First Quarter

Waxing Gibbous

Full Moon

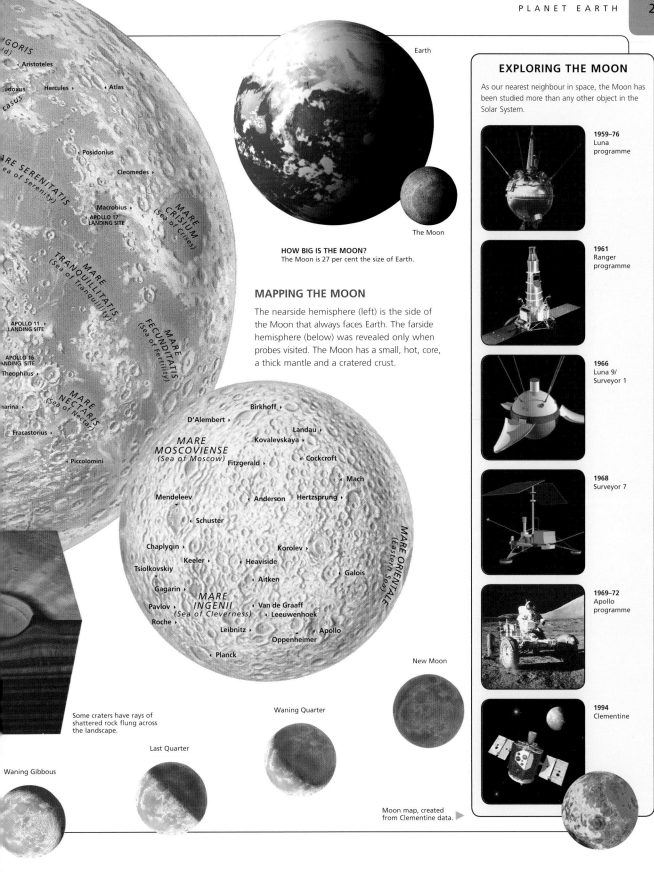

IGORIS
Aristoteles
Eudoxus    Hercules
Atlas
casus
Posidonius
Cleomedes
MARE SERENITATIS (Sea of Serenity)
Macrobius
MARE CRISIUM (Sea of Crises)
APOLLO 17 LANDING SITE
MARE TRANQUILLITATIS (Sea of Tranquillity)
MARE FECUNDITATIS (Sea of Fertility)
APOLLO 11 LANDING SITE
APOLLO 16 LANDING SITE
Theophilus
MARE NECTARIS (Sea of Nectar)
arina
Fracastorius
Piccolomini

Earth

The Moon

**HOW BIG IS THE MOON?**
The Moon is 27 per cent the size of Earth.

## MAPPING THE MOON

The nearside hemisphere (left) is the side of
the Moon that always faces Earth. The farside
hemisphere (below) was revealed only when
probes visited. The Moon has a small, hot, core,
a thick mantle and a cratered crust.

Birkhoff
D'Alembert
Landau
Kovalevskaya
MARE MOSCOVIENSE (Sea of Moscow)    Fitzgerald    Cockcroft
Mach
Mendeleev    Anderson    Hertzsprung
Schuster
Chaplygin    Korolev
Keeler    Heaviside
Tsiolkovskiy    Galois
Aitken
Gagarin
MARE INGENII (Sea of Cleverness)    Van de Graaff    Leeuwenhoek
Pavlov
Roche
Leibnitz    Apollo
Oppenheimer
Planck
MARE ORIENTALE (Eastern Sea)

New Moon

Some craters have rays of
shattered rock flung across
the landscape.

Waning Quarter

Last Quarter

Waning Gibbous

Moon map, created
from Clementine data. ▶

## EXPLORING THE MOON

As our nearest neighbour in space, the Moon has
been studied more than any other object in the
Solar System.

**1959–76**
Luna
programme

**1961**
Ranger
programme

**1966**
Luna 9/
Surveyor 1

**1968**
Surveyor 7

**1969–72**
Apollo
programme

**1994**
Clementine

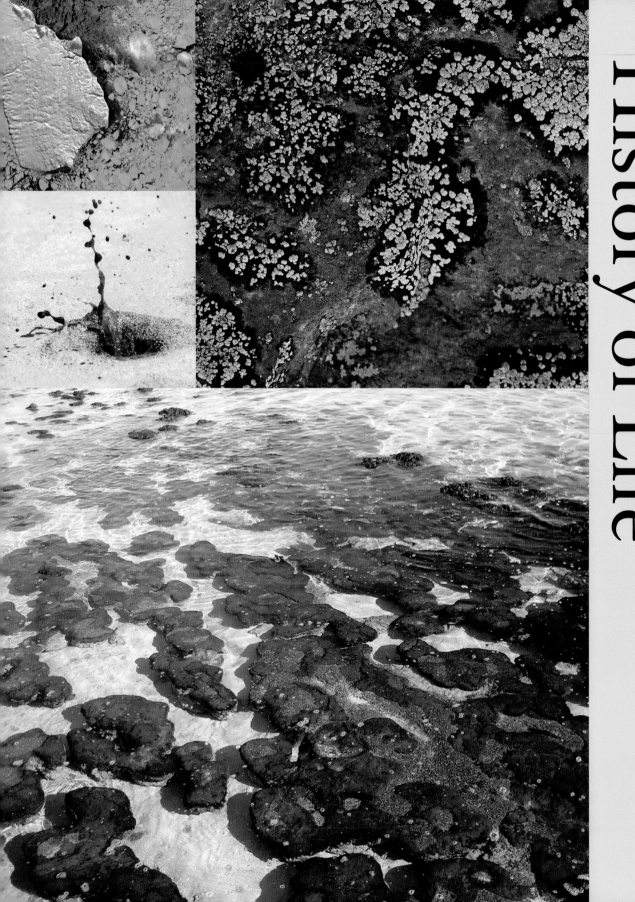

# History of Life

# Life on Earth

Simple bacteria appeared about 3.8 billion years ago, but for billions of years after that, life did not produce anything more complex than jellyfish and seaweed. About 550 million years ago, there was a dramatic increase in the number and kinds of animals, known as the "Cambrian explosion". Starting from that time, Earth's history is divided into three long eras, containing eleven shorter periods. These divisions mark changes in the environment and the kinds of plants and animals that lived at different times. During Earth's long history, there have been five mass extinctions, when much of life on our planet was destroyed.

## A HISTORY OF LIFE ON EARTH

Over the past 3.8 billion years, many different species of plants and animals have evolved, thrived and become extinct as conditions on our planet changed. Humans are latecomers to Planet Earth.

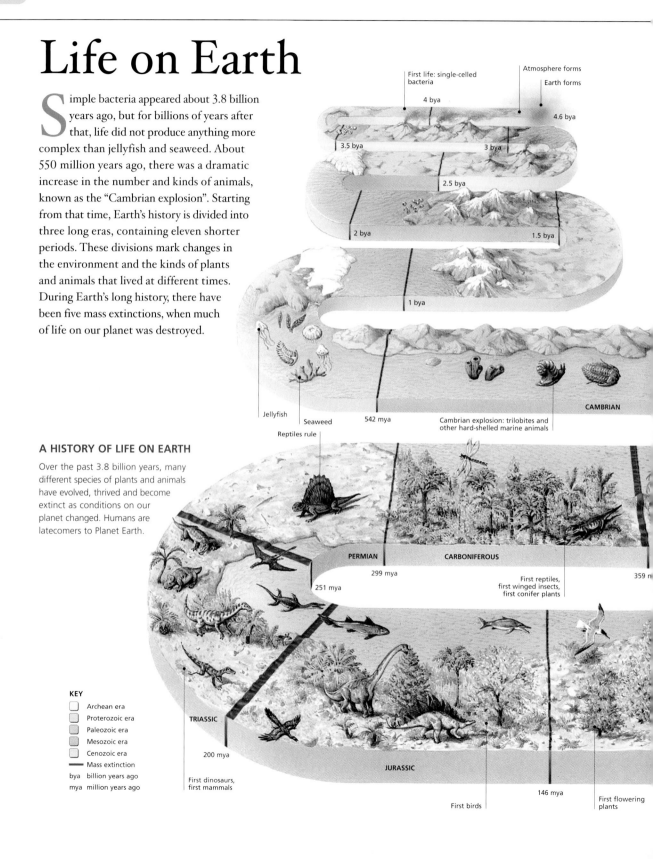

First life: single-celled bacteria
4 bya

Atmosphere forms
Earth forms
4.6 bya

3.5 bya          3 bya
2.5 bya
2 bya          1.5 bya
1 bya

Jellyfish
Seaweed
Reptiles rule
542 mya
Cambrian explosion: trilobites and other hard-shelled marine animals
CAMBRIAN

PERMIAN          CARBONIFEROUS
299 mya
251 mya
First reptiles, first winged insects, first conifer plants
359 m

TRIASSIC
200 mya
First dinosaurs, first mammals
JURASSIC
First birds
146 mya
First flowering plants

**KEY**
- Archean era
- Proterozoic era
- Paleozoic era
- Mesozoic era
- Cenozoic era
- — Mass extinction
- bya    billion years ago
- mya    million years ago

Scientists believe that Earth formed 4.6 billion years ago. The oldest rocks, in the Isua region of Greenland, are 3.8 billion years old.

## LIVING FOSSILS

Stromatolites are built up over centuries by countless blue-green bacteria that cement grains of mud together. Their shape looks a bit like a stone cauliflower. The living structure grows upward and outward, layer upon layer. Fossil stromatolites, 3.5 billion years old, are some of the oldest evidence of life on Earth.

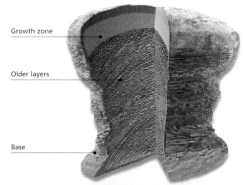

Growth zone

Older layers

Base

Living stromatolites are found today in a handful of sheltered bays. These 4,000-year-old specimens grow at Hamelin Pool in Shark Bay, Western Australia.

First jawless fish

First corals

ORDOVICIAN

488 mya

444 mya

First jawed fish

DEVONIAN

SILURIAN

416 mya

First land animals

First land plants

First insects and amphibians, first seed plants and trees

First large mammals, first primates

Early horses, camels, rodents, elephants, monkeys, whales and bats

Large browsing mammals; early apes, dogs and bears

First humans

CRETACEOUS

PALEOGENE

NEOGENE

65.5 mya

23 mya

Present

First marsupials

# Plants through time

**CARBONIFEROUS: 359–299 MILLION YEARS AGO (MYA)**
Giant horsetails, club mosse and ferns grew.

**PERMIAN: 299–251 MYA**
Seed-bearing ginkgoes and conifers thrived.

**TRIASSIC: 251–200 MYA**
Cycads flourished.

Earth is 4.6 billion years old, but for more than
1 billion years only non-living things, such as rocks and
water, could exist because of the poisonous gases in the atmosphere
and the fierce heat of the Sun. The first true plants grew in the oceans
about 550 million years ago, and the first land plants appeared about
400 million years ago. These primitive land plants grew near lakes.
They were the ancestors of the spore-bearing plants—the giant club
mosses, horsetails and ferns that formed huge forests during
the Carboniferous. Seed-bearing plants, such as conifers,
appeared 350 million years ago and flowering
plants appeared only 135 million years ago.

**Permian**
Ginkgo is the only
survivor of a group of
plants that appeared
in the Permian.

**Triassic**
Cycad

**Carboniferous**
The modern horsetail
is essentially the same
as those that existed
in the Carboniferous.

**TREE FERNS**
Ferns are land plants with woody stems
that reproduce by tiny cells called spores.
Tall tree ferns appeared and thrived
during the Carboniferous. Today they
are restricted to moist forests.

**SWAMPY CARBONIFEROUS**
Giant club mosses (1), giant horsetails (2) and cordaitales (3) grew as tall as houses.

**COOLER PERMIAN**
Ginkgoes (4) and conifers (5) shared the world with other early plants.

**DRIER TRIASSIC**
Cycads (6) flourished.

**COOLER AND WETTER JURASSIC**
New species of conifers, such as swamp cypress (7) and monkey puzzle (8), appeared in the lush, ferny undergrowth (9).

**FLOWERING CRETACEOUS**
Flowering plants, such as bulrushes (10), magnolia bushes (11) and willow trees (12), appeared.

**PALEOGENE**
Flowering plants began to rule the plant kingdom.

**Paleogene to modern day**
The strawberry is just one of more than 235,000 species of flowering plants that exist today.

**Cretaceous**
Magnolia

**JURASSIC: 200–146 MYA**
New species of conifers appeared.

**Jurassic**
Conifer

**CRETACEOUS: 146–65.5 MYA**
Flowering plants, including trees, appeared.

**PALEOGENE: 65.5–23 MYA**
Flowering plants dominated.

# Explosion of life

Before the "Cambrian explosion" about 550 million years ago, only blind, soft-bodied creatures swam in the oceans. After the "explosion", the oceans teemed with more complex animals with eyes, shells and spines. Primitive sponges built the first reefs. But while the seas were full of life, dry land remained empty and lifeless. Many Cambrian animals were arthropods, with hard, jointed cases covering the outside of their bodies. Some were predators that hunted down and ate other animals. Living arthropods include insects, spiders and crabs. The ancestors of backboned animals also appeared at this time as tiny, worm-like, jawless fish.

## ANCIENT TRILOBITES

Trilobites were a successful group of marine arthropods and were among the first animals to evolve eyes. Their bodies were covered with a hard shell that was divided into a shield-like head, a thorax or abdomen and a tail. They existed for about 300 million years.

Tail

Thorax

Head

Trilobite fossils are common and more than 15,000 species have been recorded. They became extinct at the end of the Permian.

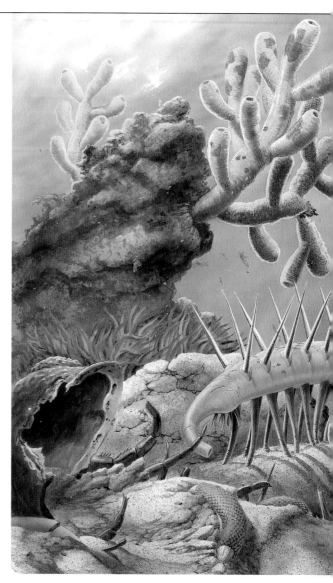

## THE CAMBRIAN SEAS

Bizarre creatures filled the Cambrian seas. The fearsome *Anomalocaris* preyed on smaller animals. On the seabed crawled trilobites, armour-plated *Wiwaxia* and the spiny *Hallucigenia*. Sponges filtered the water for edible particles. One special creature was *Pikaia*, the earliest known vertebrate, or animal with a backbone. About 490 million years ago, glaciers may have lowered temperatures and oxygen levels in the water and many of these ancient creatures became extinct.

| PALEOZOIC: AGE OF ANCIENT LIFE | | | | |
|---|---|---|---|---|
| CAMBRIAN | ORDOVICIAN | SILURIAN | DEVONIAN | CARBONIFEROUS |
| 542 mya | 488 | 444 | 416 | 359 |

## CAMBRIAN CREATURES

1 *Vauxia*, a soft-branching sponge

2 *Anomalocaris*, an arthropod relative

3 *Marella*, a primitive crustacean

4 *Pikaia*, the earliest known relative of vertebrate animals

5 Archaeocyathid, a reef-forming sponge relative

6 *Wiwaxia*, an early relative of snails

7 Trilobite, a bottom-dwelling arthropod

8 *Hallucigenia*, a 14-legged creature

9 *Halkieria*, an armour-plated, shelled creature

10 Green algae, early relatives of land plants

| | MESOZOIC: AGE OF REPTILES | | | CENOZOIC: AGE OF MAMMALS | |
|---|---|---|---|---|---|
| MIAN | TRIASSIC | JURASSIC | CRETACEOUS | PALEOGENE | NEOGENE |
| | 251 | 200 | 146 | 65.5 | 23        0 |

# Teeming oceans

While some animal groups died out when the climate changed at the end of the Cambrian, life in the oceans flourished during the next period, the Ordovician. Coral reefs appeared and provided habitats for snails, trilobites, sea lilies and other animals. Cephalopods—the same group as modern squid and octopus—became common and some evolved into giant marine predators. For protection, the small jawless fish developed hard, bony plates. Much of Earth's water was frozen into great ice sheets. About 450 million years ago, giant glaciers began to cover the land. This reduced the temperature of the oceans and lowered the sea level. Once again, many animals became extinct, including most—but not all—of the trilobites.

## THE FIRST CORAL

Coral polyps are soft animals with tentacles, related to jellyfish. Many secrete a hard outer skeleton made of calcium carbonate. Over the generations, these skeletons build up to become coral reefs. Rugose and tabulate corals were common in the Ordovician.

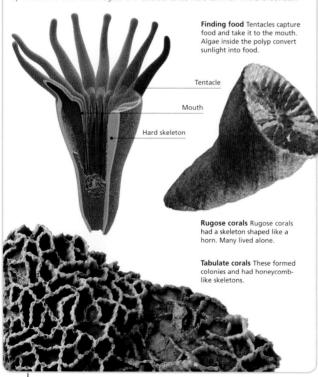

**Finding food** Tentacles capture food and take it to the mouth. Algae inside the polyp convert sunlight into food.

Tentacle

Mouth

Hard skeleton

**Rugose corals** Rugose corals had a skeleton shaped like a horn. Many lived alone.

**Tabulate corals** These formed colonies and had honeycomb-like skeletons.

## HUNTERS OF THE DEEP

Life in the seas became more complex during the Ordovician. The top predators were cephalopods, like *Cameroceras*, whose conical shell reached 9 metres (30 ft) long. Their prey tried to escape by swimming, burrowing, or rolling into a tight ball. Flexible sea lilies, called crinoids, grew on the seafloor, along with tabulate and rugose corals. These early reef communities died when the world became cold and icy towards the end of the Ordovician.

| PALEOZOIC: AGE OF ANCIENT LIFE | | | | |
|---|---|---|---|---|
| CAMBRIAN | ORDOVICIAN | SILURIAN | DEVONIAN | CARBONIFEROUS |
| 542 mya | 488 | 444 | 416 | 359 |

## ORDOVICIAN CREATURES

1 *Orthograptus*, a floating graptolite (worm-shaped sea star relative)

2 *Opipeuter*, a large-eyed, swimming trilobite

3 *Climacograptus*, a floating graptolite

4 *Sphaeragnostus*, a floating, rolled trilobite

5 *Tentaculites*, a relative of molluscs

6 *Cameroceras*, a straight-shelled nautiloid

7 *Grewingkia*, a solitary rugose coral

8 *Cyclonema bilix*, a bottom-dwelling snail relative

9 *Calapoecia*, a colonial tabulate coral

10 *Sowerbyella*, a brachiopod

11 *Ectenocrinus*, a crinoid

12 *Xenocrinus*, a crinoid

13 *Nemograptus gracilus*, a graptolite

| MESOZOIC: AGE OF REPTILES | | | | CENOZOIC: AGE OF MAMMALS | |
|---|---|---|---|---|---|
| MIAN | TRIASSIC | JURASSIC | CRETACEOUS | PALEOGENE | NEOGENE |
| | 251 | 200 | 146 | 65.5 | 23 | 0 |

# Age of fish

In the Silurian period, giant scorpions hunted in the seas while primitive plants grew on land. One group of fish developed the first jaws with teeth. Arthropods, including sea scorpions, took the first steps out of the water to scavenge along the beaches and riverbanks. Fish took over in the Devonian. Early sharks hunted in the rivers and seas. Some armour-plated fish called placoderms grew to gigantic sizes. Others developed fleshy pairs of fins that were supported by sturdy bones. These were called lobe-finned fish. One group of air-breathing lobe-finned fish developed legs. They crawled out of the water into the first forests, which teemed with primitive insects.

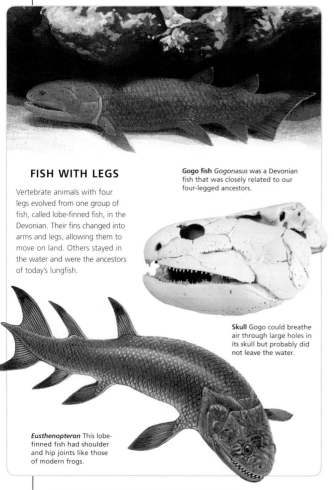

## FISH WITH LEGS

Vertebrate animals with four legs evolved from one group of fish, called lobe-finned fish, in the Devonian. Their fins changed into arms and legs, allowing them to move on land. Others stayed in the water and were the ancestors of today's lungfish.

**Gogo fish** *Gogonasus* was a Devonian fish that was closely related to our four-legged ancestors.

**Skull** Gogo could breathe air through large holes in its skull but probably did not leave the water.

**Eusthenopteron** This lobe-finned fish had shoulder and hip joints like those of modern frogs.

## WHEN FISH RULED

*Dunkleosteus*, measuring 9 metres (30 ft), was the mightiest predator of the Devonian seas. This bony-plated giant was the first of the jawed fish. A primitive shark called *Stethacanthus* had a flat-topped back fin and a flat head, both covered with tooth-shaped scales. Spiny trilobites called *Huntonia* scavenged for food on the seafloor, among brachiopods, sponges and corals. Most of these marine animals were wiped out at the end of the Devonian.

| PALEOZOIC: AGE OF ANCIENT LIFE | | | | |
|---|---|---|---|---|
| CAMBRIAN | ORDOVICIAN | SILURIAN | DEVONIAN | CARBONIFEROUS |
| 542 mya | 488 | 444 | 416 | 359 |

## DEVONIAN CREATURES

1 *Dunkleosteus*, an armoured jawed fish

2 *Stethacanthus*, a primitive shark

3 *Cladoselache*, a primitive shark with three-pointed teeth

4 *Huntonia*, a trilobite

5 Colonial rugose coral, a reef-forming coral

6 Solitary rugose coral, a large, tube-shape coral

7 *Ctenacanthus*, a primitive shark with two back fins

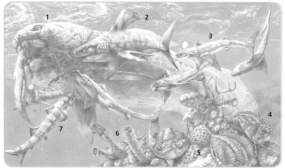

| | MESOZOIC: AGE OF REPTILES | | | CENOZOIC: AGE OF MAMMALS | |
|---|---|---|---|---|---|
| RMIAN | TRIASSIC | JURASSIC | CRETACEOUS | PALEOGENE | NEOGENE |
| 251 | 200 | 146 | | 65.5 | 23 | 0 |

# End of an era

Swampy forests of huge club mosses and horsetails thrived during the Carboniferous. Much of the coal we use today comes from the remains of those ancient plants. Predatory amphibians lurked underwater; giant millipedes scuttled through the undergrowth; and insects took to the air. Land became drier in the Permian and reptiles thrived in this more arid world. The most important reptiles were the mammal-like therapsids, some of which grew to huge sizes. At the end of the Permian, around 251 million years ago, a mass extinction killed more than 90 per cent of marine life and 75 per cent of all vertebrates on land. Coral reefs were wiped out. It took 10 million years for them to recover.

## CATASTROPHE!

One of Earth's greatest mass extinctions took place about 251 million years ago. Huge volcanic eruptions in Siberia may have poured poison gases into the atmosphere, or maybe the climate changed drastically and rainfall declined. It took 150 million years to regain the diversity of life Earth had experienced in the Permian.

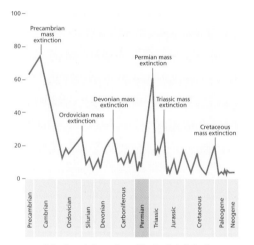

— Extinction rate (percentage of families that died out)

**GONE FOREVER**
Large predators, such as *Dinogorgon rubidgei*, did not survive the Permian extinction. Fortunately, some smaller mammal-like reptiles, including our ancestors, did.

## FIGHTING FOR SURVIVAL

During the Permian, the atmosphere was thick with volcanic dust. In the oceans, the strange, spiral-toothed shark *Helicoprion* hunted rays and smaller fish. On the bottom of the sea, the last of the trilobites hunted among the brachiopods. Saber-toothed mammal-like therapsids preyed on bony-plated reptiles in the parched deserts. But for all their size and strength, these creatures were helpless against the catastrophe that made them extinct at the end of the Permian.

| PALEOZOIC: AGE OF ANCIENT LIFE | | | | |
|---|---|---|---|---|
| **CAMBRIAN** | **ORDOVICIAN** | **SILURIAN** | **DEVONIAN** | **CARBONIFEROUS** |
| 542 mya | 488 | 444 | 416 | 359 |

## PERMIAN CREATURES

1 *Palaeoniscum*, a ray-finned fish
2 *Menapsis armata*, a shark-like ray
3 *Helicoprion*, a shark with whorled teeth
4 *Inostrancevia*, meat-eating therapsid

5 *Araucaria*, a monkey puzzle tree
6 *Scutosaurus*, a bony-plated reptile
7 Crinoid, a sea lily
8 *Phillipsia*, the last trilobite

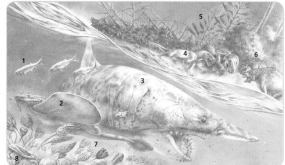

| | MESOZOIC: AGE OF REPTILES | | | CENOZOIC: AGE OF MAMMALS | |
|---|---|---|---|---|---|
| RMIAN | TRIASSIC | JURASSIC | CRETACEOUS | PALEOGENE | NEOGENE |
| | 251 | 200 | 146 | 65.5 | 23 | 0 |

# Rise of reptiles

By the beginning of the Triassic, 251 million years ago, all the world's landmasses had joined to form one giant continent called Pangaea. The climate over much of Pangaea was hot and dry. New kinds of reptiles evolved, walking on land, swimming in water and flying in the skies. Primitive turtles and crocodiles appeared. One group of reptiles developed legs and hips that allowed them to walk erect on their back legs; they were the first dinosaurs. At about the same time, the first mammals evolved from small therapsids. Towards the end of the Triassic, many large land-dwelling reptiles became extinct and the dinosaurs seized control of Planet Earth.

## PANGAEA, THE SUPERCONTINENT

Pangaea formed in the Permian when all the landmasses on Earth united in a single supercontinent. It began to break apart in the Jurassic. The land beneath our feet is still moving, and a new supercontinent may form in the distant future.

**TRIASSIC PLANTS**
Triassic flora, including cycads, ferns and conifers, were suited to the harsh environment.

Eurasia

Laurasia

**Triassic**
Pangaea is joined together.

**Jurassic**
Pangaea splits into supercontinents. Laurasia and Eurasia drift apart.

Gondwana

**Cretaceous**
The supercontinents break up into smaller chunks.

## DINOSAURS ARRIVE

The lush riverbanks of the Triassic provided a welcome retreat against the hot, dry conditions of Pangaea. The armoured plant eater *Desmatosuchus* and the terrifying *Postosuchus* were relatives of modern crocodiles. *Paracyclotosaurus*, one of the last giant amphibians, regulated its body temperature by basking in the sun. The first dinosaurs were small, lightly-built predators, such as the swift *Coelophysis* that hunted in packs.

| PALEOZOIC: AGE OF ANCIENT LIFE | | | | |
|---|---|---|---|---|
| CAMBRIAN | ORDOVICIAN | SILURIAN | DEVONIAN | CARBONIFEROUS |
| 542 mya | 488 | 444 | 416 | 359 |

## TRIASSIC CREATURES

1 *Ornithosuchus*, primitive crocodile relative

2 *Eudimorphodon*, a pterosaur (flying reptile)

3 *Auracarioxylon arazonicum*, a conifer tree

4 *Postosuchus*, an armoured, meat-eating reptile

5 *Coelophysis*, an early meat-eating dinosaur

6 *Placerias*, a tusked mammal-like reptile

7 *Desmatosuchus*, a horned plant-eating reptile

8 *Lariosaurus*, a nothosaur (aquatic reptile)

9 *Palaeocycas*, a primitive cycad plant

10 *Paracyclotosaurus*, a giant amphibian

| | MESOZOIC: AGE OF REPTILES | | | CENOZOIC: AGE OF MAMMALS | |
|---|---|---|---|---|---|
| RMIAN | TRIASSIC | JURASSIC | CRETACEOUS | PALEOGENE | NEOGENE |
| | 251 | 200 | 146 | 65.5 | 23 | 0 |

# Dinosaurs rule

Dinosaurs dominated the Jurassic and Cretaceous. The early mammals, our ancestors, were small furry creatures that hid in the shadows. Giant marine reptiles cruised beneath the waves, and pterosaurs soared overhead. Some dinosaurs grew to be the largest animals ever to walk on land. Small meat-eating dinosaurs evolved feathers for warmth, and some learned to fly, becoming the first birds. Flowers evolved early in the Cretaceous, along with the insects that pollinated them. Earth's second largest mass extinction occurred 65.5 million years ago when a huge meteorite struck the planet and 85 per cent of all life was wiped out. Most of the dinosaurs and all the marine reptiles died.

## FROM DINOSAUR TO BIRD

Many features found in modern birds, like feathers and wishbones, first appeared in small meat-eating dinosaurs. The oldest known bird, *Archaeopteryx*, had feathered wings and could probably glide efficiently.

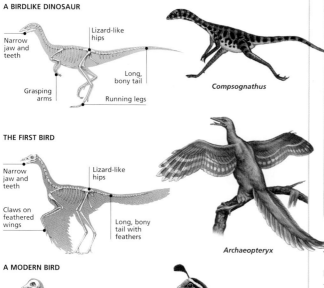

**A BIRDLIKE DINOSAUR**

Narrow jaw and teeth

Lizard-like hips

Grasping arms

Long, bony tail

Running legs

*Compsognathus*

**THE FIRST BIRD**

Narrow jaw and teeth

Lizard-like hips

Claws on feathered wings

Long, bony tail with feathers

*Archaeopteryx*

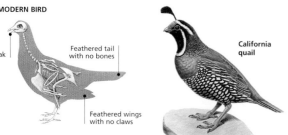

**A MODERN BIRD**

Beak

Feathered tail with no bones

California quail

Feathered wings with no claws

## THE AGE OF DINOSAURS

Dinosaurs reached their peak towards the end of the Cretaceous. Most terrifying were the giant meat eaters *Tyrannosaurus*, shadowed by scavenging *Troodon* looking for leftovers. Some plant eaters, such as *Styracosaurus*, had protective horns or armour. Other reptiles ruled the seas—long-necked *Elasmosaurus* and fish-eating *Plotosaurus*. Soaring overhead were the pterosaur *Quetzalcoatlus*, the largest flying animal ever to have lived, and the smaller *Pteranodon*.

| PALEOZOIC: AGE OF ANCIENT LIFE | | | | |
|---|---|---|---|---|
| CAMBRIAN | ORDOVICIAN | SILURIAN | DEVONIAN | CARBONIFEROUS |
| 542 mya | 488 | 444 | 416 | 359 |

## CRETACEOUS CREATURES

1  *Pteranodon*, a pterosaur (flying reptile)

2  *Tyrannosaurus*, a large meat-eating dinosaur

3  *Quetzalcoatlus*, the largest pterosaur

4  *Parasaurolphus*, a duck-billed dinosaur

5  *Carnotaurus*, a meat-eating dinosaur

6  *Nodosaurus*, an armoured plant-eating dinosaur

7  *Belemnites*, a large, coiled ammonite

8  *Plotosaurus*, a fish-eating mosasaur (marine reptile)

9  *Elasmosaurus*, a long-necked plesiosaur (marine reptile)

10  *Hesperornis*, a flightless aquatic bird

11  *Styracosaurus*, a horned plant-eating dinosaur

12  *Troodon*, a small, intelligent, meat-eating dinosaur

| MESOZOIC: AGE OF REPTILES | | | | CENOZOIC: AGE OF MAMMALS | |
|---|---|---|---|---|---|
| MIAN | TRIASSIC | JURASSIC | CRETACEOUS | PALEOGENE | NEOGENE |
| | 251 | 200 | 146 | 65.5 | 23 |

0

# Age of mammals

After the giant dinosaurs died out, mammals began to expand
in size and move into new environments during the Paleogene
period. This was when whales conquered the oceans and bats
took to the air. One group to appear was the primates. The first
primates were small tree dwellers with large brains, grasping
limbs and complex social behaviour. Today's monkeys, apes and
humans are descended from those early primates. For much of
the Paleogene, the world was warm and humid. Grasses, which
first grew on riverbanks and lake edges, began to spread into
drier areas. Dense forests extended to the polar regions. Late
in the period, the planet slowly cooled, as Antarctica froze over
and the ocean currents became colder.

## FROM REPTILES TO EARLY MAMMALS

The earliest reptile ancestors of mammals
had long bodies and did not look much like
mammals. They then developed specialized
teeth and compact bodies covered with
fur. The first true mammals appeared
at the end of the Triassic period and
developed special bones in the ear
that gave them sensitive hearing.

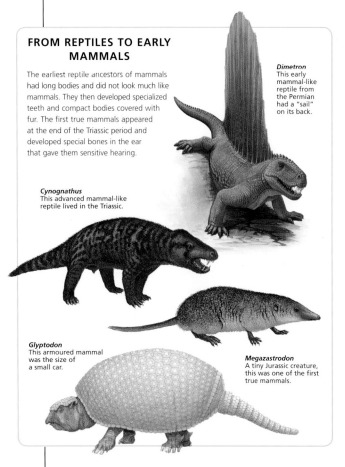

**Dimetron**
This early
mammal-like
reptile from
the Permian
had a "sail"
on its back.

**Cynognathus**
This advanced mammal-like
reptile lived in the Triassic.

**Glyptodon**
This armoured mammal
was the size of
a small car.

**Megazastrodon**
A tiny Jurassic creature,
this was one of the first
true mammals.

## UNDER ATTACK

This mother *Arsinoitherium* desperately tries to defend her baby against
a pack of marauding *Hyaeonodon*. *Arsinoitherium* was a plant eater
with giant horns that lived on the plains of northern Africa 35 million
years ago. It was a distant cousin of today's elephants, but looked
more like a rhinoceros. *Hyaeonodon* were fierce predators with sharp
fangs. They had hooves on their toes instead of claws.

| | PALEOZOIC: AGE OF ANCIENT LIFE | | | |
|---|---|---|---|---|
| CAMBRIAN | ORDOVICIAN | SILURIAN | DEVONIAN | CARBONIFEROUS |
| 542 mya | 488 | 444 | 416 | 359 |

**GINKGO**
Only one species of
ginkgo survives today.
It is sometimes called
a living fossil because
it provides clues to the
plant life of long ago.

This ginkgo leaf fossil was discovered in North Dakota, USA, in rocks from the Paleogene.

| MESOZOIC: AGE OF REPTILES | | | | CENOZOIC: AGE OF MAMMALS | |
|---|---|---|---|---|---|
| MIAN | TRIASSIC | JURASSIC | CRETACEOUS | PALEOGENE | NEOGENE |
| | 251 | 200 | 146 | 65.5 | 23 | 0 |

# Home to humans

When the world's climate became cooler and drier between 23 million and 2 million years ago, vast areas of grassy plains replaced the lush tropical forests of southern Africa. Newly formed mountain chains like the Himalaya disrupted global weather patterns. Plant-eating mammals roamed in huge nomadic herds eating the grasses and developed grinding teeth and stomachs. Many modern mammals can trace their ancestry to smaller animals from this time. Apes left the trees to forage on the ground and learned to walk upright. This made it easier to see food and predators and freed their arms to carry their young. The first humans evolved about 2 million years ago. They learned to make stone tools, and they mastered the use of fire. Several forms evolved and died out before our own species, *Homo sapiens*, appeared about 200,000 years ago.

**LUCY**
Humans evolved from upright-walking apes called australopithecines that lived 4 million years ago. A female australopithecine skeleton, nicknamed "Lucy", was discovered in Ethiopia in 1974.

**STONE-AGE BURIAL**
These two stone-age humans appear to have been buried together, with their bodies curled around each other. The skull of the right-hand body is crowned with a headdress made from shells. The remains were discovered in Liguria, Italy.

| PALEOZOIC: AGE OF ANCIENT LIFE | | | | |
|---|---|---|---|---|
| CAMBRIAN | ORDOVICIAN | SILURIAN | DEVONIAN | CARBONIFEROUS |
| 542 mya | 488 | 444 | 416 | 359 |

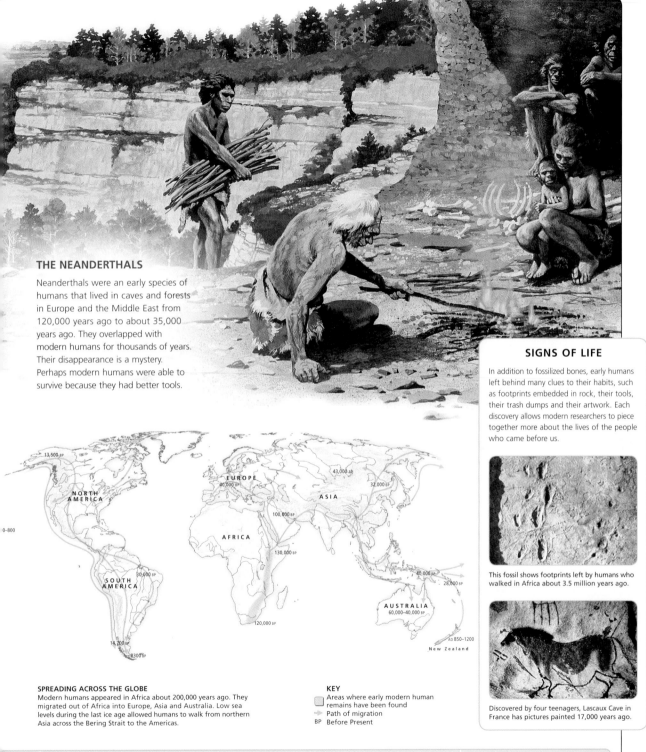

## THE NEANDERTHALS

Neanderthals were an early species of
humans that lived in caves and forests
in Europe and the Middle East from
120,000 years ago to about 35,000
years ago. They overlapped with
modern humans for thousands of years.
Their disappearance is a mystery.
Perhaps modern humans were able to
survive because they had better tools.

### SIGNS OF LIFE

In addition to fossilized bones, early humans
left behind many clues to their habits, such
as footprints embedded in rock, their tools,
their trash dumps and their artwork. Each
discovery allows modern researchers to piece
together more about the lives of the people
who came before us.

This fossil shows footprints left by humans who
walked in Africa about 3.5 million years ago.

Discovered by four teenagers, Lascaux Cave in
France has pictures painted 17,000 years ago.

**SPREADING ACROSS THE GLOBE**
Modern humans appeared in Africa about 200,000 years ago. They
migrated out of Africa into Europe, Asia and Australia. Low sea
levels during the last ice age allowed humans to walk from northern
Asia across the Bering Strait to the Americas.

**KEY**
Areas where early modern human
remains have been found
→ Path of migration
BP Before Present

| MESOZOIC: AGE OF REPTILES | | | | CENOZOIC: AGE OF MAMMALS | |
|---|---|---|---|---|---|
| TRIASSIC | JURASSIC | | CRETACEOUS | PALEOGENE | NEOGENE |
| 251 | 200 | | 146 | 65.5 | 23      0 |

MIAN

Inside Earth

# Journey to the Centre

A river of lava flows down a valley. When a volcano erupts, lava forces its way to the surface from the mantle.

About 4.6 billion years ago, Earth was a fiery ball of liquid melted rock. As it slowly cooled, the strength of Earth's own gravity pulled the heaviest elements, such as iron, towards its centre while lighter elements, including oxygen and silicon, floated to the surface. Eventually, Earth separated into layers. At the centre is a heavy iron core, made up of two distinct parts: a solid inner core and a liquid outer core. Around the core is a lighter mantle layer made mainly of a green gemstone called olivine, which is often carried from the mantle up to the surface by erupting lava. A brittle rocky crust floats on top of the mantle. The crust and the thin, upper part of the mantle are called the lithosphere.

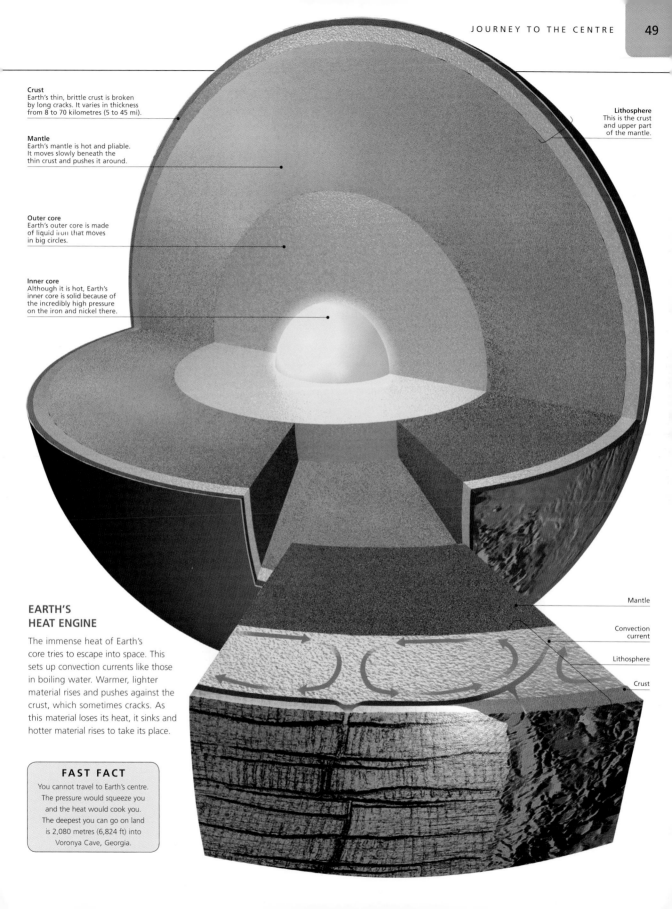

**Crust**
Earth's thin, brittle crust is broken by long cracks. It varies in thickness from 8 to 70 kilometres (5 to 45 mi).

**Mantle**
Earth's mantle is hot and pliable. It moves slowly beneath the thin crust and pushes it around.

**Outer core**
Earth's outer core is made of liquid iron that moves in big circles.

**Inner core**
Although it is hot, Earth's inner core is solid because of the incredibly high pressure on the iron and nickel there.

**Lithosphere**
This is the crust and upper part of the mantle.

Mantle

Convection current

Lithosphere

Crust

## EARTH'S HEAT ENGINE

The immense heat of Earth's core tries to escape into space. This sets up convection currents like those in boiling water. Warmer, lighter material rises and pushes against the crust, which sometimes cracks. As this material loses its heat, it sinks and hotter material rises to take its place.

### FAST FACT
You cannot travel to Earth's centre. The pressure would squeeze you and the heat would cook you. The deepest you can go on land is 2,080 metres (6,824 ft) into Voronya Cave, Georgia.

# Restless Earth

At Earth's centre lies a tremendous powerhouse, a blistering hot core. Heat from the core bakes the rock directly above it, in the mantle. As the mantle cooks, hot liquid rocks—called magma—rise like bubbles in boiling water. Cooler parts sink, but they are reheated by the core and soon rise again. This constant cycle forms convection currents. Magma moving in a convection current pushes and tugs at Earth's crust. After Earth formed, these movements cracked the crust and turned it into a giant jigsaw puzzle. The puzzle pieces are called tectonic plates, and they carry the world's oceans and landmasses. When magma oozes up between two plates, the plates separate. But they can travel only so far before they crash into other plates. These collisions cause earthquakes and volcanic eruptions.

This waterfall on the Genesee River, New York, USA, wears down Earth's landscape in an endless battle against the forces that push the land upward.

Geysers, such as these in Black Rock Desert, Nevada, USA, are explosive spouts of superheated water. They occur only where superheated rocks lie just below the surface.

## UNDER THE SURFACE

Convection currents (indicated by red arrows) stretch and squeeze the crust. Where plates separate, ocean ridges and rift valleys appear. Where plates smash into each other, mountains, volcanoes and undersea valleys form.

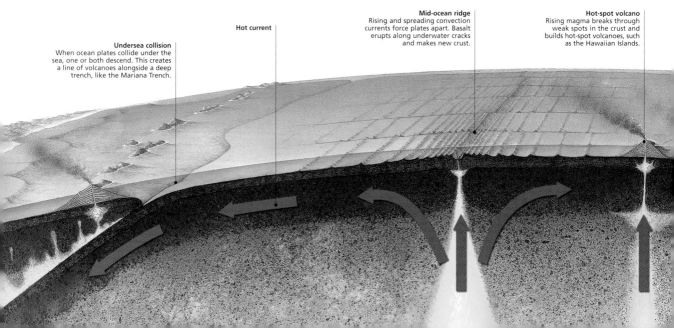

**Undersea collision**
When ocean plates collide under the sea, one or both descend. This creates a line of volcanoes alongside a deep trench, like the Mariana Trench.

**Hot current**

**Mid-ocean ridge**
Rising and spreading convection currents force plates apart. Basalt erupts along underwater cracks and makes new crust.

**Hot-spot volcano**
Rising magma breaks through weak spots in the crust and builds hot-spot volcanoes, such as the Hawaiian Islands.

Rivers of lava pour out of deep cracks or vents beneath Hawaii's surface and build giant volcanoes. Volcanoes are common wherever there are weaknesses in Earth's crust.

Hot springs are common around the edges of tectonic plates. In Yellowstone National Park, USA, underground water is heated as it flows along cracks in the hot rocks.

## BELOW THE CRUST

Earth's crust is thin and floats above the mantle. Oceanic crust is made of heavy basalt rock. The thicker continental crust floats higher because it is made of lighter granite rock. So the continents are above sea level, and most of Earth's water lies in the deeper ocean basins.

**OCEANIC CRUST**
The oceanic crust is made from basalt, a volcanic rock that hardens when magma erupts at mid-ocean ridges.

**CONTINENTAL CRUST**
The continental crust forms landmasses and is composed of older, lighter rocks, such as granite, gneiss and sandstone.

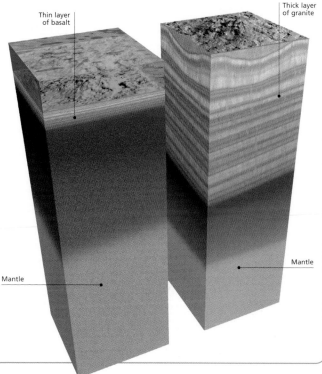

Thin layer of basalt

Thick layer of granite

Mantle

Mantle

**Coastal collision**
When ocean and continent collide, the heavier oceanic plate is pushed under. Magma rises to the surface, creating volcanoes and mountains.

**Sliding plates**
Plates sliding sideways alongside one another form long straight fault lines, such as the San Andreas Fault. The jerky movement releases energy as earthquakes.

**Continental rift**
Rising currents lift and separate continents, and form deep rift valleys. These widen and eventually are flooded by the sea.

**Folding crust**
When continental crusts collide they cannot push beneath one another. Their edges buckle and fold into giant ranges, such as the Himalaya Mountains.

# Continents on the Move

Earth's crust is on the move. Until about 50 years ago, geologists could not prove this, and early theories of "drifting continents" fell on deaf ears. Nevertheless, there were many things that could not be explained unless the continents were once joined, such as finding similar plants and animals on all the southern continents, or the surprising jigsaw fit of South America and Africa. In 1912, a German scientist, Alfred Wegener, noticed that the rocks in America and Africa were very similar and suggested they once formed a single continent. In the 1960s, scientists using underwater mapping equipment discovered long ridges under the ocean where Earth's crust had been pulled apart. The idea of continental drift began to be accepted.

**A MOVING HISTORY**
For millions of years, the movements of Earth's tectonic plates have been shrinking and enlarging seas, and separating and joining continents.

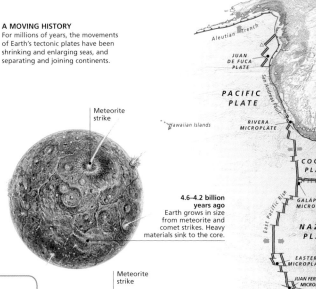

Meteorite strike

**4.6–4.2 billion years ago**
Earth grows in size from meteorite and comet strikes. Heavy materials sink to the core.

Meteorite strike

**4.2–3.8 billion years ago**
As the impacts lessen, Earth cools and forms a solid crust. Water vapour from volcanoes and comets condenses to form oceans.

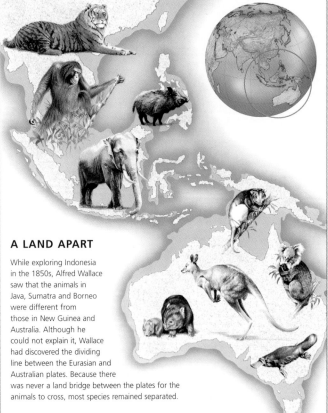

## A LAND APART

While exploring Indonesia in the 1850s, Alfred Wallace saw that the animals in Java, Sumatra and Borneo were different from those in New Guinea and Australia. Although he could not explain it, Wallace had discovered the dividing line between the Eurasian and Australian plates. Because there was never a land bridge between the plates for the animals to cross, most species remained separated.

The coastlines of the Red Sea and the Gulf of Aden started moving apart only about 25 million years ago.

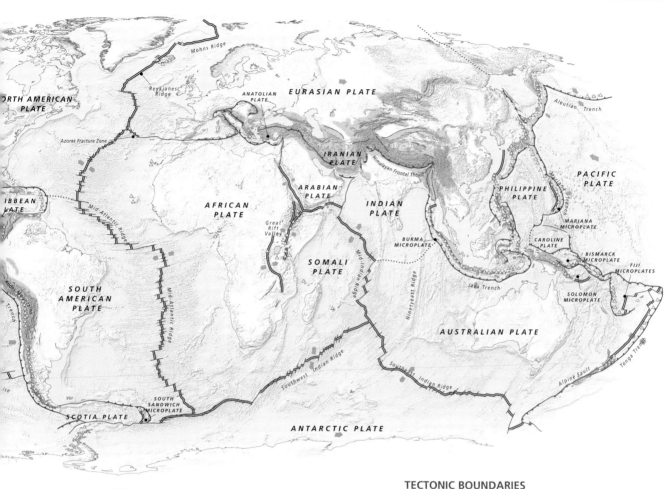

NORTH AMERICAN PLATE

Mohns Ridge

Reykjanes Ridge

EURASIAN PLATE

ANATOLIAN PLATE

Aleutian Trench

Azores Fracture Zone

IRANIAN PLATE

Himalayan Frontal Thrust

PACIFIC PLATE

CARIBBEAN PLATE

Mid Atlantic Ridge

AFRICAN PLATE

ARABIAN PLATE

Great Rift Valley

INDIAN PLATE

PHILIPPINE PLATE

Mariana Trench

MARIANA MICROPLATE

BURMA MICROPLATE

CAROLINE PLATE

BISMARCK MICROPLATE

SOUTH AMERICAN PLATE

Mid Atlantic Ridge

SOMALI PLATE

Mid-Indian Ridge

Ninetyeast Ridge

Java Trench

FIJI MICROPLATES

SOLOMON MICROPLATE

AUSTRALIAN PLATE

Southwest Indian Ridge

Southeast Indian Ridge

Alpine Fault

Tonga Trench

SCOTIA PLATE

SOUTH SANDWICH MICROPLATE

ANTARCTIC PLATE

## KEY

 Earthquake zone
△ Volcanic zone
Colliding plates
Separating plates

— Sideways-moving plates
···· Uncertain
 Direction of movement

## TECTONIC BOUNDARIES

Volcanoes, ocean trenches, mountain ranges and earthquakes mark where Earth's tectonic plates meet. The Pacific Plate's edge, called the "Ring of Fire", is the most active. Arrows indicate the way each plate moves.

**270 million years ago**
The landmasses join in the enormous supercontinent, Pangaea, surrounded by a single ocean.

**200 million years ago**
Pangaea starts to break up, first into two supercontinents and then into smaller chunks.

**Today**
The Atlantic Ocean is widening and the Americas are drifting away from Europe and Africa.

**50 million years from now**
The Atlantic continues to widen and the Pacific closes, bringing North America closer to Asia. Africa collides with Europe, closing the Mediterranean.

# Folds and Faults

The immense pressure of plate movements under the surface can snap even the toughest rocks. Cracks between shifting rock layers are called faults. You can see small ones in rock faces and road cuts. Large faults extend for hundreds of miles. The type of fault that forms depends on the way the rocks move. When rocks pull apart, one side slips downward. This is called a normal fault. When rocks push together, one side usually rides up over the other, creating a reverse fault. Sometimes rocks slide past each other in opposite directions or at different speeds. This creates a lateral, or transform, fault. All three may occur along a major fault line.

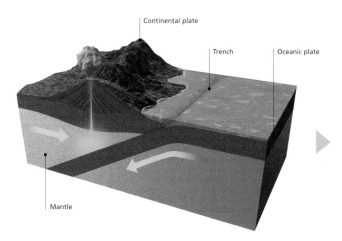

Continental plate

Trench          Oceanic plate

Mantle

## OCEAN MEETS CONTINENT

When an oceanic plate collides with a continental plate, it slides underneath the continent and melts. Rising molten rock pushes through the continental plate and forms volcanoes.

The Torres del Paine, in Chile, are part of the Andes. The mountains grew when the Pacific Plate slid beneath the South American Plate.

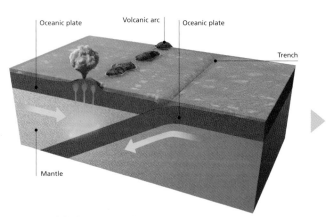

Oceanic plate     Volcanic arc     Oceanic plate

Trench

Mantle

## OCEAN MEETS OCEAN

When two oceanic plates collide, the denser one slides underneath the other. The sinking plate melts and rising molten rock builds a line of islands called a volcanic arc.

Gunung Semeru is one of hundreds of volcanoes in the Indonesian island arc. They were formed when the Australian Plate melted beneath the Pacific Plate.

This giant scar in the ground is the San Andreas Fault, in California, USA. On the left side, the Pacific Plate moves slowly northwest—towards the top and left of the photo. On the right, the North American Plate slides southeast—towards the bottom and right of the photo.

## KINDS OF FAULTS

Tectonic plates meet one another in different ways—pushing together (converging), sliding side by side, or moving away (diverging).

**Himalaya Mountains** When two continents crash together, they do not sink. Their edges buckle high in the air as mountain ranges.

**San Andreas Fault** If two plates slide alongside one another, the sliding movement is rough, and sudden slips cause big earthquakes.

**East African Rift Valley** When a continent is pulled apart, deep cracks slowly widen into long rift valleys. Rivers and lakes form in these valleys.

**Mid-Atlantic Ridge** As continents move apart, basalt lava flows through underwater cracks in the crust. Eventually, an ocean forms with a spreading ridge down its middle.

# Rocks

The rocks around you are on a slow-motion roller coaster. Geological forces thrust them up as mountains, throw them into the air as molten rock, break them into bits and pieces and plunge them deep underground. During this turbulent ride, three kinds of rocks appear. When molten rock cools, igneous rocks form. When rocks on Earth's surface are pummelled to pieces by waves, broken up by ice or scoured to bits by other rocks, the fragments settle in layers and become sedimentary rocks. Meanwhile, deep inside Earth, fierce temperatures and intense pressure cook and squeeze rocks, tranforming them into metamorphic rocks.

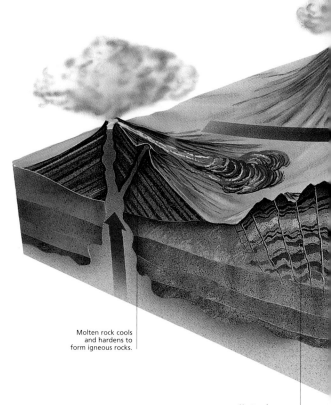

## HOW ROCKS FORM

Rocks are made, destroyed and rebuilt in a perpetual "rock cycle". Erosion wears down mountains and volcanoes, then rivers carry the sediment to the sea. Sediment on the seafloor is pushed into subduction zones, where it melts and provides lava for volcanoes to complete the cycle.

Molten rock cools and hardens to form igneous rocks.

Heat and pressure underground create metamorphic rocks.

## NAME THAT ROCK

Look at the rocks around you. Do they have big or small crystals? Do they lie in flat, straight beds, or are the layers folded and twisted? These are all clues to the rock's origin.

Conglomerate

Milky quartz

Granite

Quartz

Mica

Feldspar

Gneiss

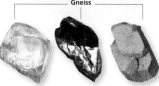

Quartz

Biotite

Feldspar

**SEDIMENTARY ROCK**
Conglomerate is a sedimentary rock. It is made up of pebbles of milky quartz surrounded by sand, clay and iron oxide.

**IGNEOUS ROCK**
Granite, an igneous rock, includes large crystals of quartz, mica and feldspar. Other igneous rocks, such as basalt, have much finer crystals.

**METAMORPHIC ROCK**
The metamorphic rock gneiss has a coarse texture. It looks rather like granite but contains layers of crystals rather than scattered pieces.

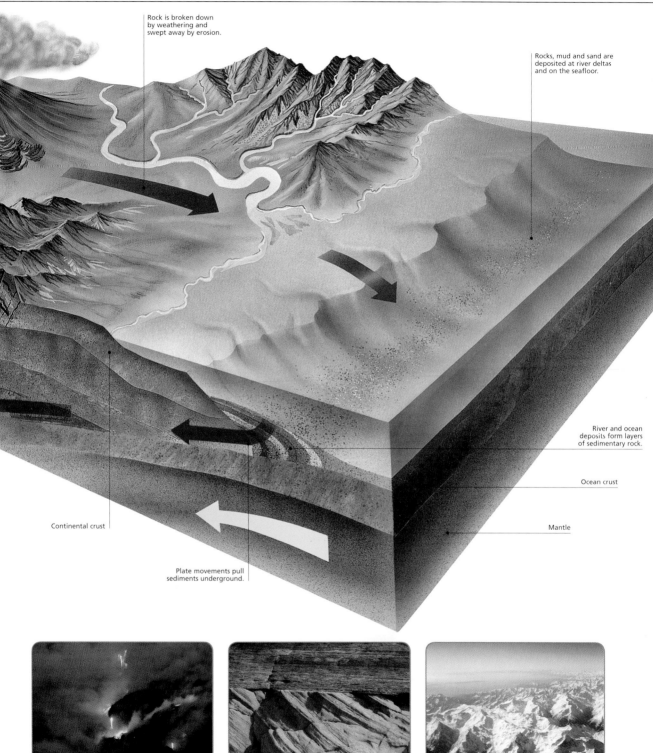

Rock is broken down by weathering and swept away by erosion.

Rocks, mud and sand are deposited at river deltas and on the seafloor.

River and ocean deposits form layers of sedimentary rock.

Ocean crust

Mantle

Continental crust

Plate movements pull sediments underground.

Newborn igneous rock is cooled by the ocean as lava flows to the edge of the Kilauea volcano, Hawaii, USA.

This sedimentary rock in Arizona, USA, shows tilted rocks laid below flat ones. These indicate ancient sand dunes.

The Alps formed when the Tethys Sea squeezed against the Eurasian Plate and the rocks changed with pressure.

# Igneous rock

Igneous rock, or "fire rock", comes from cooling magma. As the molten rock cools, tiny crystals grow, then get bigger. The more time igneous rock has to cool, the bigger the crystals become. Some are even bigger than a car. However, lava that erupts onto Earth's surface and cools quickly has tiny crystals that can be seen only with a microscope. Igneous rock can be tough, and it is often used for buildings and roads.

**Gabbro**
Gabbro is found on the Moon as well as Earth.

**Pumice**
This light, porous rock is used for cleaning, polishing and scouring.

**Andesite**
This rock is named after the Andes mountain range.

**Banded obsidian**
Obsidian may be banded if the thick lava flows a bit before cooling.

**Ignimbrite**

**Obsidian**
Glassy and brittle, obsidian breaks into pieces with razor-sharp edges.

**Volcanic tuff**
Tuff is made from volcanic ash that has solidified and compressed.

**Kimberlite**
Kimberlite erupts from deep in Earth's mantle and sometimes brings diamond crystals with it.

**Rhyolite**
Made of the same materials as granite, rhyolite has smaller crystals because the lava cooled quickly.

**Vesicular basalt**
This common fine-grained grey rock is cooled lava. Sometimes it is full of gas bubbles.

**Obsidian lava**
Obsidian lava is high in silica. This makes it flow slowly like thick soup.

## LOOKING INSIDE

**Basalt** When sliced and backlit, basalt shows both short and long crystals surrounded by fine-grained minerals.

**Gabbro** This has the same composition as basalt, but with much bigger crystals because it cooled slowly underground.

**Pegmatite** Pegmatite cools very slowly and so can have large crystals of minerals and gems.

**Serpentine** Serpentine is a green rock that has been squeezed up along the edges of colliding continents.

◄ **Gabbro**
This dark-coloured rock is made of coarse crystals.

► **Granite**
Granite is made of large crystals that cooled slowly from magma below Earth's surface.

◄ **Andesite**
Andesite is formed from thick, soup-like lava that erupted from volcanoes on the edges of tectonic plates.

◄ **Granite**
Pretty pink feldspar crystals make this granite look different from white granite.

◄ **Pallasite meteorite**
Rich in nickel and iron, this meteorite came from the core of an exploded planet.

## VOLCANIC PLUGS

Plugs and dikes are columns of igneous rock that were once part of a volcano. Molten rock that cools in an old volcano's vent is much harder than the soft ash of the volcano's cone. As the ash erodes away, the volcano's insides are exposed.

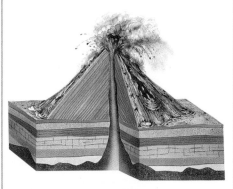

**Eruption** Magma rises to the surface and erupts through the active volcano's main vent to build a steep-sided cone of ash layers and lava.

**Extinction** The volcano eventually becomes extinct, and magma cools inside the vent, hardening from the top down into solid igneous rock.

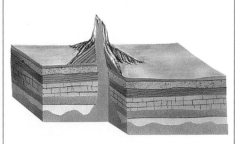

**Erosion** Rainfall erodes the extinct volcano's sides. The runoff carries away soft ash from the cone and uncovers hard lava formations, called plugs and dikes.

# Sedimentary rock

Sedimentary rock is made from grains of rock or mineral from older rocks that are broken by the forces of weathering and erosion. This loose material is called sediment. Running water, wind and ice carry large amounts of sediment. Large rivers can even move boulders. If their journey in a river is long, rocks can end up quite rounded. Eventually the sediment reaches a lake or ocean where it settles in layers, with fine, light pieces travelling further. Sediment that arrives later buries the original layers and, in time, all the material is naturally cemented together or compressed into solid rock.

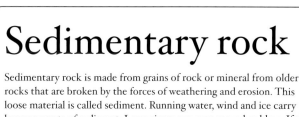

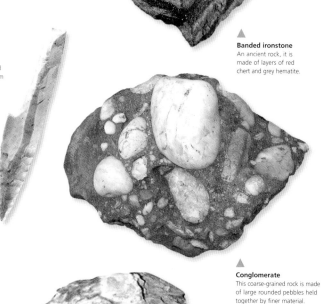

**Banded ironstone**
An ancient rock, it is made of layers of red chert and grey hematite.

**Flint spearheads**
Spearheads were chipped carefully from flint to form a sharp edge.

**Pisolitic ironstone**
Minerals are clumped together in this rock.

**Conglomerate**
This coarse-grained rock is made of large rounded pebbles held together by finer material.

**Chert**
Chert is a tough, fine-grained rock made from material deposited on the ocean floor.

## LOOKING INSIDE

This thin slice of sandstone is seen through a polarizing microscope. It is composed of partly rounded quartz sand grains.

**Breccia**
This breccia consists of sharp rock pieces that erupted from a volcano and then cemented into rock.

**Shale**
Sheets of shale sometimes have brown bands caused by rusty water seeping inward.

**Breccia pebble**
This rounded river pebble of breccia is perhaps on its way to becoming part of a conglomerate.

**Banded jasper**
This mineral is made from quartz and is a banded ironstone rock.

# FORMING A CANYON

Canyons, like the Grand Canyon cut by the Colorado River, Arizona, USA, are excellent places to see layers of sedimentary rock. Harder layers stand out clearly as steep cliffs, while the softer layers erode to more gentle slopes.

**Canyon forms** Tectonic activity lifts the land surface above sea level, giving rivers plenty of energy to cut downward through the rocks.

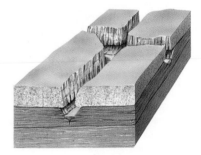

**Canyon deepens** The river cuts down through the sedimentary layers to form a deep, narrow canyon with steep sides.

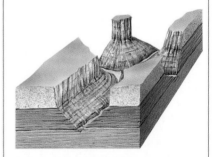

**Canyon widens** Softer layers of rock erode and are undercut, widening the canyon. This also causes the harder layers on top to collapse.

**Flint tools**
Early humans used flint to make useful tools, including knives, spears and arrows.

**Limestone**
The calcium carbonate shells of tiny sea creatures are clearly seen in this piece.

**Evaporite**
When minerals like salt and gypsum crystallize as lakes and seas dry out, they are called evaporites.

**Chert**
Chert, like flint, was used by Stone-Age people to make tools.

**Shale**
Shale is mined to make tiles, bricks and cement.

**Breccia**
Sharp edges on these grains show they have not been carried far from their source.

**Sandstone**
This common rock is made of cemented sand grains, usually quartz.

# Metamorphic rock

Below the surface, rocks are continually changing from one kind to another in Earth's giant pressure cooker. They do not melt, but change slowly while staying solid. This is called metamorphism. Not much seems to happen at first, but then crystals in heated rocks join and grow larger. Metamorphic rocks like quartzite and marble are tougher and stronger than the rocks that formed them. Flat minerals such as mica regrow, turning their flat sides towards the pressure to form slate, phyllite and banded schists. At very high temperatures and pressures, new minerals such as garnet grow.

**Quartzite**
This rock is tougher than its sandstone parent because the quartz grains are joined together by heat.

**Amphibolite**
This consists of volcanic basalt with black amphibole minerals that have been heated and squeezed.

**Blue marble**
The blue-green colours in this marble come from serpentine that mixed with the limestone.

**Banded gneiss**
Easily recognized, this rock has thick, strongly folded bands of black mica and white feldspar.

**Skarn**
The ray-like crystals in this skarn formed when sandy limestone was strongly heated.

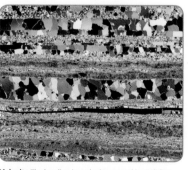

**Micaceous quartzite**
When clay mixed in the original quartz sandstone, it caused mica to grow in this quartzite.

## LOOKING INSIDE

**Gneiss** Under a microscope, this slice shows interlocking crystals of white, black and grey quartz and brown mica.

**Mylonite** The banding in mylonite, caused by a sliding fault, is clearly seen in this magnified rock slice.

**Anthracite coal**
Anthracite is the highest quality coal and has been heated as well as squeezed.

**Phyllite**
The original flat layers of shale rock were bent by pressure into tightly folded bands of phyllite.

**Skarn**
Skarn contains calcite and metal-bearing minerals such as copper.

**Ruby-studded marble**
This marble contains the rare mineral, ruby.

**White marble**
Formed from superheated limestone, marble is used for buildings and carvings.

**Garnet schist**
Minerals such as garnets grow in this rock.

**Granulite**
Its coarse, granular crystals are caused by the minerals heated and squeezed to near melting point.

**Biotite schist**
Layered rock formed by pressure forced these mica crystals to grow in one direction.

# METAMORPHISM

There are two ways that rock can metamorphose, or change: by intense pressure, like being squeezed in a giant vice; or by intense heat, like being cooked by a blowtorch.

## SQUEEZING
Sometimes rocks change when they are squeezed and pushed up into mountains by forces deep within Earth.

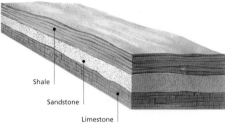

Shale
Sandstone
Limestone

**Flat layers** Sedimentary layers lie flat and straight as squeezing begins.

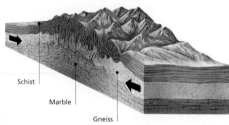

Schist
Marble
Gneiss

**Folds** Intense squeezing folds the layers tightly, like a rumpled carpet.

## BAKING
Magma rises to the surface and cooks the surrounding rock. The rock is hardened and new minerals grow.

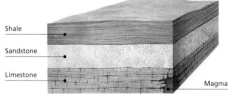

Shale
Sandstone
Limestone
Magma

**Heating** Hot magma begins to rise through the sedimentary rocks.

Hornfels
Quartzite
Marble
Magma

**Baking** Heat from the magma bakes the rocks and changes them.

# Rocks in the landscape

The different kinds of rocks in the landscape are easy to recognize. Flat sedimentary rock layers in canyon cliffs look different from the pointed cones of volcanoes or the folded metamorphic cliffs of a mountain range. Water, wind and ice change the landscape by eroding softer rocks away from harder ones. Granite is polished into smooth, rounded hills and mountains, while old basalt volcanic necks and lava flows form spectacular cliffs of straight, pipe-like columns.

## THE GRAND CANYON

Cut in the landscape by the Colorado River, the Grand Canyon in Arizona, USA, is the largest desert canyon. The layered canyon walls are like the pages of a giant book that dates back more than 2 billion years. To follow the canyon's history, read the labels from the bottom of the illustration to the top.

Granite can weather into smooth, rounded shapes that look like a stack of giant marbles.

Molten basalt from volcanoes cools and shrinks, forming beautiful six-sided columns.

Glaciers have carved steep cliffs out of solid granite mountains in Yosemite National Park, California, USA.

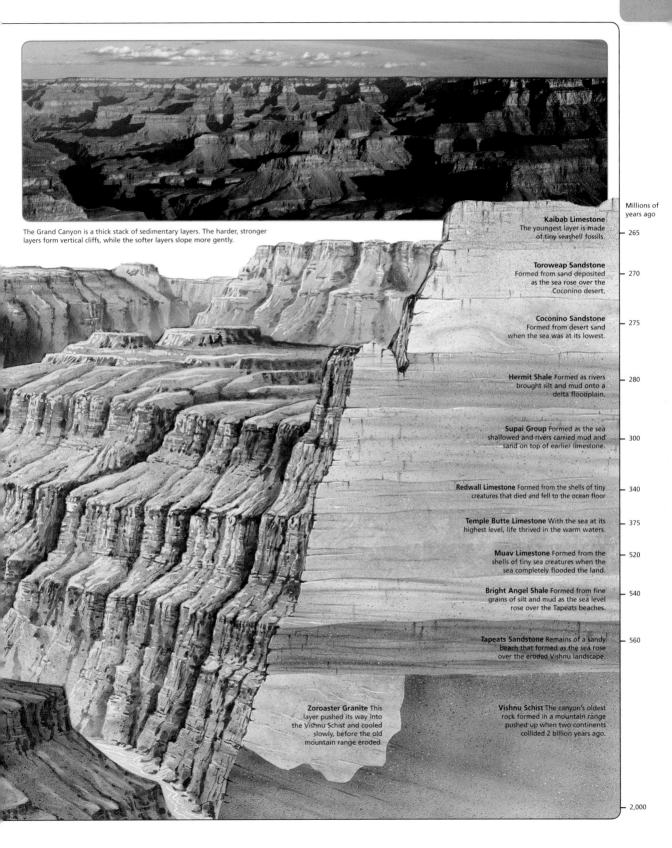

The Grand Canyon is a thick stack of sedimentary layers. The harder, stronger layers form vertical cliffs, while the softer layers slope more gently.

Millions of years ago

**Kaibab Limestone** The youngest layer is made of tiny seashell fossils. — 265

**Toroweap Sandstone** Formed from sand deposited as the sea rose over the Coconino desert. — 270

**Coconino Sandstone** Formed from desert sand when the sea was at its lowest. — 275

**Hermit Shale** Formed as rivers brought silt and mud onto a delta floodplain. — 280

**Supai Group** Formed as the sea shallowed and rivers carried mud and sand on top of earlier limestone. — 300

**Redwall Limestone** Formed from the shells of tiny creatures that died and fell to the ocean floor — 340

**Temple Butte Limestone** With the sea at its highest level, life thrived in the warm waters. — 375

**Muav Limestone** Formed from the shells of tiny sea creatures when the sea completely flooded the land. — 520

**Bright Angel Shale** Formed from fine grains of silt and mud as the sea level rose over the Tapeats beaches. — 540

**Tapeats Sandstone** Remains of a sandy beach that formed as the sea rose over the eroded Vishnu landscape. — 560

**Zoroaster Granite** This layer pushed its way into the Vishnu Schist and cooled slowly, before the old mountain range eroded.

**Vishnu Schist** The canyon's oldest rock formed in a mountain range pushed up when two continents collided 2 billion years ago.

— 2,000

# Using rocks

Humans have long used rocks for tools and for building. Flint and volcanic rock are ideal for making tools because they break with sharp cutting edges. Great monuments, such as pyramids, palaces and temples, were built with granite, marble, slate, sandstone and limestone. Slate can be split into thin sheets and used for roofs or paving. Clay and shale are mined, shaped and fired in ovens to make bricks. Recently, other building materials have been developed, including glass and steel, to replace stone and brick in modern structures. However, polished slabs of granite and marble still decorate important buildings.

## MAKING FLINT TOOLS

Early humans began making stone tools 2.5 million years ago to help them hunt animals for food. Their thumbs let them grip, hold and chip the rocks to make tools such as knives, spear points and axe heads. About 50,000 years ago, humans learned to make better tools with fire.

1. Suitable rocks for tools are selected by smashing river pebbles.

2. The rocks are buried in sand and a fire is lit over the top.

3. Slow heating and cooling make the stone easier to work.

4. Striking the rock with another breaks off thin, sharp flakes.

5. Sharp edges are made when the stone is split in two.

6. Small pieces are sometimes wrapped to protect the fingers.

7. Small pointed flakes are suitable for cutting and shaping.

### FAST FACT

Well-made knives and other tools were highly prized by early humans. The flaked edges of flint chips can be as sharp as steel. They are not as long lasting, however, because flint is brittle and the edges break.

## BUILDING STONEHENGE

England's early inhabitants created the stone rings of Stonehenge about 5,000 years ago. The first pillars and lintels were cut from hard, local sandstone; later ones were made from dolerite brought from Wales.

Levers were used to lift and slide the pillars into holes.

The pillars were pulled with ropes to stand perfectly straight.

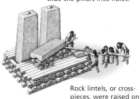

Rock lintels, or cross-pieces, were raised on wooden platforms.

The lintel was shifted from the platform to the upright pillars.

### PYRAMID OF THE MAGICIAN

The Maya started building the Pyramid of the Magician in Uxmal, Mexico, about 1,400 years ago. It was made of stone in five stages over 300 years—each time, a new and bigger pyramid was built on top of the older one.

India's Taj Mahal, made of white marble and decorated with gems, was built in the mid-1600s by Emperor Shah Jahan as a monument to his wife.

The pyramid has an unusual oval shape, steep sides and two temples on the top.

# Minerals

Look closely at a rock and you may notice that it is made up of tiny pieces of one or more minerals. Minerals are the building blocks of rocks. They are solid chemical substances that occur naturally in Earth's crust. They are made up of chemicals called elements. A mineral that contains only one element is called a native element. There are thousands of different minerals, and they come in all colours, shapes and sizes. They include metals such as gold and silver, as well as valuable gemstones such as diamonds. Minerals may form regular, flat-sided shapes called crystals. Often, crystals of different minerals grow together, forming rocks. When minerals have plenty of space to grow, they form large, beautiful crystals.

Fluorite

## COLOUR
Some minerals are always one unmistakable colour, while others, such as fluorite, may have many. Different elements or impurities in the mineral can cause colour variations.

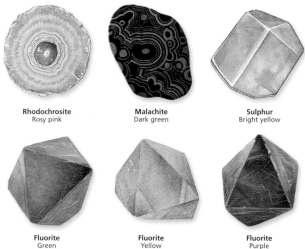

**Rhodochrosite**
Rosy pink

**Malachite**
Dark green

**Sulphur**
Bright yellow

**Fluorite**
Green

**Fluorite**
Yellow

**Fluorite**
Purple

## LUSTRE
Lustre describes how the surface of a mineral looks. It may be silky, metallic, glassy, waxy or just plain dull. The brightest lustre is that of a diamond.

**Kaolinite**
Dull

**Asbestos**
Silky

**Galena**
Metallic

## HABIT
Habit is the shape formed by a mineral's crystals. Like a person, crystals can be short and fat, tall and thin, or somewhere in between.

**Copper**
Tree-like

**Labradorite**
Rock-like

**Garnet**
Equal-sided

**Calcite**
Glassy

**Turquoise**
Waxy

**Amazonite**
Glassy

Strontianite

## FLUORESCENT MINERALS

A few minerals, such as fluorite, strontianite, willemite and calcite, glow beautifully when an ultraviolet light is shone on them.

**EARTH'S CRUST**
About 90 per cent of all the minerals found at Earth's surface are silicates—the building blocks of rocks.

Silicates 90%

Non-silicates 10%

**CRYSTAL SYSTEMS**
Minerals are grouped into six systems, based on the shape of their crystals.

Willemite (green) and calcite (red)

**Vesuvianite**
Tetragonal

**Pyrite**
Cubic

**Amazonite**
Triclinic

**Selenite**
Monoclinic

**Beryl**
Hexagonal

**Barite**
Orthorhombic

**TRANSPARENCY**
Transparency refers to how easy it is to see through a mineral. Many pure minerals are completely see-through. Opaque minerals cannot be seen through at all.

**Quartz**
Transparent

**Moonstone**
Semi-transparent

**Chrysoprase**
Translucent

**Malachite**
Opaque

## MOHS SCALE OF HARDNESS

The Mohs scale of hardness uses 10 minerals, soft to hard, to help determine the hardness of other materials. If you scratch quartz against an unknown material and the quartz leaves a mark, then the mystery material is softer than quartz. You can also use the items on the right-hand side to test for hardness.

1 Talc

2 Gypsum

2.5 Fingernail

3 Calcite

3.5 Copper coin

4 Fluorite

5 Apatite

5.5 Glass

6 Orthoclase

6.5 Steel knife

7 Quartz

8 Topaz

8.5 Emery board

9 Corundum

10 Diamond

# Ornamental minerals and crystals

Ornamental is the name given to attractive minerals and rocks that are not considered precious. These minerals, including agate, chalcedony, hematite and lapis lazuli, are frequently used for carvings and jewelry. Minerals mined to extract metals are called ores, and some, like the silvery cubes of galena (lead ore), can be very pretty. Ores are found in old mine dumps or collected with permission from working mines. Some collectors specialize in beautiful crystals, common minerals like quartz or rare ones like rhodochrosite. Other collectors prefer miniature specimens that are best seen with a microscope.

**Kyanite**
The gem mineral kyanite grows as long, light blue crystals in metamorphic rock.

**Cinnabar**
This mineral is a mercury ore and was used for red pigment called vermilion.

**Desert roses**
These flower-like crystal clusters of gypsum are often found in dry desert lakes.

**Selenite gypsum**
This soft mineral breaks along two cleavage planes.

**Aragonite**
Mollusc and coral shells are made from this mineral, which is a form of calcium carbonate.

**Sulphur**
This pretty mineral, too soft to be a gemstone, is used to make sulphuric acid.

**Lapis lazuli**
This is treasured for its rich blue colour.

**Rhodochrosite**
Crystals of this mineral are rare collectors' items.

## LAPIS LAZULI

Lapis lazuli was crushed to a fine powder and mixed with oil to make a highly prized blue pigment used in early paintings, jewelry, and ornaments. Ancient Egyptians used the powder as eye shadow.

Rare and expensive lapis lazuli was used rarely in paintings, unless it was paid for by the wealthy. In this detail of *The Coronation of the Virgin*, painted in 1430, the robes of church officials contain the pigment.

**Malachite**
This delicately banded, deep green ornamental mineral is an ore of copper.

## SALT LAKES

The mineral we call "salt" and use to flavour food is halite. Before refrigerators were invented, salt was used to preserve food and was as valuable as gold. Halite is deposited on the floor of lakes when salty water evaporates.

This dry lake in Death Valley, California, USA, has a crust of evaporated salt. As the lake water dries up, salt is easily mined by just scraping it up.

**Kaolinite**
This clay mineral is used in ceramics and toothpaste.

**Cuprite**
This attractive copper mineral is an important source of copper metal.

**Wulfenite**
Its crystals may also appear thin and table-like.

**Wulfenite**
This ore forms heavy, yellow crystals.

**Talc**
One of the softest minerals, talc is crushed into fine flakes for talcum powder.

**Galena**
This heavy lead ore forms silvery blocks. The ancient Egyptians used it in eye makeup.

**Rock salt**
This mineral grows in cubic crystals.

**Amazonite**
This blue-green mineral is named for the Amazon River.

**Pegmatite**
This igneous rock, shown here with mica and fluorite, often has large gem crystals.

# Precious and semi-precious minerals

In order to be called a precious gemstone, a mineral must satisfy three conditions: It must be beautiful, durable and rare. Diamond, ruby, sapphire and emerald are the four best-known precious gemstones. Amethyst was once a gemstone and worn by royalty, but when large deposits were found in Brazil, it became too common. Sulphur is a striking yellow colour, but it would break if it were worn. Alexandrite is perhaps the rarest and most prized gemstone because of its strange ability to change colour from vivid green in the day to intense red at night. Semi-precious minerals, like tourmaline and quartz, are beautiful but quite common.

**Azurite**
This intense blue ore of copper is often polished for ornamental use.

**Sapphires**
Blue is the most common colour for sapphires, but orange and yellow stones are also found.

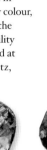

**Diamond**
This precious carbon mineral is the hardest of all gemstones.

**Cat's-eye chrysoberyl**
Fine needle-like fibres in this gem reflect a single bright line of light.

## MAKING DIAMONDS

For carbon to form diamond crystals, it needs extremely high pressure. This is only found more than 150 kilometres (90 mi) below Earth's surface.

**RISING TO THE SURFACE**
Kimberlite magma, formed in the mantle, moves up into the crust, bringing diamonds with it. It must travel quickly or else the diamonds will turn back to black carbon.

**EXPLODING BUBBLES**
Gas bubbles form as the magma nears the surface and begins to boil. Water in the surrounding rocks boils, too, causing an explosion like a shotgun blast.

**AWAITING DISCOVERY**
Afterward, broken rock and magma harden in the volcano's funnel-shaped throat. Erosion carries some of the diamonds to nearby rivers.

**Diamonds** These come from explosive volcanoes that have burst through Earth's crust. Diamond locations are shown in purple.

**Emeralds** Emeralds are mined in several countries, but most come from Colombia in South America. Emerald locations are green.

**Sapphires and rubies** These heavy minerals are found in rivers near corundum-rich rocks. Sapphire locations are blue; rubies, red.

**Fosterite**
A form of olivine, fosterite is the most abundant mineral in Earth's mantle.

**Pyrite**
This iron sulphide mineral, often called fool's gold, is made into beads and jewelry.

**Amethyst**
This is a violet or purple form of quartz.

**Aquamarine**
This delicate blue gemstone is related to emeralds.

**Tourmaline**
With a variable chemical makeup, tourmaline comes in many kinds and colours.

**Imperial topaz**
Deep orange crystals such as this are much harder to find than the pale blue variety.

**Star ruby**
Light shining off tiny needles in this ruby creates a floating star-like reflection.

**Quartz**
Perfectly formed crystals like this are prized by collectors.

**Emerald**
The most valuable emeralds have a rich green colour.

**Quartz**
This transparent gem also occurs in colours such as purple and yellow.

**Galaxy opal**
The colours in this huge opal, discovered in Australia in 1989, cover the spectrum, from red to violet.

## BIRTHSTONES

Birthstones go back to the time of Moses. He made a breastplate for his brother Aaron, a high priest, which was set with 12 coloured gemstones, representing the tribes of Israel. Gemstones later became associated with the months of the year and the zodiac. Birthstones were once believed to have magical power.

**JANUARY**
Garnet

**FEBRUARY**
Amethyst

**MARCH**
Aquamarine

**APRIL**
Diamond

**MAY**
Emerald

**JUNE**
Pearl

**JULY**
Ruby

**AUGUST**
Peridot

**SEPTEMBER**
Sapphire

**OCTOBER**
Opal

**NOVEMBER**
Topaz

**DECEMBER**
Turquoise

# Metals

Native metals, such as gold, tin and copper, are found naturally in their pure form. The discovery that lumps of metal could be beaten or cast made it possible for people to create better tools and weapons. Gold was first worked about 8,000 years ago, but in its pure form it is too soft to be very useful. About 6,000 years ago, people in Mesopotamia discovered that when tin was added to molten copper, a stronger metal called bronze was formed. This metal mixture, or alloy, was durable and long-lasting. When people learned to extract iron from its rocky ore, it replaced bronze.

## WORKING IN BRONZE

Over 3,000 years ago in China, people of the Shang dynasty traded bronze objects. They used clay moulds to mass-produce ornately decorated vases and urns.

Hematite, the most important ore of iron, is heated to extract the metal. It typically has a kidney-like shape.

# NATIVE METALS

## NATIVE METALS

Gold, silver and copper are called native metals because they are found in their pure form. They sometimes occur in the ground as a lump of pure metal, so they are easy to recognize and collect. Other metals, such as aluminium or iron, have to be extracted from ores. Native metals do not break down or weather easily. They can be beaten and shaped into tools, weapons and ornaments.

**GOLD**
Native gold is often found with quartz. It typically has tree-like crystals and a bright metallic lustre.

Gold has long been a precious metal. This death mask was made for Tutankhamun, an Egyptian king who began his reign in 1361 BC at age 9 and died at age 18. The mask is decorated with precious stones.

**COPPER**
Native copper is generally found in branching crystals. It is covered with a blue-green film where it has come in contact with the air.

The Hopewell culture of Ohio, USA, flourished from 300 BC to AD 500. Craftsmen used copper to make artefacts, such as this raven.

Peru was once a rich source of silver. This pendant, engraved with a god wearing a feathered-axe headdress, is from the Chimu people. Their culture reached its peak in the 1400s.

**SILVER**
Native silver forms long, thin crystal branches with a black tarnished skin.

# Fossils

Most of what we know about life on Earth comes from the study of the fossilized remains of living things. Fossils are created over a long period of time. For a plant or animal to become a fossil, it must die in the right place to be covered by sediment and to escape decay, scavenging animals and erosion. The fossil record has many gaps. Organisms with hard body parts— such as shells, skeletons and teeth—are more readily fossilized than soft-bodied animals, and water dwellers are more readily fossilized than land dwellers. The fossil record makes exciting reading. As well as the stories of individual species, it charts the history of the whole living world, showing dead-end lines, periods of rapid growth, and devastating mass extinctions.

**CAUGHT IN SAP**
These gnats were trapped about 40 million years ago by sticky tree sap that hardened to become amber. Many are missing legs and wings, which they lost as they struggled to free themselves.

**NEOGENE**
Humans appear

Bivalve mollusc

*Tyrannosaurus rex*

*Archaeopteryx*

Cycad leaves

Discosauriscus (amphibian)

PALEOGENE

23 mya

65.5 mya

CRETACEOUS

146 mya

JURASSIC

200 mya

TRIASSIC

251 mya

PERMIA

## FROM BONE TO STONE

All living things die, but few become fossils. Fossils form when the hard remains of living creatures are buried and protected beneath sediment. Soft-bodied creatures decompose too quickly to preserve well.

**SAFE FROM SCAVENGERS**
A dinosaur dies. Its body sinks to the bottom of a still lake. The soft parts decay, leaving the hard parts.

**COVERED BY SAND**
The dinosaur's hard parts are preserved, preventing them from decaying or washing away.

# FOSSIL TIMELINE

In this spiralling timeline, each period after the long Precambrian era is highlighted by a fossil typical of that time. Fossils show us how life has changed over the ages, from simple cells to complex creatures like ourselves.

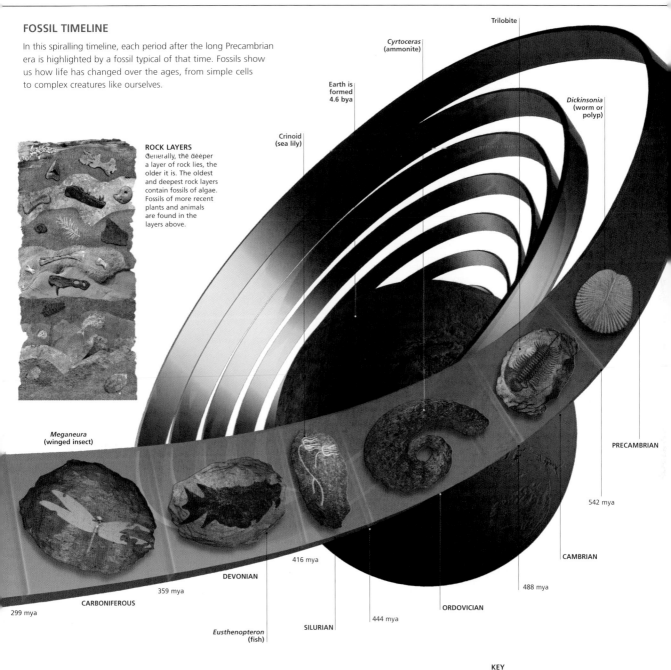

Trilobite

Cyrtoceras (ammonite)

Earth is formed 4.6 bya

Dickinsonia (worm or polyp)

Crinoid (sea lily)

**ROCK LAYERS**
Generally, the deeper a layer of rock lies, the older it is. The oldest and deepest rock layers contain fossils of algae. Fossils of more recent plants and animals are found in the layers above.

PRECAMBRIAN

Meganeura (winged insect)

542 mya

CAMBRIAN

416 mya

DEVONIAN

488 mya

359 mya

CARBONIFEROUS

SILURIAN

ORDOVICIAN

299 mya

444 mya

Eusthenopteron (fish)

**KEY**
**bya** billion years ago    **mya** million years ago

**COMPRESSED LAYERS**
Layers of sediment build up and flatten the skeleton; this slowly hardens into solid rock.

**UPLIFT AND EROSION**
After millions of years, the rock rises again to the surface and the bones are exposed.

# Plants and invertebrates

When plants become fossils, they are petrified, or turned to stone. The fine details of delicate leaves can be preserved in mudstone. More durable plant parts, such as tree trunks and branches, can survive rough conditions. These are found in sandstone and volcanic ash. Invertebrates—animals without backbones—that have hard body parts like shells or spines are more commonly found as fossils than their soft-bodied relatives. Molluscs make up one of the largest groups in the animal kingdom, and their fossils are common. These include clams and mussels, snails, and ammonites. Coral fossils may be found in limestone.

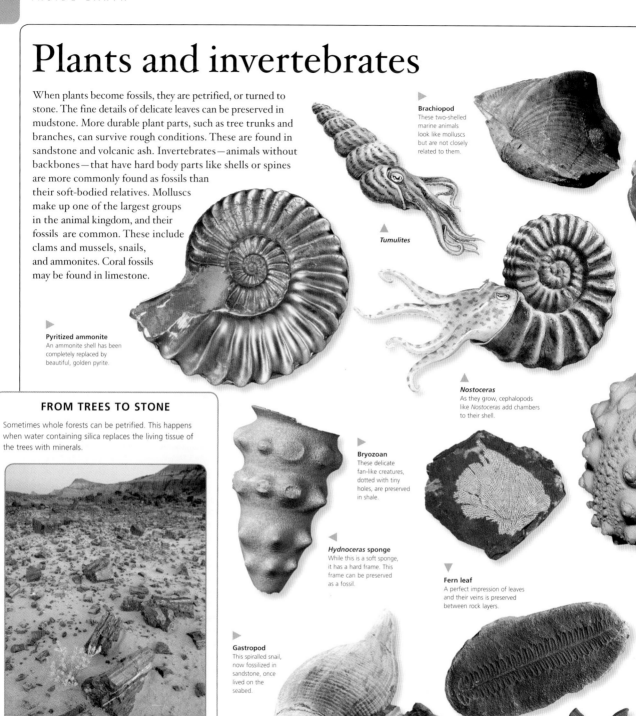

**Brachiopod**
These two-shelled marine animals look like molluscs but are not closely related to them.

*Tumulites*

**Pyritized ammonite**
An ammonite shell has been completely replaced by beautiful, golden pyrite.

**Nostoceras**
As they grow, cephalopods like *Nostoceras* add chambers to their shell.

**Bryozoan**
These delicate fan-like creatures, dotted with tiny holes, are preserved in shale.

**Hydnoceras sponge**
While this is a soft sponge, it has a hard frame. This frame can be preserved as a fossil.

**Fern leaf**
A perfect impression of leaves and their veins is preserved between rock layers.

**Gastropod**
This spiralled snail, now fossilized in sandstone, once lived on the seabed.

**Hexactinellid sponge**
This is a fragment of hard sponge skeleton.

## FROM TREES TO STONE

Sometimes whole forests can be petrified. This happens when water containing silica replaces the living tissue of the trees with minerals.

Pieces of petrified wood from the Triassic are scattered over the ground at Petrified Forest National Park, Arizona, USA.

**Trilobites**
Trilobites lived in the oceans. They had well-defined body sections.

**Burgess shale crinoid**
This animal used tentacles to bring food towards its central mouth.

*Coeloptychium* sponge

Ammonite

**Ginkgo wood**
This section of fossilized wood from an ancient ginkgo tree shows its growth rings.

**Spiny urchin**
Sea urchin spines usually fall off before the shell is fossilized.

**Amber**
These gnats, now preserved in amber, flew in a coniferous forest 40 million years ago.

*Mawsonites*
Jellyfish are rarely found as fossils because their soft bodies decompose quickly.

Ammonite

Crinoids, or sea lilies, had spiny skin and were attached to the seabed by a stem.

This fossilized maple leaf in stone shows a clear picture of its structure.

Fossilized stems and berries can reveal a lot about this basswood tree.

Growth chambers are clearly visible inside these ammonite shell fossils.

# Vertebrates

Vertebrates are animals with an internal skeleton of hard bones. The oldest known specimens appeared about 500 million years ago. Vertebrate fossils include fish, amphibians, reptiles, dinosaurs, birds, mammals and humans. Vertebrates, especially complete specimens, are not found as often as plant or invertebrate fossils. This is because their remains were usually eaten by scavengers soon after they died, and the bones were scattered.

*Archaeopteryx*, the first bird, lived during the Jurassic. Like its modern descendants it had light, hollow bones for speed and agility.

This squirrel-like rodent, an early mammal, ate seeds and leaves like today's squirrels.

This frog lived 49 million years ago. The fossil was found in the Grube Messel quarry, Germany.

The fossil of this ancient python shows that it was very similar to modern pythons.

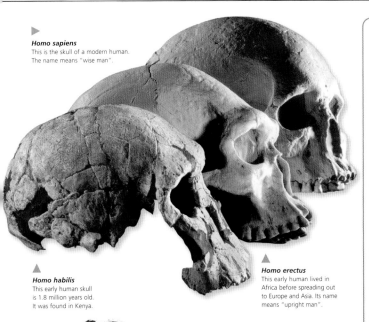

**Homo sapiens**
This is the skull of a modern human. The name means "wise man".

▲
**Homo habilis**
This early human skull is 1.8 million years old. It was found in Kenya.

▲
**Homo erectus**
This early human lived in Africa before spreading out to Europe and Asia. Its name means "upright man".

▶
**Tyrannosaurus rex**
This massive, meat-eating dinosaur roamed North America more than 65 million years ago. Its skull could reach 1.2 metres (4 ft) in length.

▼
**Jurassic fish**
So many fossils together usually means something killed these fish at once. Perhaps a volcano erupted or their lake evaporated.

## FROZEN IN TIME

Whole animals can be perfectly preserved in ice if they freeze quickly and remain frozen. Woolly mammoths, rhinoceros and bison from 10,000 years ago have been found in Siberia. Their last meal remains in their stomachs.

**Iceman** The frozen body of a 45-year-old man, nicknamed Otzi the Iceman, was found in a melting glacier in the Austrian Alps in 1991. He lived about 5,300 years ago and died in a fight.

**Inuit baby** This Inuit baby died 500 years ago and was left in an icy cave in Greenland. The child's body and clothes were perfectly preserved in the dry, cold air of the cave.

# Reconstructing fossils

Recreating an animal from its fossilized remains is like putting together a big jigsaw puzzle. It takes a lot of patience to find the fossil pieces of the puzzle. Vertebrates can have more than 200 bones, the fossils of which may be spread over a large area. Each piece must be numbered and its location mapped before it can be prised free from the rock. Delicate fossils need to be coated in plaster to protect them before they are moved. In the laboratory, it takes many hours of work to clean and prepare the fossils. Only then can the jigsaw pieces be put together, and missing pieces added, to reconstruct the original animal.

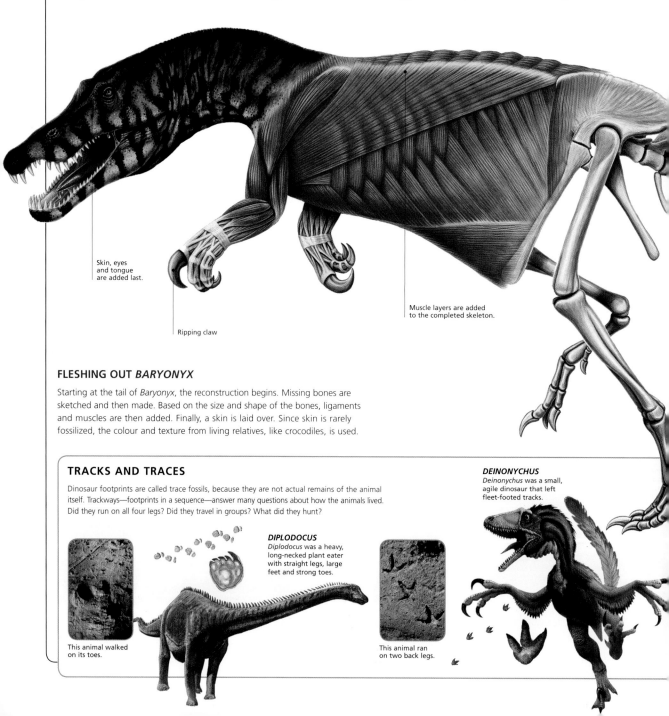

Skin, eyes and tongue are added last.

Ripping claw

Muscle layers are added to the completed skeleton.

## FLESHING OUT *BARYONYX*

Starting at the tail of *Baryonyx*, the reconstruction begins. Missing bones are sketched and then made. Based on the size and shape of the bones, ligaments and muscles are then added. Finally, a skin is laid over. Since skin is rarely fossilized, the colour and texture from living relatives, like crocodiles, is used.

## TRACKS AND TRACES

Dinosaur footprints are called trace fossils, because they are not actual remains of the animal itself. Trackways—footprints in a sequence—answer many questions about how the animals lived. Did they run on all four legs? Did they travel in groups? What did they hunt?

### DIPLODOCUS
*Diplodocus* was a heavy, long-necked plant eater with straight legs, large feet and strong toes.

This animal walked on its toes.

This animal ran on two back legs.

### DEINONYCHUS
*Deinonychus* was a small, agile dinosaur that left fleet-footed tracks.

# FOSSIL DETECTIVES

*Parasaurolophus* was a plant-eating dinosaur that lived in the late Cretaceous, between about 83 and 65 million years ago. It lived at a dangerous time when huge predators, such as *Tyrannosaurus*, were at large. It probably lived in herds for protection.

Air flowed through the hollow crest.

Scientists have studied the fossil to work out how *Parasaurolophus* used its unusual bony crest. They believe it was like a trumpet that warned others when predators were near.

The first fossil skeleton of *Parasaurolophus* was discovered in 1921 in Alberta, Canada. It is one of the most complete dinosaur fossils ever found and has been carefully preserved.

Missing bones are replaced with plaster.

## THE FOSSIL SITE
The bones of *Baryonyx* were dug out of a clay pit in southern England. They were laid out in an outline of the animal so the missing pieces could be reconstructed.

Location of *Baryonyx* fossils

Original fossil remains

## CHASMOSAURUS
This heavy, plant-eating dinosaur had horns and an armour-plated head for protection.

## ALLOSAURUS
It was a large, but agile hunter with long, muscular legs for fast running.

This heavy animal walked on four legs.

This three-toed animal ran on two legs.

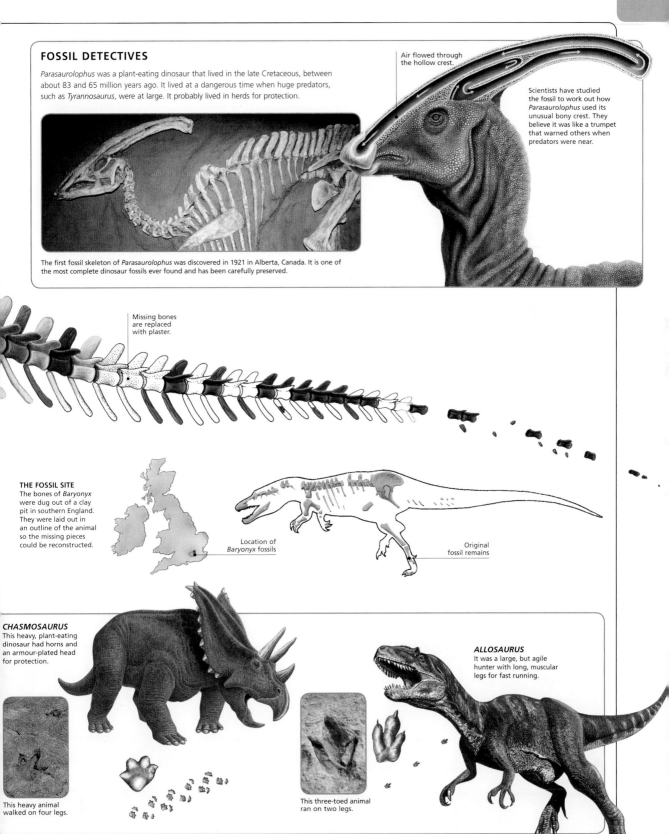

Dynamic Earth

# Volcanoes

Ash cloud

Lava erupts
through crater

Pyroclastic flow:
torrent of hot lava,
ash and gas

Fissure

Dike: a vertical
channel of magma

Lava flow
from side vent

Laccolith: a mass
of magma that pushes
rock layers upward

Sill: a sheet of magma
that forms between
layers of rock

Lava rises through
central vent

Extinct magma
chamber

Magma rises from pool
of molten rock called
magma chamber

**ANATOMY OF A VOLCANO**
A volcano consists of the
magma chamber or reservoir
that is the source of the
magma under the surface,
the vents by which the magma
reaches the surface and the
lava and other material ejected
by eruptions.

Volcanoes form where magma—incredibly hot, liquid rock—rises from Earth's upper mantle and collects in a chamber just below the crust. As more magma arrives, the pressure inside the chamber increases until the magma rises through fissures and overflows in an eruption. When it reaches the surface, magma becomes lava.

The type of eruption depends on the composition of the lava. If it is thick and contains large amounts of gas, the eruption releases cinders and clouds of ash in an explosion. If the lava is thin with little gas, it flows across the surface. If the magma comes into contact with water underground, the volcano explodes violently.

## KINDS OF VOLCANOES

A fissure volcano forms where lava erupts along a fracture in Earth's surface. A shield volcano occurs when erupted material builds a low-angle hill. A cinder cone is made from cinders and ash erupted from a central vent. A composite volcano is made from layers of lava, ash and material eroded from the sides of the cone.

**FISSURE VOLCANO**
Fracture
Fissure

**SHIELD VOLCANO**
Magma chamber
Low-angle cone

**CINDER CONE**
Steep cone
Vent

**COMPOSITE VOLCANO**
Steep cone

### HOW A LAVA TUBE FORMS
Lava hardens on exposure to air, but it continues to flow through tunnels beneath the surface. When lava stops flowing, the tunnels remain as hollow lava tubes up to 30 metres (100 ft) wide and 15 metres (50 ft) high.

**1 Lava rivers** These develop a hard skin soon after the lava starts flowing.
Cooling skin
Hot interior

**2 Hard skin** This becomes harder and forms a tube through which the lava keeps flowing.
Lava river
Hard tube

**3 Hollow tube** A hollow tube is left when the lava stops flowing.
Hollow lava tube

Lava tube

### FLOWING LAVA

Magma is hot. When it reaches the surface, its temperature is usually about 1,200°C (2,200°F), which is why it glows red. Lava flowing down the sides of a volcano and across the nearby land is a mixture of molten rock and blocks of solid rock. Gases bubble out of cooling lava.

**Pahoehoe**
Lava that forms a smooth, flowing surface

**A'a**
Lava that hardens into lumps

# Hot-spot volcanoes

Beneath Earth's crust, and far from the edges of tectonic plates, there are places where very hot
material in the mantle rises all the way to the base of the crust. These are known as hot spots.
The mantle rock is so hot it melts the solid rock and forms a magma chamber. Eventually,
the magma erupts to the surface as a volcano. Tectonic plates move, but hot spots remain
in the same place. When the plates move over a hot spot, a chain of volcanoes is created.
An ocean hot spot can produce a line of volcanic islands. The volcanoes closest to the
hot spot are active; those further away are extinct.

## THE HOT-SPOT CYCLE

This diagram illustrates the birth, life and death of hot-spot volcanoes.
At the front, active volcanoes are erupting above the hot spot. Behind
lie older volcanoes that have been worn down by erosion. Those whose
rims are fringed with coral are called atolls. Those that lie underwater
are called seamounts.

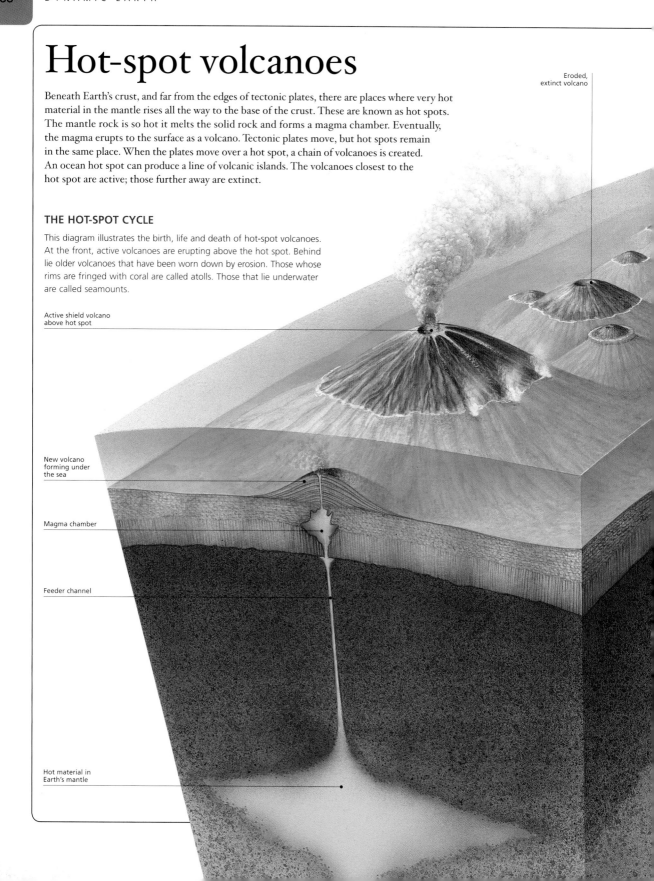

Eroded,
extinct volcano

Active shield volcano
above hot spot

New volcano
forming under
the sea

Magma chamber

Feeder channel

Hot material in
Earth's mantle

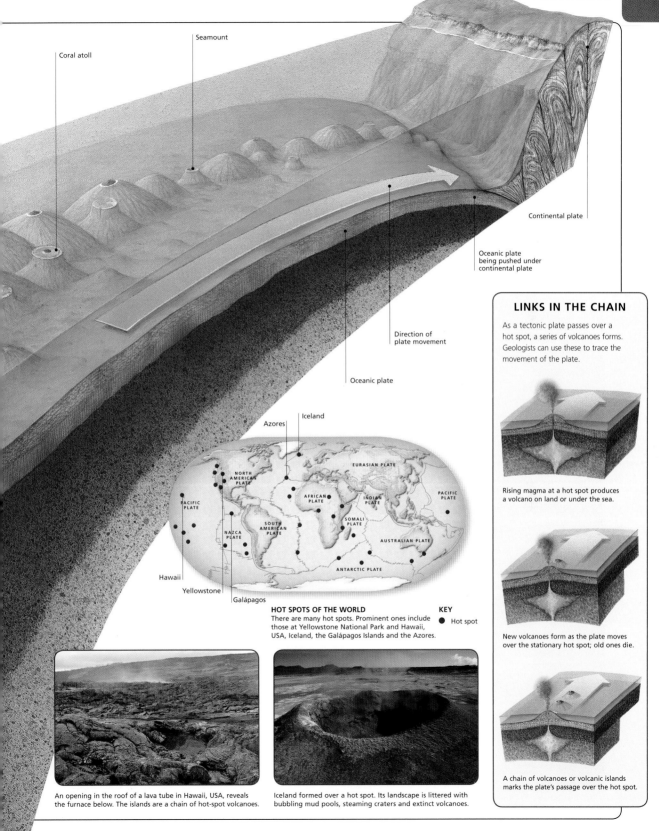

Coral atoll

Seamount

Continental plate

Oceanic plate
being pushed under
continental plate

Direction of
plate movement

Oceanic plate

## LINKS IN THE CHAIN

As a tectonic plate passes over a
hot spot, a series of volcanoes forms.
Geologists can use these to trace the
movement of the plate.

Rising magma at a hot spot produces
a volcano on land or under the sea.

New volcanoes form as the plate moves
over the stationary hot spot; old ones die.

A chain of volcanoes or volcanic islands
marks the plate's passage over the hot spot.

Azores   Iceland

EURASIAN PLATE

NORTH
AMERICAN
PLATE

AFRICAN
PLATE

INDIAN
PLATE

PACIFIC
PLATE

PACIFIC
PLATE

SOMALI
PLATE

SOUTH
AMERICAN
PLATE

NAZCA
PLATE

AUSTRALIAN PLATE

ANTARCTIC PLATE

Hawaii

Yellowstone

Galápagos

### HOT SPOTS OF THE WORLD

**KEY**
● Hot spot

There are many hot spots. Prominent ones include
those at Yellowstone National Park and Hawaii,
USA, Iceland, the Galápagos Islands and the Azores.

An opening in the roof of a lava tube in Hawaii, USA, reveals
the furnace below. The islands are a chain of hot-spot volcanoes.

Iceland formed over a hot spot. Its landscape is littered with
bubbling mud pools, steaming craters and extinct volcanoes.

# Kilauea

Kilauea, on the Big Island of Hawaii, is one of the world's most active volcanoes. It may have started erupting 600,000 years ago and has been erupting continuously since 1983. It can throw fountains of lava up to 600 metres (2,000 ft) into the air. The volcano makes up more than 13 per cent of the area of the island, and its plumbing reaches 60 kilometres (37 mi) deep into Earth. Because it is constantly erupting, Kilauea is still growing. But it is also falling apart as landslides carry huge amounts of debris away from the centre of the volcano towards the sea. According to Hawaiian legend, Kilauea is home to Pele, the volcano goddess.

### HAWAII'S BIG ISLAND

Kilauea is located on Hawaii's Big Island. It is one of five volcanoes on the island. It is not the largest of these volcanoes—that honour goes to Mauna Loa—but it is the most active. Kilauea is also the most visited volcano on the planet.

Fountains of lava erupt from one of Kilauea's many craters and vents. Kilauea has been erupting constantly for more than 25 years.

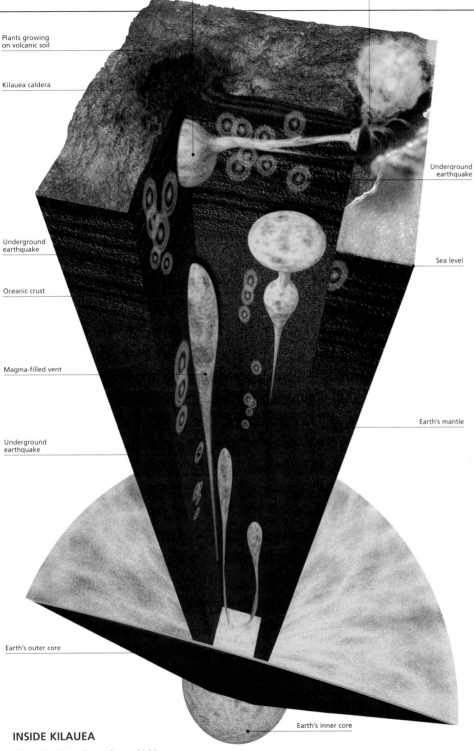

Magma chamber
near Earth's surface

Site of current
eruption

Plants growing
on volcanic soil

Kilauea caldera

Underground
earthquake

Underground
earthquake

Oceanic crust

Sea level

Magma-filled vent

Earth's mantle

Underground
earthquake

Earth's outer core

Earth's inner core

## INSIDE KILAUEA

Kilauea is a Hawaiian-style, or shield,
volcano. It shoots out almost continuous
eruptions of lava that can travel up to
10 kilometres per hour (6 mph).

## TYPES OF ERUPTIONS

There are five main kinds of volcanic eruptions.
Scientists name and describe them as follows:

**Hawaiian** Large amounts of runny lava erupt
and produce wide, low volcanoes.

**Peléean** Blocks of thick, sticky lava are
followed by a burning cloud of ash and gas.

**Strombolian** Small, sticky lava bombs and
blocks, ash, gas and glowing cinders erupt.

**Vulcanian** Violent explosions shoot out very
thick lava and large lava bombs.

**Plinian** Cinders, gas and ash are thrown high
into the air.

# Volcanoes around the world

Most volcanoes occur along the edges of tectonic plates. Where oceanic and continental plates collide, the denser oceanic plate is pushed under the lighter continental plate, a process known as "subduction". As well, new crust is continually formed by magma that rises to the surface and forces oceanic plates to separate. Both types of interaction between plates produce volcanoes and earthquakes. All the boundaries to the Pacific Plate are active and form a nearly continuous line of oceanic volcanic mountains extending in a horseshoe shape for 40,000 kilometres (25,000 mi). The volcanoes surrounding the ocean are often described as a "Ring of Fire". The ring includes many famous volcanoes—Fuji, Pinatubo, Tambora, Krakatau and Mount St. Helens.

## DANGER ZONES

Three-quarters of the world's active volcanoes, including some of the most violent, occur in the ring that surrounds the Pacific Ocean. The northward movement of the African Plate into the Eurasian Plate has created volcanoes in southern Europe, and in 1963 a volcano on the Mid-Atlantic Ridge produced the island of Surtsey, Iceland.

**DUST AND ASH**
Clouds of gas, dust and ash from extremely violent volcanic eruptions can sometimes rise above the troposphere and reach the stratosphere, where they can remain for months. They stop sunlight reaching Earth, and the world's climate becomes colder.

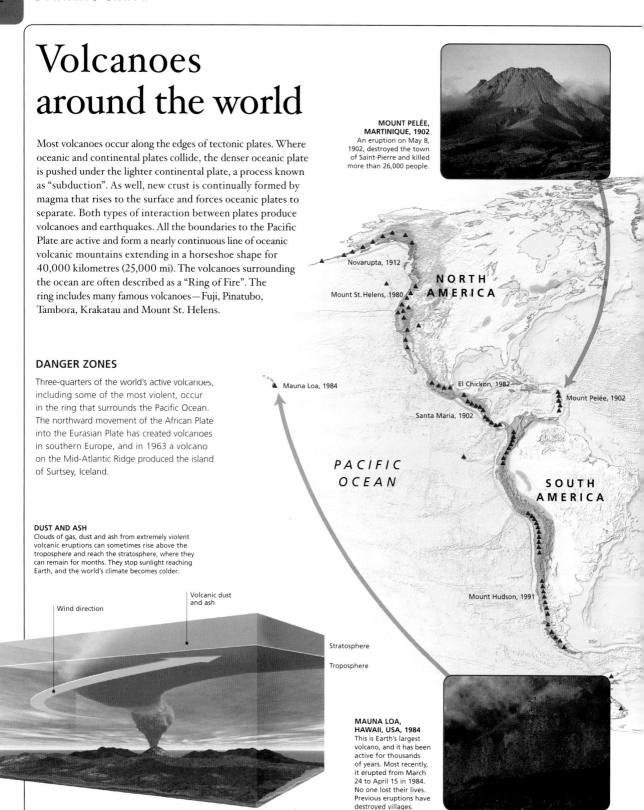

**MOUNT PELÉE, MARTINIQUE, 1902**
An eruption on May 8, 1902, destroyed the town of Saint-Pierre and killed more than 26,000 people.

Novarupta, 1912

**NORTH AMERICA**

Mount St. Helens, 1980

Mauna Loa, 1984

El Chickon, 1982

Mount Pelée, 1902

Santa Maria, 1902

**PACIFIC OCEAN**

**SOUTH AMERICA**

Mount Hudson, 1991

Wind direction

Volcanic dust and ash

Stratosphere

Troposphere

**MAUNA LOA, HAWAII, USA, 1984**
This is Earth's largest volcano, and it has been active for thousands of years. Most recently, it erupted from March 24 to April 15 in 1984. No one lost their lives. Previous eruptions have destroyed villages.

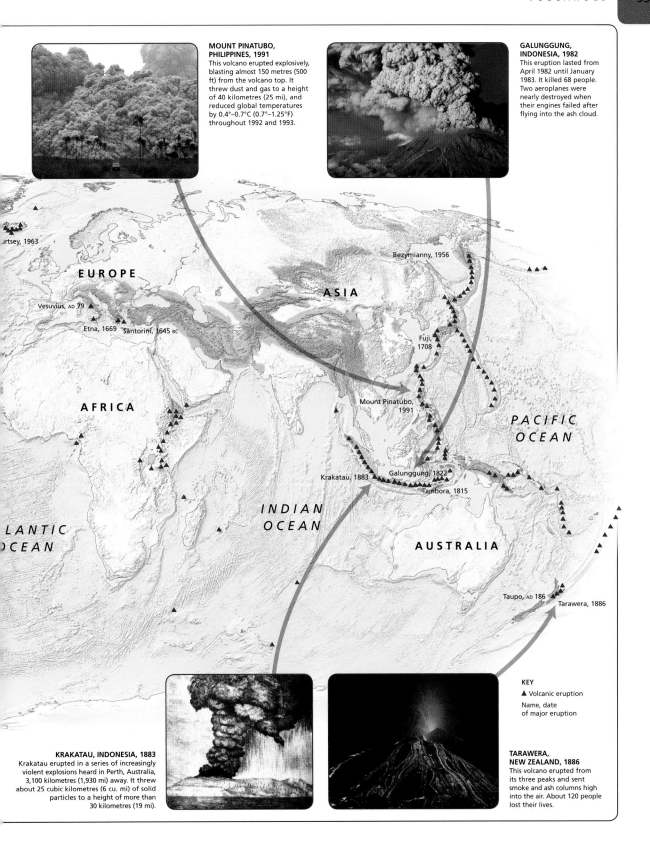

**MOUNT PINATUBO, PHILIPPINES, 1991**
This volcano erupted explosively, blasting almost 150 metres (500 ft) from the volcano top. It threw dust and gas to a height of 40 kilometres (25 mi), and reduced global temperatures by 0.4°–0.7°C (0.7°–1.25°F) throughout 1992 and 1993.

**GALUNGGUNG, INDONESIA, 1982**
This eruption lasted from April 1982 until January 1983. It killed 68 people. Two aeroplanes were nearly destroyed when their engines failed after flying into the ash cloud.

EUROPE

ASIA

AFRICA

PACIFIC OCEAN

INDIAN OCEAN

AUSTRALIA

ATLANTIC OCEAN

urtsey, 1963

Vesuvius, AD 79

Etna, 1669     Santorini, 1645 BC

Bezymianny, 1956

Fuji, 1708

Mount Pinatubo, 1991

Krakatau, 1883     Galunggung, 1822

Tambora, 1815

Taupo, AD 186     Tarawera, 1886

**KEY**
▲ Volcanic eruption
  Name, date
  of major eruption

**KRAKATAU, INDONESIA, 1883**
Krakatau erupted in a series of increasingly violent explosions heard in Perth, Australia, 3,100 kilometres (1,930 mi) away. It threw about 25 cubic kilometres (6 cu. mi) of solid particles to a height of more than 30 kilometres (19 mi).

**TARAWERA, NEW ZEALAND, 1886**
This volcano erupted from its three peaks and sent smoke and ash columns high into the air. About 120 people lost their lives.

# Volcanic landscapes

When volcanoes spill molten rock across Earth's surface, they remake the surrounding landscape. The Deccan Plateau in India consists of a sheet of volcanic basalt rock that covers more than 500,000 square kilometres (193,000 sq. mi) and is more than 1.6 kilometres (1 mi) thick. The plateau was formed when, over a period of a million years, lava from a hot-spot volcano spread across a third of India and hardened. Eroded volcanoes are dramatic landscape features. Calderas, which are created when the top of a volcano collapses into its empty magma chamber, often fill with water and form distinctive lakes, called crater lakes, that may be tens of kilometres across. Volcanic gases often give these lakes unusual bluish green colours.

With the active volcano Gunung Semeru (the highest point on Java, Indonesia) in the distance and the smoking Gunung Bromo caldera in the foreground, this landscape is entirely volcanic.

## READING THE CLUES

Landscapes contain evidence of past volcanic activity. The erosion of softer rocks exposes volcanic basalt, plugs of solidified lava and dikes of hardened magma. Sills are small lava sheets, usually up to approximately 30 metres (100 ft) thick. Calderas may have small cinder cones, or craters, from later eruptions. When a caldera floods, its cinder cone becomes an island.

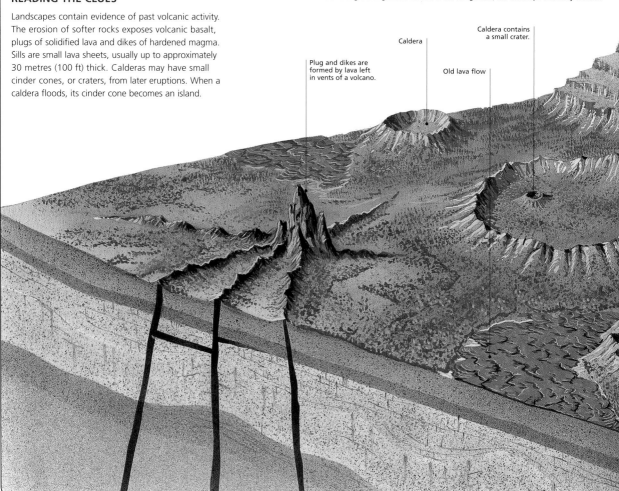

Plug and dikes are formed by lava left in vents of a volcano.

Caldera

Old lava flow

Caldera contains a small crater.

# THE GIANT'S CAUSEWAY AND SHIP ROCK

### MAKING COLUMNS

**Cooling lava**
Lava cools from the surface downward and shrinks as it hardens.

**Vertical cracks**
Cracks appear and grow towards each other and the hot centre.

**Columns**
These form when the cracks join up with each other.

The Giant's Causeway in Northern Ireland is an exposure of basalt columns.

### MAKING PLUGS

**Active volcano**
Magma rises through a vent in the volcano.

**Eruption ends**
When the magma chamber is empty, any magma still in the vent solidifies.

Ship Rock

**Plug forms**
Erosion removes the outer layers of the volcano and exposes the lava as a plug.

Ship Rock, New Mexico, USA, is a plug that formed inside a volcano.

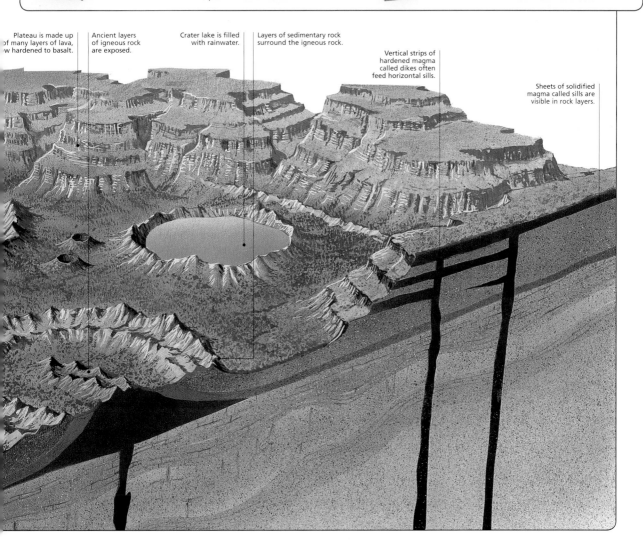

Plateau is made up of many layers of lava, now hardened to basalt.

Ancient layers of igneous rock are exposed.

Crater lake is filled with rainwater.

Layers of sedimentary rock surround the igneous rock.

Vertical strips of hardened magma called dikes often feed horizontal sills.

Sheets of solidified magma called sills are visible in rock layers.

# Craters and calderas

Craters are the funnel-shaped hollows or cavities that form at the openings, or vents, of volcanoes. The simplest craters occur on the top of volcanic vents and usually have a diameter of about 1 kilometre (½ mi) or less. Sometimes, magma melts some of the rock around the mouth and carries it away, to create a crater at the side of the volcano. A caldera is formed when an eruption empties the magma chamber and its roof caves in because it is not strong enough to support the weight of the volcano above. Later the volcano may become active again, erupting through the same vent to form a cinder cone inside the caldera.

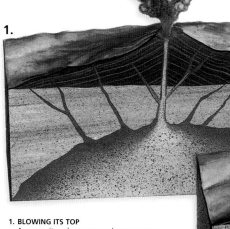

1.

**1. BLOWING ITS TOP**
A composite volcano grows above a magma chamber beneath the surface. Ash, gases and lava erupt through a central vent.

**2. VIOLENT ERUPTION**
The eruption becomes more violent, throwing ash and gas high into the air. The eruption reduces the amount of magma in the chamber.

2.

## HOW A CALDERA FORMS

Calderas are huge craters formed by a massive volcanic eruption. They are often more than 5 kilometres (3 mi) in diameter. The world's largest, Mount Aso, Japan, is 27 kilometres (17 mi) long and 16 kilometres (10 mi) wide.

Mount Aso in Japan is the country's largest active volcano, standing 1,592 metres (5,223 ft) above sea level. Its caldera measures 114 kilometres (71 mi) if you walk around the rim.

A lake fills the caldera of Hare Shetan, Ethiopia. The aerial view reveals its circular shape and steep sides.

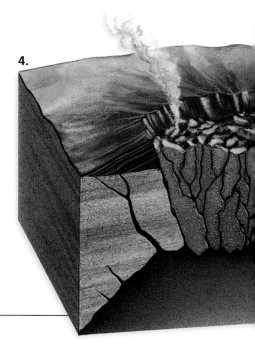

4.

**3.**

**3. THE CLIMAX**
The magma chamber is partly emptied.
Magma sinks below the roof of the magma
chamber, leaving an empty space.

**4. THE COLLAPSE**
The roof of the magma chamber can no longer
support the weight of the volcano. It collapses
downward along faults around the central vent.

## VOLCANOES ON OTHER PLANETS

Space probes have found nine volcanoes on Mars; five on Venus; four on Io, a moon of Jupiter; and many on Neptune's moon Triton.
Not all of these resemble volcanoes on Earth. Some erupt sulphur, and volcanoes on Triton erupt liquid nitrogen or methane.

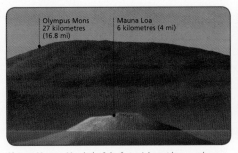

Olympus Mons
27 kilometres
(16.8 mi)

Mauna Loa
6 kilometres (4 mi)

Olympus Mons on Mars is the Solar System's largest known volcano,
more than four times higher than Mauna Loa, Hawaii.

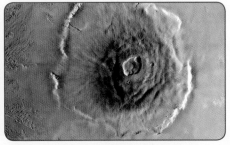

From above, the extent of Olympus Mons' lava flows can be seen. It is
500 kilometres (310 mi) across, with a caldera 80 kilometres (50 mi) wide.

# Earthquakes

An earthquake is a violent release of energy in Earth's crust. When large rock masses move suddenly along faults below ground, the movement shakes the ground above. Earthquakes often happen because rocks are being pushed in two directions, usually due to the movement of tectonic plates. Volcanic activity can also cause earthquakes. The place in the crust where the break happens is called the hypocentre. The place on the surface immediately above the hypocentre is the epicentre. A shallow earthquake has a hypocentre less than 70 kilometres (44 mi) below the surface, intermediate ones occur 70–300 kilometres (44–186 mi) below, and deep earthquakes happen at depths greater than 300 kilometres (186 mi).

People in Izmit, Turkey, search through the rubble for their possessions after the 1999 earthquake. This quake killed more than 17,000 people.

## MEASURING EARTHQUAKES

The magnitude of an earthquake is usually measured by the Richter scale, developed by Charles Richter in 1935, based on the amount of energy released. The Mercalli scale is an alternative measure, devised in 1897 by Giuseppe Mercalli. It divides earthquakes into 12 categories, according to observations of the damage caused.

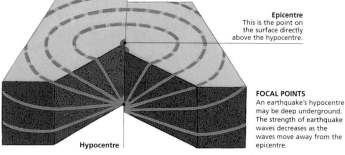

**Epicentre**
This is the point on the surface directly above the hypocentre.

**Hypocentre**

**FOCAL POINTS**
An earthquake's hypocentre may be deep underground. The strength of earthquake waves decreases as the waves move away from the epicentre.

## MERCALLI SCALE

I   People feel no movement beneath them.

II  People on upper floors feel slight movement.

III Hanging objects swing, everyone feels the movement.

IV  Windows and doors rattle, stationary cars rock.

V   Sleeping people wake, doors swing, dishes break.

VI  Walking difficult, trees shake, slight structural damage.

VII Standing difficult, damage to poorly constructed buildings.

VIII Chimneys fall, tree branches break, furniture overturns.

IX  Structural damage to most buildings, ground cracks.

X   Large ground cracks, landslides, most buildings damaged.

XI  Buildings collapse, underground pipes fracture.

XII Ground moves in waves, widespread devastation.

I    II    III    IV    V    VI    VII

**THE RICHTER SCALE**
Each step on the scale is a tenfold increase in earthquake power. That means that magnitude 7
is 10 times stronger than magnitude 6 and 100 times stronger than magnitude 5.

# JAPANESE EARTHQUAKES

Under the islands of Japan, three tectonic plates jostle for position. To the southeast, the Philippine Plate slides beneath the Eurasian Plate. In the east, the Pacific Plate dives under the Eurasian Plate and the Philippine Plate as well. As a result, Japanese people experience regular earthquakes.

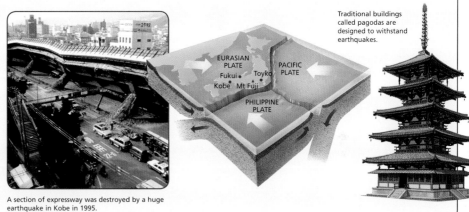

Traditional buildings called pagodas are designed to withstand earthquakes.

Traditionally, the Japanese blamed earthquakes on Namazu, a catfish. Usually the deity Kashima held Namazu down, but if he was distracted, Namazu thrashed about, shaking the ground.

A section of expressway was destroyed by a huge earthquake in Kobe in 1995.

**SEISMIC WAVES**
There are different kinds of earthquake waves. The most dangerous are surface waves.

**Surface waves**
These make the surface move from side to side like a snake, or up and down like an ocean wave.

**P-waves**
The first waves to arrive are called P-waves. They push and pull rocks in the ground.

**S-waves**
S-waves then move rocks up and down and from side to side.

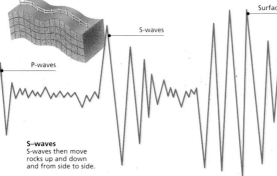
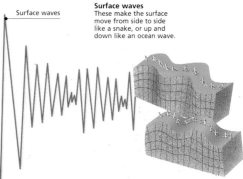
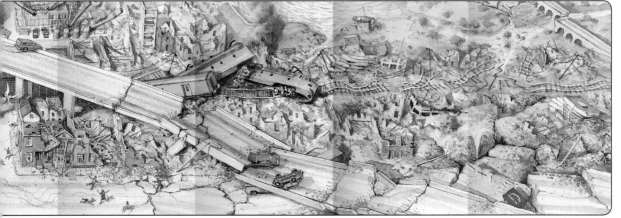

IX    X    XI    XII

# Tsunamis

A tsunami—is Japanese for "harbour wave"—begins on the ocean floor with an earthquake or a large underwater landslide. The movement of the ocean floor sends shock waves through the water, like ripples on a pond, travelling at 645 kilometres per hour (400 mph) or more, but only about 90 centimetres (3 ft) high. Sailors at sea may not even notice these waves. When the waves enter shallow water, friction with the seabed acts like a brake at the bottom of the waves and slows them to about 50 kilometres per hour (30 mph). The waves that continue to arrive push together, increasing the wave height. More waves follow. Sometimes a tsunami comes ashore as a vertical wall of water that batters and floods the coast and causes enormous damage.

## A TSUNAMI STRIKES

A tsunami has nothing to do with the tides, but it is more like a tidal movement than a breaker, hence its old name of "tidal wave". There are early warning systems to inform people of approaching tsunamis, and there are sometimes natural warning signs. Anyone seeing these signs should move to high ground immediately.

Incoming water advances further up the shore than usual and remains still for several minutes.

The water retreats away from the coast much further than normal, as if someone had pulled a giant bath plug.

A white line on the horizon marks the tsunami wave crest, now approaching very fast.

A tsunami that hit Indonesia on December 26, 2004, killed more than 280,000 people. It was caused by a Richter magnitude 9.3 earthquake.

**KILLER WAVE**

A towering tsunami is a terrifying sight. As the wave reaches land, it collapses, smacking coastal buildings and hurling boats on land. Often, tsunamis are far more destructive than the earthquakes that caused them.

# Earthquakes around the world

Earthquakes can happen almost anywhere. In most parts of the world they are rarely more than a tremor that rattles windows. But there are certain regions where earthquakes are much more violent. The shakiest parts of our planet lie on the boundaries of tectonic plates. The most active earthquake region is known as the "Ring of Fire" around the Pacific Ocean. The northward advance of the Indian Plate into the Eurasian Plate generates another earthquake zone in central Asia, Malaysia and Indonesia. A third zone runs through Africa and into southern Europe, along the boundaries of four tectonic plates.

**ALASKA, USA, 1964**
At 9.2 magnitude, this was the third strongest earthquake ever recorded. It struck Prince William Sound and lasted about 4 minutes. Amazingly, only 131 people died.

Alaska, 1964, 9.2

NORTH AMERICA

San Francisco, 1989, 7.1

ATLANTIC OCEAN

Mexico City, 1985, 8.1

Guatemala City, 1976, 7.5

PACIFIC OCEAN

Nothern Peru, 1970, 7.8

SOUTH AMERICA

Valdivia, 1960, 9.5

## RESCUE OPERATIONS

Nations respond to major earthquakes by sending emergency supplies and teams of doctors, firefighters and specialist rescue workers. Some rescuers use dogs trained to find people trapped under rubble. Others use thermal imaging equipment. Heavy-lifting gear moves pieces of buildings and rubble.

**MEXICO CITY, MEXICO, 1985**
This magnitude 8.1 earthquake lasted 3–4 minutes and was followed by a magnitude 7.5 aftershock. It killed 9,000 people, injured 30,000 more, and left 100,000 homeless.

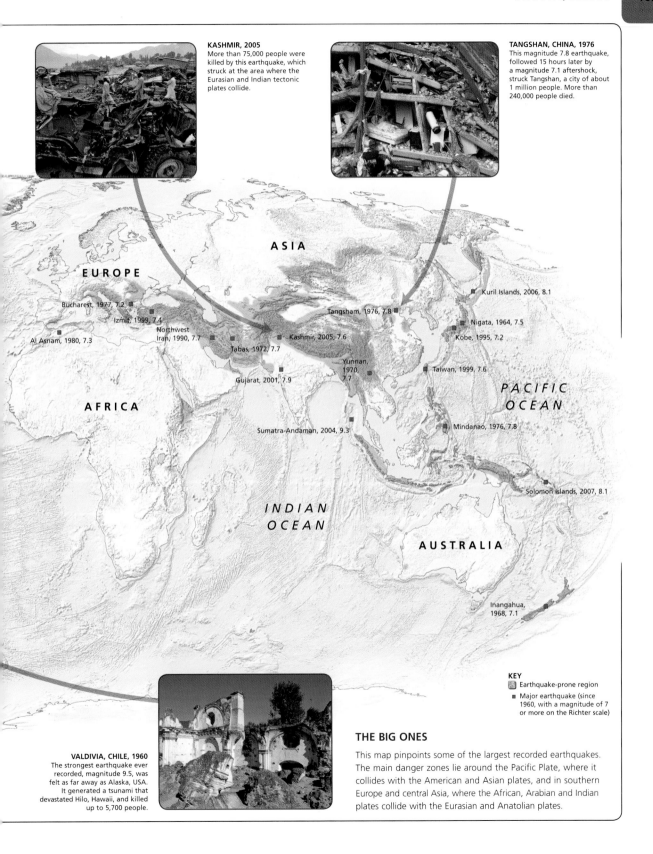

**KASHMIR, 2005**
More than 75,000 people were killed by this earthquake, which struck at the area where the Eurasian and Indian tectonic plates collide.

**TANGSHAN, CHINA, 1976**
This magnitude 7.8 earthquake, followed 15 hours later by a magnitude 7.1 aftershock, struck Tangshan, a city of about 1 million people. More than 240,000 people died.

ASIA

EUROPE

Kuril Islands, 2006, 8.1

Bucharest, 1977, 7.2

Izmit, 1999, 7.4
Tangsham, 1976, 7.8    Nigata, 1964, 7.5

Northwest
Iran, 1990, 7.7    Kashmir, 2005, 7.6    Kobe, 1995, 7.2

Al Asnam, 1980, 7.3

Tabas, 1972, 7.7

Gujarat, 2001, 7.9    Yunnan, 1970, 7.7    Taiwan, 1999, 7.6

AFRICA

PACIFIC
OCEAN

Sumatra-Andaman, 2004, 9.3    Mindanao, 1976, 7.8

Solomon Islands, 2007, 8.1

INDIAN
OCEAN

AUSTRALIA

Inangahua, 1968, 7.1

**KEY**
Earthquake-prone region
Major earthquake (since 1960, with a magnitude of 7 or more on the Richter scale)

**VALDIVIA, CHILE, 1960**
The strongest earthquake ever recorded, magnitude 9.5, was felt as far away as Alaska, USA. It generated a tsunami that devastated Hilo, Hawaii, and killed up to 5,700 people.

## THE BIG ONES

This map pinpoints some of the largest recorded earthquakes. The main danger zones lie around the Pacific Plate, where it collides with the American and Asian plates, and in southern Europe and central Asia, where the African, Arabian and Indian plates collide with the Eurasian and Anatolian plates.

# Geysers and Hot Springs

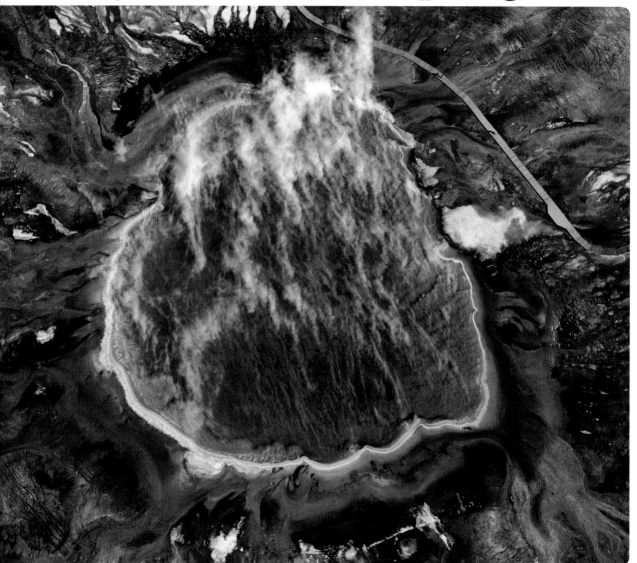

The Grand Prismatic Spring in Yellowstone National Park is the largest hot spring in North America. Layers of bacteria create the bright colours around the edges of the hot pool.

Thousands of years after its last eruption, the area beneath a volcano may still be hot. In these areas, known as geothermal regions, heat rising from ancient magma chambers meets water trickling down through the ground. Water deep under the ground can be twice as hot as normal boiling water, but the pressure of the cooler water on top stops it from boiling. When water overflows at the surface, the pressure is released and the deeper, hotter water turns to steam and explodes upward. Depending on the pressure, the water and steam may explode as a giant fountain—a geyser—or bubble out gently as a hot spring.

When water at a hot spring mixes with soil and dissolved minerals, the result is a lake of boiling mud.

Japanese macaques relax in the warmth of a hot spring on the island of Honshu, Japan, escaping winter temperatures below –15ºC (5°F).

People bathe in Iceland's hot springs, even in winter, to soothe sore muscles and benefit from the water's minerals.

**Draining**
Cold water drains down and meets hot rock. Its temperature increases to above 100°C (212°F), but pressure prevents it from boiling.

**Expanding**
Hot water expands, rising through the fissures and pushing cold water upward. This relieves the pressure on the superheated water.

**Boiling over**
Hot water boils with the pressure relieved, pushing cold water upward. The water boils explosively, ejecting a column of water and steam.

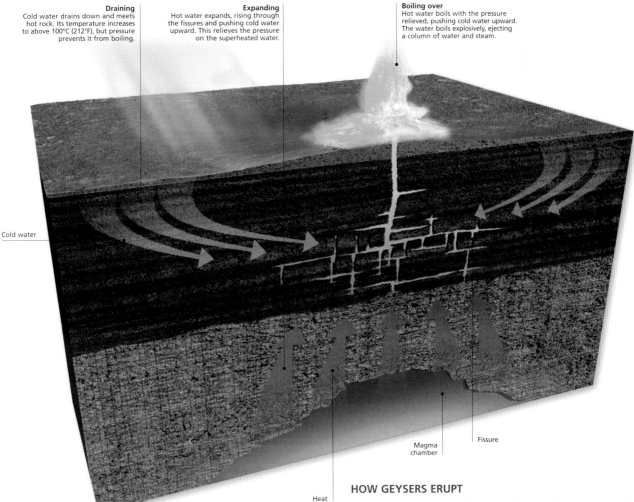

Cold water

Heat

Magma chamber

Fissure

## HOW GEYSERS ERUPT

Rainwater drains through rock fissures until contact with hot rock heats it to more than 100°C (212°F). Because of the weight of cold water above, high pressure prevents the water from boiling. The hot water expands, pushing cold water upward through the fissures. This relieves the pressure and the hot water boils, violently expelling a column of water and steam.

# Glaciers and Ice Sheets

Antarctica's ice sheet is the largest in the world. It holds approximately 70 per cent of the world's fresh water. If melted, it would raise the sea level by more than 55 metres (180 ft).

A glacier is a huge amount of ice formed by the buildup of snow. When snow falls every year in a place where the temperature rarely or never rises above freezing, the pressure from newly fallen snow packs older snowflakes together and compresses them into solid ice. Each year's snowfall forms a layer and scientists can tell the age of the ice by counting the layers. Because the ice is so heavy, a glacier flows very slowly downhill. If it is contained between the sides of a valley, it is called a valley glacier. Ice sheets are dome-shaped glaciers that form when winter snowfall exceeds the amount of snow that melts away in the warmer months.

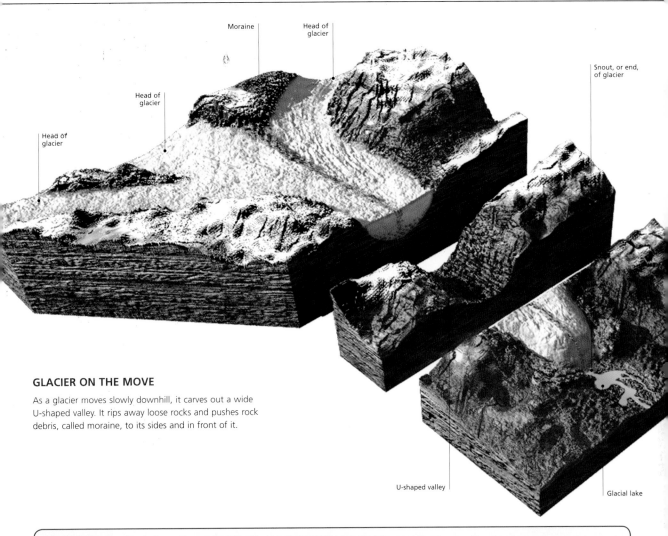

Moraine

Head of glacier

Head of glacier

Head of glacier

Snout, or end, of glacier

U-shaped valley

Glacial lake

## GLACIER ON THE MOVE

As a glacier moves slowly downhill, it carves out a wide U-shaped valley. It rips away loose rocks and pushes rock debris, called moraine, to its sides and in front of it.

## SHAPING THE LAND

As they flow, glaciers scour away all the soil, then carve the underlying rocks into shapes an expert eye can recognize thousands of years later, long after the ice has disappeared. Glaciers cut U-shaped valleys, often with waterfalls entering high on their sides. They leave moraines and carry loose rocks long distances.

Between ice ages, the climate is warm and a range of mountains is covered by vegetation. Valleys are V-shaped, with steep sides, and the mountains are rugged.

During an ice age, the climate is too cold for plants and they disappear. Only the tops of the mountains are visible above the ice sheet. Ice flows through the valleys.

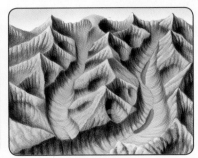

When the ice retreats, the valleys that remain are U-shaped. This is because they have been carved out by the slowly moving ice of glaciers.

# Avalanches and Landslides

An avalanche tumbles down from Shispar Peak in the Huza region of Pakistan. The sides of the mountain are too steep for snow to form deep layers.

Mountain slopes and hillsides are not always stable. When rock, soil or mud start to move downhill, a landslide can occur. When snow slips from a slope or cliff, an avalanche occurs. The sliding material may move slowly or quickly. Gravity pulls it straight downward, but part of the weight is directed downhill, along the edge of the slope. An avalanche or landslide occurs when the downhill force is greater than the strength of the material. A solid rock cliff face is perfectly stable, but material not firmly attached to it may move, especially if water makes the surface slippery. Landslides, rock falls, mudslides and avalanches can cause appalling damage. They can demolish buildings and bury entire villages.

# MUDFLOWS

## AFTER AN ERUPTION

In November 1985, the eruption of Nevado del Ruiz in Colombia melted ice and snow, which caused a devastating mudflow. Armero, 50 kilometres (31 mi) away, was engulfed in a 40-metre (131-ft) wall of mud and ash, which killed more than 23,000 people.

**Nevado del Ruiz**
This volcano is known by locals as the "sleeping lion".

**Path of the mudflow**
Mud streamed into the Lagunella River valley. It ended up spreading over 40 square kilometres (16 sq. mi).

**Town of Armero**
Bodies were discovered here up to three weeks after the volcano erupted.

# Weathering and Erosion

Wind has driven sand grains onto the solid rock of the Colorado Plateau, USA. This sandblasting has revealed the layers by eroding the softer rock faster than the hard rock.

When rock is exposed to the atmosphere, wind, rain and ice begin to wear it away. This is known as physical weathering. It grinds rocks into soil particles and grains of sand and can reduce mountain ranges to level plains. Another type of physical weathering happens when extreme pressure and heat deep underground cause rocks to break apart.

Minerals in soil and bedrock can also be broken down when acidic rainwater soaks downward. When a chemical reaction takes place, it is called chemical weathering. Rainwater reacts with granite—which consists mainly of feldspar, mica and quartz— to change the feldspar and mica to clay, but does not affect the quartz. Erosion is the removal of the products of weathering by wind or water.

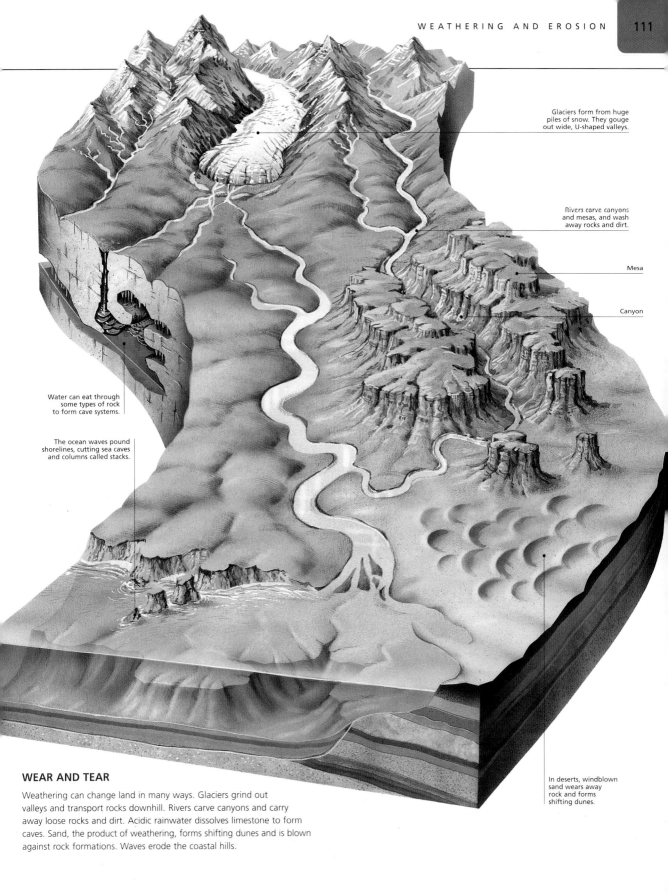

Glaciers form from huge piles of snow. They gouge out wide, U-shaped valleys.

Rivers carve canyons and mesas, and wash away rocks and dirt.

Mesa

Canyon

Water can eat through some types of rock to form cave systems.

The ocean waves pound shorelines, cutting sea caves and columns called stacks.

In deserts, windblown sand wears away rock and forms shifting dunes.

## WEAR AND TEAR

Weathering can change land in many ways. Glaciers grind out valleys and transport rocks downhill. Rivers carve canyons and carry away loose rocks and dirt. Acidic rainwater dissolves limestone to form caves. Sand, the product of weathering, forms shifting dunes and is blown against rock formations. Waves erode the coastal hills.

# Eroded landscapes

Weathering and erosion reshape landscapes. At present, the world's fastest rate of erosion is found in the Himalaya. This mountain range, the highest in the world, is still rising as India pushes into Eurasia, but it is wearing away almost as fast. Over hundreds of millions of years, weathering and erosion will level these mountains until the region is a flat plain. Northern Canada, now a vast plain with a few low mountains, was once very mountainous. Ocean waves are powerful agents of coastal erosion. Their action produces coastal cliffs, caves and stacks. In deserts, wind erosion creates strange landforms and salt weathering produces oddly shaped rocks.

## PINNACLES

Rain seldom falls in the desert, but when it does it is often heavy and powerful. Erosion removes surface material, but in some places a covering of resistant rock shields the rock beneath, which is left as a column.

1. Thin cracks crisscrossing the rock are opened by falling water.

## CANYONS

The force of water in rivers cuts canyons in the land, sometimes very quickly. The world's deepest canyon, Yarlung Zangbo Canyon in Tibet, cuts 5.3 kilometres (3.3 mi) into the surface.

1. A river and its tributaries erode channels along the least resistant parts of sedimentary rock.

## SEA STACKS

Where coastal cliffs are made from rocks with vertical joints or faults, waves can eat away at the cliffs, first creating then eroding a headland to make sea-level caves. This produces an arch in the rock, which can collapse and leave a stack.

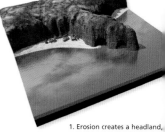

1. Erosion creates a headland, which juts out into the ocean.

## KARST

Karst describes a hilly landscape, usually made of limestone, which has been eroded by acidic rainwater. Much of the surface rock has dissolved to form rugged, cone-shape peaks, and there are large underground caves, lakes and rivers.

1. Massive beds of limestone are formed from the decaying skeletons of marine creatures.

2. Acidic rainwater dissolves surface limestone and carries it away.

## INSIDE A LIMESTONE CAVE

**A CAVE FORMS**
Acidic rainwater dissolves the calcium carbonate of limestone and carries it away, leaving behind a space that becomes a cave as the water erodes more and more material.

Stalactite

**STALACTITES AND STALAGMITES**
Water dripping from a cave roof contains dissolved calcium carbonate. As some of the water evaporates, it forms pointy stalactites hanging from the roof. As water drips down, calcium carbonate collects below and stalagmites grow upward from the cave floor.

Column

Stalagmite

**COLUMNS AND PILLARS**
Stalactites and stalagmites grow 2.5 centimetres (1 in) on average every 1,000 years. It is a very slow process, but eventually stalactites and stalagmites meet, forming pillars inside the cave. Over time, the pillars thicken and become columns.

he cap rock breaks into sections
nd erosion widens the cracks.

3. Erosion removes the material between
   the pinnacles and they become thinner.

Pinnacles in Monument Valley, Arizona, USA, are made from layers of shale
and sandstone and range in height from 120 to 300 metres (400 to 1,000 ft).

e great force of fast-flowing
ter deepens the channels
ster than it widens them.

3. Rocks fall from the nearly
   vertical sides of the river valleys,
   widening them into canyons.

The riverbed of the Rio Grande on the US–Mexico border is so deep it is
almost level with the land beyond the canyon.

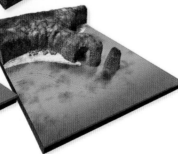

2. Waves batter the headland, making
   back-to-back caves either side.
   These meet in an arch.

3. The arch collapses, leaving
   a stack, separated from
   the headland.

The Twelve Apostles are limestone stacks in Victoria, Australia. Several
have fallen since they were named, and there are now only eight.

3. Erosion continues to sharpen karst
   peaks, widen the channels into
   valleys, and create a network of
   caves and underground waterways.

4. Water floods in and the karst peaks
   stand above sea level.

The landscape of Guanxi, China, consists of steep-sided hills of karst.

Oceans

# World Oceans

Oceans and seas cover 71 per cent of Earth's surface. The average depth of the world's five oceans is approximately 3,730 metres (12,240 ft), and combined they contain about 1,370 million cubic kilometres (329 million cu. mi) of water. Continents extend for an average of 72 kilometres (45 mi) beyond their coasts as gently sloping continental shelves beneath the water. At the edge of the continental shelves, the water is about 152 metres (500 ft) deep. Beyond that the ocean floor slopes more steeply. The deepest point is at the bottom of the Mariana Trench, about 11 kilometres (6.8 mi) below the surface of the Pacific Ocean.

**WATER ON EARTH**
Oceans hold 97.5 per cent of Earth's water. Of the remaining 2.5 per cent, 79 per cent is frozen in ice caps and glaciers, 20 per cent is below ground, and only 1 per cent—0.00025 per cent of all the water on Earth—exists as fresh water.

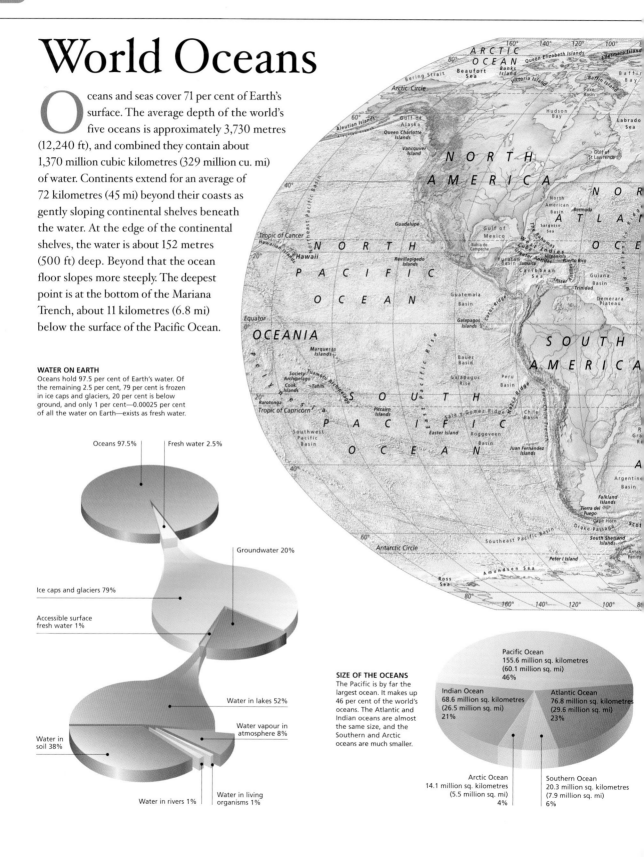

Oceans 97.5%     Fresh water 2.5%

Groundwater 20%

Ice caps and glaciers 79%

Accessible surface
fresh water 1%

Water in lakes 52%

Water in
soil 38%

Water vapour in
atmosphere 8%

Water in rivers 1%    Water in living
organisms 1%

**SIZE OF THE OCEANS**
The Pacific is by far the largest ocean. It makes up 46 per cent of the world's oceans. The Atlantic and Indian oceans are almost the same size, and the Southern and Arctic oceans are much smaller.

Pacific Ocean
155.6 million sq. kilometres
(60.1 million sq. mi)
46%

Indian Ocean
68.6 million sq. kilometres
(26.5 million sq. mi)
21%

Atlantic Ocean
76.8 million sq. kilometres
(29.6 million sq. mi)
23%

Arctic Ocean
14.1 million sq. kilometres
(5.5 million sq. mi)
4%

Southern Ocean
20.3 million sq. kilometres
(7.9 million sq. mi)
6%

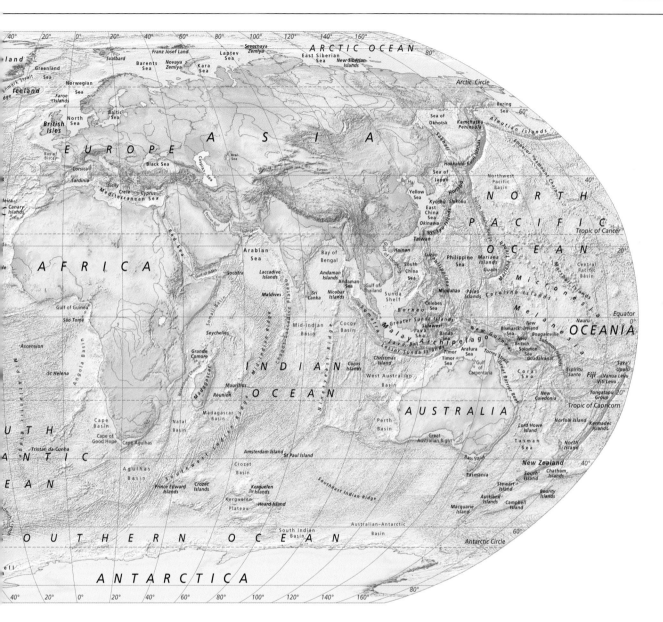

**NORTHERN HEMISPHERE**

**SOUTHERN HEMISPHERE**

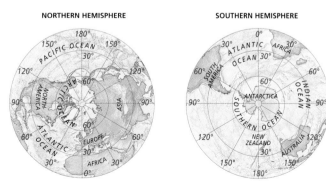

## THE HEMISPHERES

Water is not distributed evenly on Earth because tectonic plate movements have carried the continents northward into the Northern Hemisphere. More than two-thirds of Earth's land area is found here, while oceans cover nearly 80 per cent of the Southern Hemisphere. At present the Atlantic Ocean is growing wider and the Pacific Ocean is getting narrower.

# Pacific Ocean

The world's largest ocean extends from the Aleutian Islands in the north to the border of the Southern Ocean at 60°S latitude in the south. As well as having the largest area, covering about one-third of Earth's surface, the Pacific is the deepest ocean. It is also the coldest, with an average water temperature of 3.4°C (38.1°F), and the least saline, or salty. Its salt content averages 34.7 parts per thousand. Its vast area and depth mean the Pacific provides a wide variety of habitats for living organisms. Intense tectonic plate activity surrounding the Pacific has produced many volcanic islands.

## NATURAL RESOURCES

The upward flow of nutrient-rich water off the Peruvian coast sustains one of the world's largest fisheries. The North Pacific also supports important commercial fisheries for cod, sea bass, salmon and tuna. There are mineral, oil and gas reserves on continental shelves around the ocean.

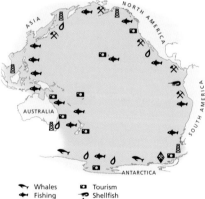

Whales
Fishing
Oil
Gas
Tourism
Shellfish
Precious metals and minerals
Mining

Marine iguanas are sea-dwelling lizards that live only on the Galápagos Islands.

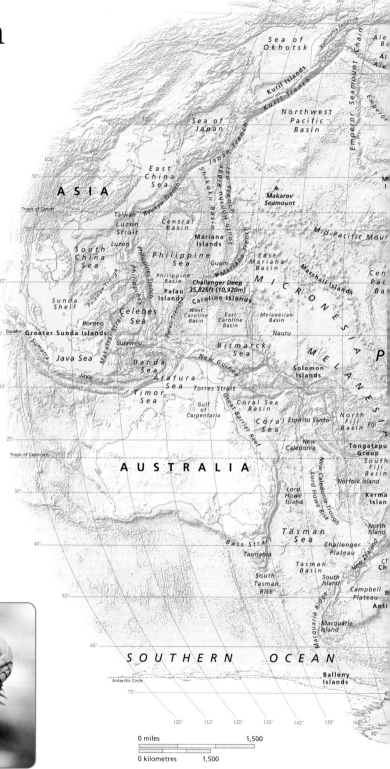

Sea of Okhotsk
Kamchatka Peninsula
Ale
B
Al
Ale
Emperor
Kuril Islands
Kuril Trench
Northwest Pacific Basin
Emperor Seamount Chain
Sea of Japan
Japan Trench
Izu-Ogasawara Trench
Shikoku Basin
ASIA
East China Sea
Tropic of Cancer
Makarov Seamount
M
Taiwan
Ryukyu Trench
Central Basin
Mid-Pacific Mour
Luzon Strait
Luzon
Mariana Islands
South China Sea
Philippine Sea
East Mariana Basin
Cen
Pac
Bas
Philippine Basin
Guam
Challenger Deep 35,826ft (10,920m)
Marshall Islands
MICRONESIA
Philippine Trench
Palawan Trough
Philippines Trench
Sunda Shelf
Palau Islands
Caroline Islands
West Caroline Basin
East Caroline Basin
Melanesian Basin
Borneo
Celebes Sea
Nauru
Equator
Greater Sunda Islands
Sulawesi
Makassar Strait
Sumatra
Java Sea
Bismarck Sea
MELANESIA
P
Java
Banda Sea
New Guinea
Solomon Islands
Arafura Sea
Timor Sea
Torres Strait
Coral Sea Basin
North Fiji Basin
Fiji
Gulf of Carpentaria
Great Barrier Reef
Coral Sea
Espiritu Santo
Tropic of Capricorn
New Caledonia
Tongatapu Group
AUSTRALIA
New Caledonia Trough
Lord Howe Rise
South Fiji Basin
Norfolk Island
Kerma
Islan
Lord Howe Island
Tasman Sea
North Island
Bass Strait
Tasmania
Challenger Plateau
New Zealand
Ch
Ch
Tasman Basin
South Tasman Rise
South Island
Campbell Plateau
Anti
Macquarie Ridge
Macquarie Island
SOUTHERN    OCEAN
Balleny Islands
Antarctic Circle

0 miles    1,500
0 kilometres    1,500

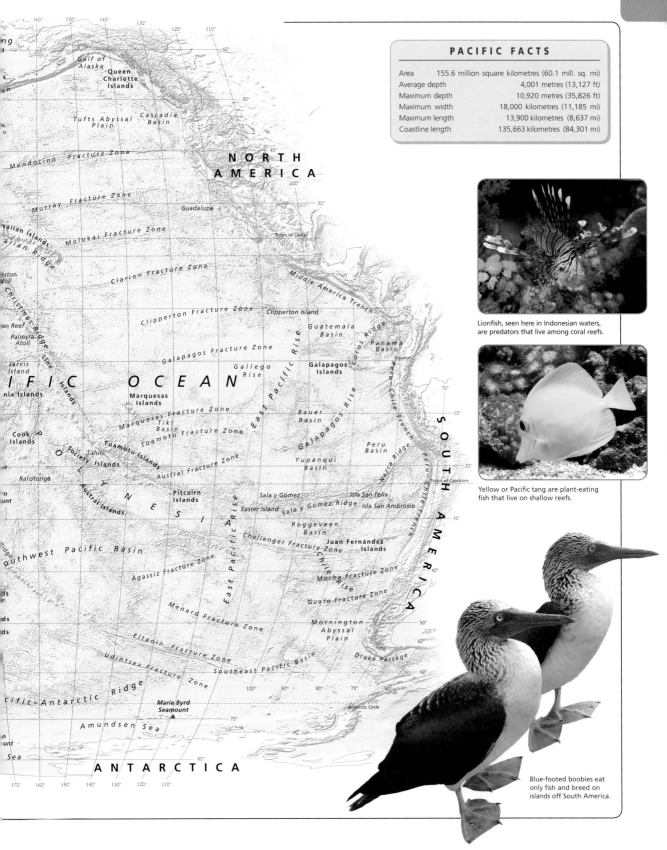

## PACIFIC FACTS

| | |
|---|---|
| Area | 155.6 million square kilometres (60.1 mill. sq. mi) |
| Average depth | 4,001 metres (13,127 ft) |
| Maximum depth | 10,920 metres (35,826 ft) |
| Maximum width | 18,000 kilometres (11,185 mi) |
| Maximum length | 13,900 kilometres (8,637 mi) |
| Coastline length | 135,663 kilometres (84,301 mi) |

Lionfish, seen here in Indonesian waters, are predators that live among coral reefs.

Yellow or Pacific tang are plant-eating fish that live on shallow reefs.

Blue-footed boobies eat only fish and breed on islands off South America.

NORTH AMERICA

SOUTH AMERICA

PACIFIC OCEAN

POLYNESIA

ANTARCTICA

Gulf of Alaska
Queen Charlotte Islands
Tufts Abyssal Plain
Cascadia Basin
Mendocino Fracture Zone
Murray Fracture Zone
Guadalupe
Molokai Fracture Zone
Tropic of Cancer
Clarion Fracture Zone
Middle America Trench
Clipperton Fracture Zone
Clipperton Island
Galapagos Fracture Zone
Guatemala Basin
Cocos Ridge
Panama Basin
Gallego Rise
Galapagos Islands
Equator
Marquesas Islands
East Pacific Rise
Bauer Basin
Galapagos Rise
Marquesas Fracture Zone
Tiki Basin
Tuamotu Fracture Zone
Tahiti
Society Islands
Tuamotu Islands
Austral Fracture Zone
Yupanqui Basin
Peru Basin
Peru–Chile Trench
Nazca Ridge
Cook Islands
Rarotonga
Austral Islands
Pitcairn Islands
Sala y Gómez
Easter Island
Sala y Gómez Ridge
Isla San Felix
Isla San Ambrosio
Tropic of Capricorn
Roggeveen Basin
Juan Fernández Islands
Challenger Fracture Zone
East Pacific Rise
Southwest Pacific Basin
Agassiz Fracture Zone
Mocha Fracture Zone
Chile Rise
Guafo Fracture Zone
Menard Fracture Zone
Mornington Abyssal Plain
Eltanin Fracture Zone
Southeast Pacific Basin
Drake Passage
Udintsev Fracture Zone
Pacific–Antarctic Ridge
Marie Byrd Seamount
Antarctic Circle
Amundsen Sea
Christmas Ridge
Palmyra Atoll
Jarvis Island
Line Islands
Phoenix Islands
Hawaiian Islands
Hawaiian Ridge

# Atlantic Ocean

The world's second-largest ocean, covering approximately one-fifth of Earth's surface, is the warmest, with an average water temperature of 3.7°C (38.7°F). It is also the saltiest; Atlantic Ocean water contains 34.9 parts per thousand of salt. Its deepest point is 8,605 metres (28,233 ft) below the surface, at Milwaukee Deep in the Puerto Rico Trench. Along the ocean floor, from Iceland to about 58°S, a large underwater mountain range, called the Mid-Atlantic Ridge, divides the ocean into two sections, each consisting of several basins. The ocean is widening by about 2.5 centimetres (1 in) a year as the seafloor spreads at the Mid-Atlantic Ridge.

## NATURAL RESOURCES

The Atlantic has some of the world's richest shallow-water fisheries, although many have been over-exploited. There are oil and gas reserves off the African, Caribbean and Gulf of Mexico coasts and mineral reserves—including precious stones—off North and South America and Africa.

- Fishing
- Whales
- Shellfish
- Precious metals and minerals
- Mining
- Oil
- Gas
- Tourism

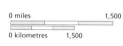

Atlantic walrus feed mainly on molluscs. They live in eastern Canada and the high Arctic.

Atlantic spotted dolphins inhabit tropical and subtropical Atlantic waters, and live in social groups called pods.

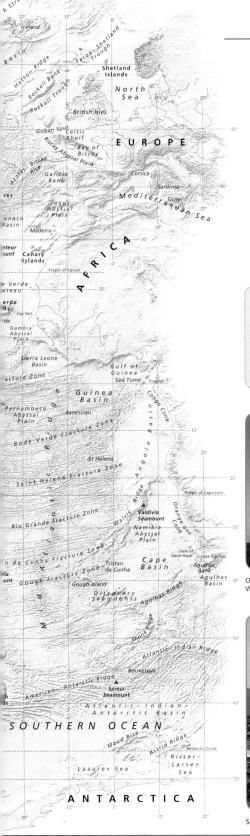

Hawksbill turtles inhabit tropical and subtropical oceans, including the western Atlantic and Caribbean.

### ATLANTIC FACTS

| | |
|---|---|
| Area | 76.8 million square kilometres (29.6 mil. sq. mi) |
| Average depth | 3,605 metres (11,828 ft) |
| Maximum depth | 8,605 metres (28,233 ft) |
| Maximum width | 7,900 kilometres (4,909 mi) |
| Maximum length | 14,120 kilometres (8,774 mi) |
| Coastline length | 111,866 kilometres (69,514 mi) |

The Azores are a group of Portuguese islands in the North Atlantic.

Offshore oil rigs drill for oil found deep under the ocean bed. Workers can access the rig by ship or helicopter.

Sperm whales live in all the oceans. This pair, photographed near the Azores, is about to dive.

# Indian Ocean

The Indian Ocean is the third-largest ocean and
occupies 21 per cent of the total world ocean area.
It is bounded by Africa to the west, the Arabian
Sea and Bay of Bengal to the north, Indonesia
and Australia to the east, and the Southern
Ocean to the south. The Indian Ocean is
divided from the Atlantic at 20°E, and
it is separated from the Pacific at 147°E.
North of the equator, the Indian Ocean
climate is dominated by the monsoon
winds. Tropical cyclones sometimes
develop in the Bay of Bengal.

## NATURAL RESOURCES

Warm waters restrict the growth of the marine algae
on which fish feed. Fishing is therefore limited, aside
from shrimp and tuna. There are large offshore oil
and gas reserves. Beach sands contain minerals that
several countries are exploiting.

Fishing
Shellfish
Whales
Oil
Gas
Mining
Precious metals and minerals
Tourism

Seychelles giant tortoises, once thought to be extinct, now survive only in captivity.

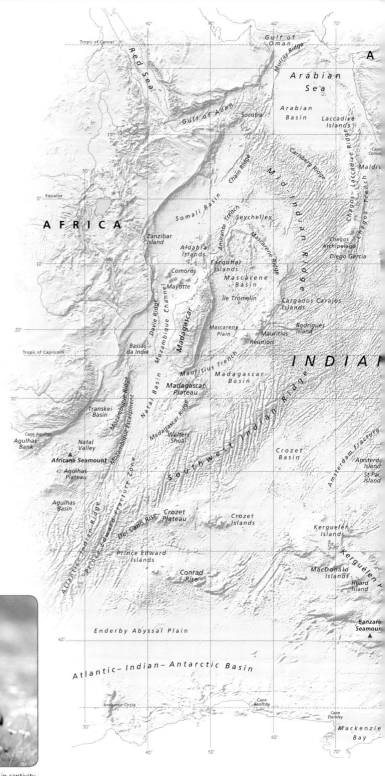

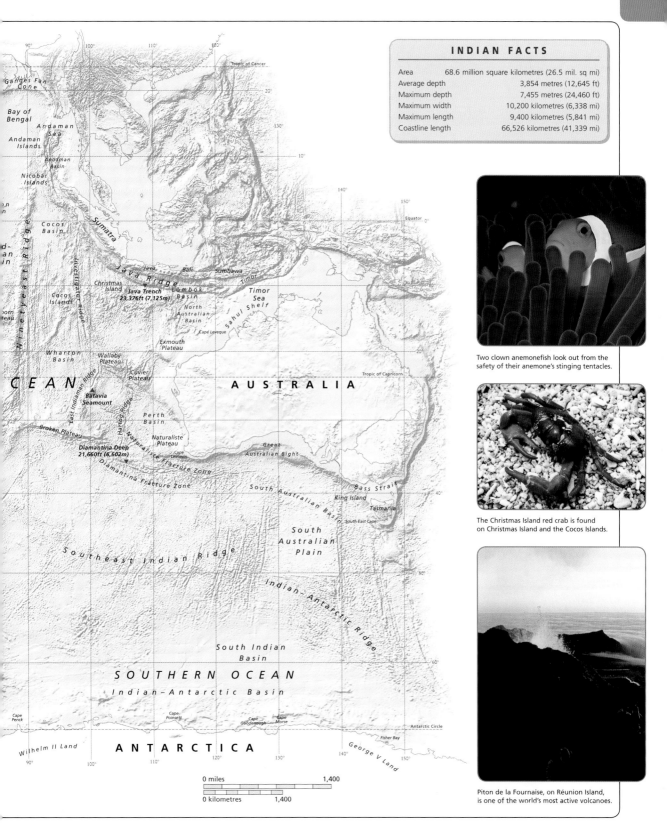

**INDIAN FACTS**

| | |
|---|---|
| Area | 68.6 million square kilometres (26.5 mil. sq mi) |
| Average depth | 3,854 metres (12,645 ft) |
| Maximum depth | 7,455 metres (24,460 ft) |
| Maximum width | 10,200 kilometres (6,338 mi) |
| Maximum length | 9,400 kilometres (5,841 mi) |
| Coastline length | 66,526 kilometres (41,339 mi) |

Two clown anemonefish look out from the safety of their anemone's stinging tentacles.

The Christmas Island red crab is found on Christmas Island and the Cocos Islands.

Piton de la Fournaise, on Réunion Island, is one of the world's most active volcanoes.

# Arctic Ocean

The Arctic Ocean is the smallest and shallowest of the world's five oceans. It is almost completely landlocked by North America, Europe and Asia and is connected to the Pacific through the Bering Strait and to the Atlantic through the Greenland and Labrador seas. The ocean is roughly circular and divided by a mid-ocean ridge into two basins, the Eurasian and North American. Most of the ocean is covered in ice during winter, and some areas remain frozen in summer. In recent years the thickness and area of sea ice have been decreasing. The salt content of the Arctic Ocean varies seasonally as sea ice expands and retreats.

### ARCTIC FACTS

| | |
|---|---|
| Area | 14.0 million square kilometres (5.4 mil. sq mi) |
| Average depth | 1,430 metres (4,690 ft) |
| Maximum depth | 5,669 metres (18,599 ft) |
| Maximum width | 3,200 kilometres (1,988 mi) |
| Maximum length | 5,000 kilometres (3,107 mi) |
| Coastline length | 45,389 kilometres (28,205 mi) |

0 miles                                   1,000

0 kilometres                   1,000

**KEY**
▲ Mountain

The thick fur of the polar bear helps to protect it during the harsh Arctic winters.

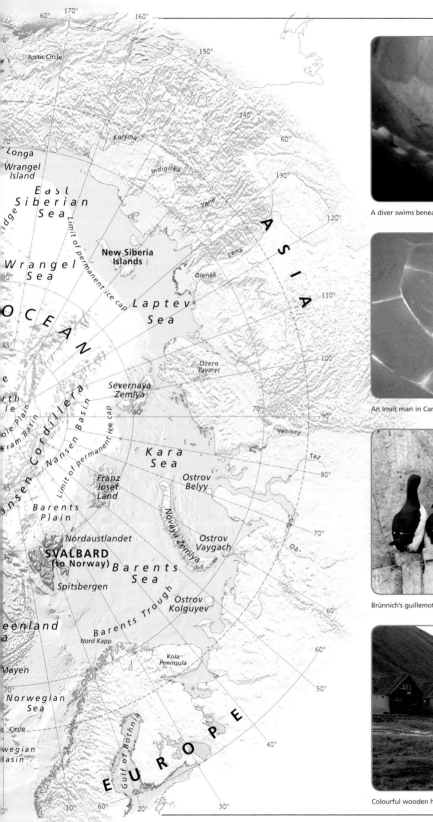

A diver swims beneath the pack ice in the Canada Basin, off North America.

An Inuit man in Canada completes an igloo made from blocks of ice.

Brünnich's guillemots perch on a ledge on the island of Svalbard, Norway.

Colourful wooden houses are typical at Longyearbyen on Spitsbergen island.

# Southern Ocean

The Southern Ocean did not officially exist until 2000, when the International Hydrographic Organization formally defined its boundaries as the waters between latitude 60˚S and the continent of Antarctica. Sometimes called the circumpolar sea or the Antarctic Ocean, it is the world's fourth-largest ocean. Surface sea temperatures range from about –2˚ to 10˚C (28˚ to 50˚F). With no continent to slow and deflect them, the winds in the Southern Ocean blow without interruption right around the world. The region is known for ferocious winds and high waves. Sea ice is widespread and the area and thickness of winter ice has increased in recent decades.

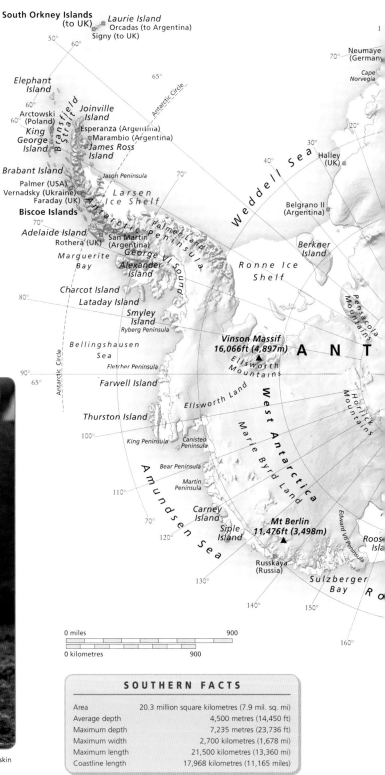

King penguins incubate their eggs on their feet under a warm fold of skin and waterproof feathers. Older chicks may try to snuggle back under.

0 miles 900
0 kilometres 900

## SOUTHERN FACTS

| | |
|---|---|
| Area | 20.3 million square kilometres (7.9 mil. sq. mi) |
| Average depth | 4,500 metres (14,450 ft) |
| Maximum depth | 7,235 metres (23,736 ft) |
| Maximum width | 2,700 kilometres (1,678 mi) |
| Maximum length | 21,500 kilometres (13,360 mi) |
| Coastline length | 17,968 kilometres (11,165 mi) |

This pair of wandering albatrosses perform a courtship "dance". They mate for life.

This seal stretches out to rest on the snow covering Brown Bluff, on the Antarctic Peninsula.

The Argentine research station and settlement Esperanza is home to about 50 people over winter.

Map labels:

Maitri (India), Novolazarevskaya (Russia), Asuka (Japan), Syowa (Japan), Mizuho (Japan), Molodezhnaya (Russia), Riiser-Larsen Peninsula, Lützow-Holm Bay, Antarctic Circle, Thorshavnheiane, Queen Maud Land, East, Enderby Land, Law Promontory, Kemp Land, Mawson (Australia), Mac Robertson Land, Prince Charles Mountains, Cape Darnley, Amery Ice Shelf, Mackenzie Bay, Zhongshan (China), Davis (Australia), Davis Sea, Princess Elizabeth Land, Kaiser Wilhelm II Land, Mirny (Russia), Queen Mary Land, Shackleton Ice Shelf, Mill Island, Bowman Island, Vostok (Russia), South Geomagnetic Pole, South Pole, Amundsen-Scott (USA), Transantarctic Mountains, Kirkpatrick 14,856ft (4,528m), ANTARCTICA, Vincennes Bay, Casey (Australia), Cape Poinsett, Cape Waldron, Wilkes Land, Scott Base (NZ), Ross Island, McMurdo (USA), Victoria Land, Terra Nova Bay (Italy), Mt Minto 13,665ft (4,165m), Cape Adare, George V Land, Adélie Land, Porpoise Bay, Cape Keltie, Leningradskaya (Russia), Cape Cheetham, Mawson Peninsula, Cape Freshfield, Cape Gray, Dumont d'Urville (France), Dumont d'Urville Sea, Balleny Islands, SOUTHERN OCEAN

# The Spreading Seas

Ocean basins, or underwater depressions, cover about 65 per cent of Earth's surface. Layers of sediment cover the ocean floor, but beneath the sediment the oceanic crust is made from basaltic rocks. Continents contain rocks that are billions of years old, but no oceanic crust is more than 200 million years old. Mid-ocean ridges that run through all oceans mark the boundaries between tectonic plates that are moving apart. Oceans expand as magma pushes through the crust at these ridges. The oceanic crust does not remain intact because as some basins expand, others are shrinking to compensate. Dense oceanic crust is pulled beneath lighter continental crust where the two collide, and the oceanic crust sinks into Earth's mantle.

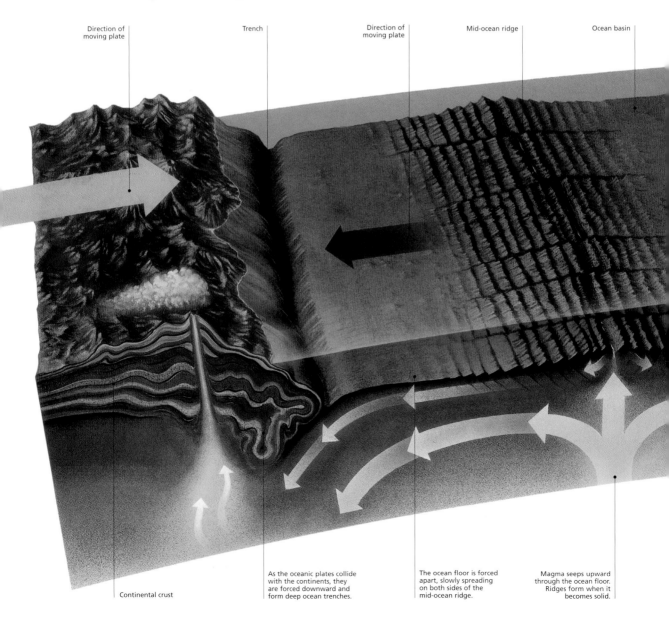

Direction of moving plate

Trench

Direction of moving plate

Mid-ocean ridge

Ocean basin

Continental crust

As the oceanic plates collide with the continents, they are forced downward and form deep ocean trenches.

The ocean floor is forced apart, slowly spreading on both sides of the mid-ocean ridge.

Magma seeps upward through the ocean floor. Ridges form when it becomes solid.

## PARTING THE LANDSCAPE

An ocean begins when plates move apart along a margin below a continent. This forms a rift valley that floods when the rifting crosses the coast, allowing seawater to enter.

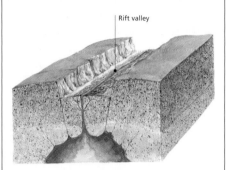

Rift valley

**Rifting** This occurs when a section of crust falls between two sets of parallel faults, forming a rift valley.

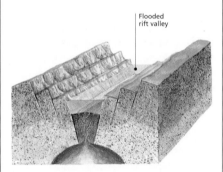

Flooded rift valley

**Flooding** When the rift crosses the coast, it floods. As plates continue to move apart, the rift widens. Rising magma hardens and forms the rift valley floor.

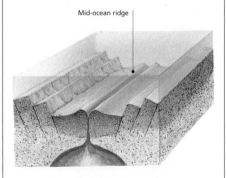

Mid-ocean ridge

**Spreading** As spreading continues, the flooded rift valley widens until it is a narrow sea, such as the Red Sea. Magma forms a central ridge in what will become an ocean.

## CHANGING SHAPE

Oceans expand because two plates are moving apart along a mid-ocean ridge. Rising magma solidifies and forms new crust on the floor of the ocean basin. When sediment covers the floor and buries the mountains, an abyssal plain forms.

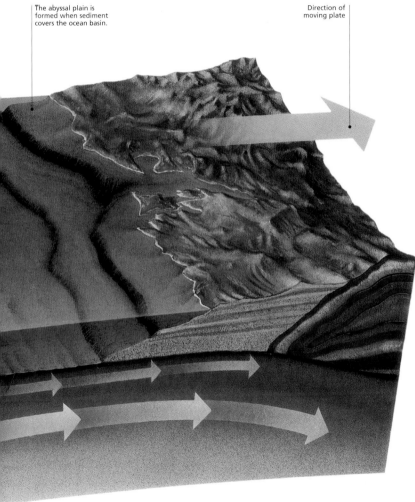

The abyssal plain is formed when sediment covers the ocean basin.

Direction of moving plate

Mid-Atlantic Ridge

South America

Africa

**ON THE OCEAN FLOOR**
The North American, Caribbean and South American tectonic plates are moving away from the Eurasian and African plates. This makes the Atlantic Ocean wider by about 2.5 centimetres (1 in) each year. The plate boundary is along the Mid-Atlantic Ridge, where rising magma fills the gap.

# Currents

This view from space shows Cape Hatteras in North Carolina, USA, looking south to where the warm current called the Gulf Stream begins to swing eastward towards Europe.

Warm air rises over the equator and falls in cooler regions to the north and south. This movement carries heat away from the equator and produces wind systems. Surface winds create ocean currents that carry warm water from the equator to the poles and cold water from the poles towards the equator.

As they approach continents, currents turn away from the equator, then continue turning, forming circular patterns called gyres in the Atlantic, Pacific and Indian oceans. In the Arctic Ocean and near Antarctica, sea ice makes some water colder and saltier. This sinks below warmer, less salty water and flows away as a deepwater current.

## SURFACE CURRENTS

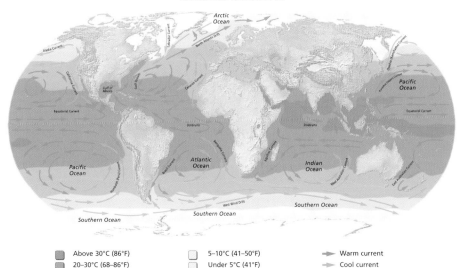

| | | |
|---|---|---|
| ■ Above 30°C (86°F) | ☐ 5–10°C (41–50°F) | ➡ Warm current |
| ■ 20–30°C (68–86°F) | ☐ Under 5°C (41°F) | ➡ Cool current |
| ■ 10–20°C (50–68°F) | | |

## DEEP-WATER CURRENTS

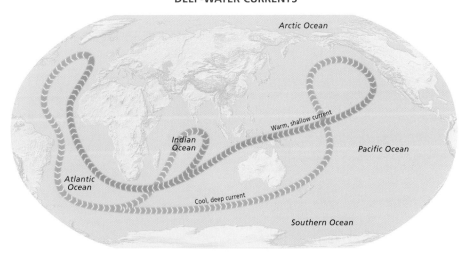

Seawater is densest when its temperature is just above freezing. When it freezes, salt is released from the ice, so water next to the ice is saltier, and therefore denser, than more distant water. The dense water sinks to form a deepwater current known as the Great Conveyor.

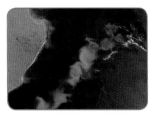

A current flowing south past the River Plate, Argentina, swirls into one heading north.

Clouds form over the Gulf of Alaska, where the warm Alaska Current meets cold air.

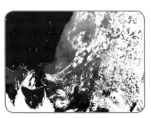

The warm East Australian Current (pink) sweeps from the Coral Sea to Tasmania.

## THE GULF STREAM

The Gulf Stream is a warm ocean current that runs up the east coast of North America before it swings across the North Atlantic to Europe. It is like a river in the sea, 80–145 kilometres (50–90 mi) wide. Also like a river, it forms curving meanders and circular eddies as it flows through the ocean.

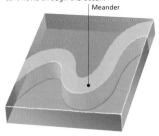

The Gulf Stream follows a curving path that eventually forms a meander.

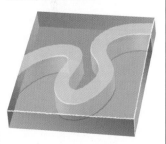

The meander keeps curving until it almost surrounds a body of warm or cool water.

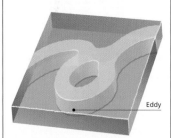

When the meander closes, it cuts off part of the current and forms an eddy.

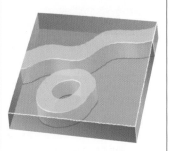

Warm-water eddies spin clockwise and cool-water eddies spin anticlockwise.

# Waves and Tides

Water at the top of a tall wave may travel faster than water at the bottom. The top then falls forward, and the wave curls as it breaks.

The gravity of the Moon works against Earth's gravity to produce two bulges—the tides—that move around Earth. The tides follow the orbit of the Moon and raise and lower the surface of the ocean. One bulge is on the part of Earth facing the Moon, and the other bulge is on the opposite side of Earth. The Moon takes 24 hours 50 minutes to complete one orbit, so high and low tides usually occur every 12 hours 25 minutes—exactly half of the Moon's orbit time. When tides pass around the coastline, their timing and magnitude—called the "reach"—may change. While tides affect waves deep in the ocean, surface waves are caused by winds.

## OCEAN TIDES

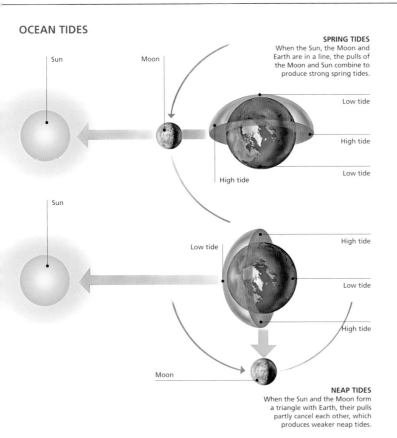

**SPRING TIDES**
When the Sun, the Moon and Earth are in a line, the pulls of the Moon and Sun combine to produce strong spring tides.

Sun

Moon

Low tide

High tide

Low tide

High tide

Sun

Low tide

High tide

Low tide

High tide

Moon

**NEAP TIDES**
When the Sun and the Moon form a triangle with Earth, their pulls partly cancel each other, which produces weaker neap tides.

The Bay of Fundy, Canada, has the world's largest tidal range. At low tide, rocks and ocean floor are visible and can be walked over.

At high tide, the ocean washes over the rocks and ocean floor of the bay.

## FORMING A WAVE

Tides and movements along the thermocline produce waves below the surface, but surface waves are caused by winds that push the water forward. Their size depends on the strength of the wind and the distance over which it blows.

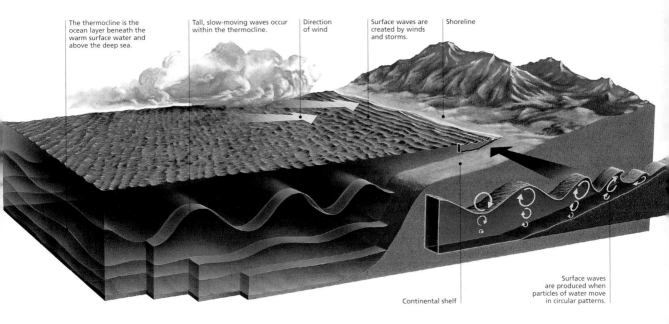

The thermocline is the ocean layer beneath the warm surface water and above the deep sea.

Tall, slow-moving waves occur within the thermocline.

Direction of wind

Surface waves are created by winds and storms.

Shoreline

Continental shelf

Surface waves are produced when particles of water move in circular patterns.

# Ocean Zones and Habitats

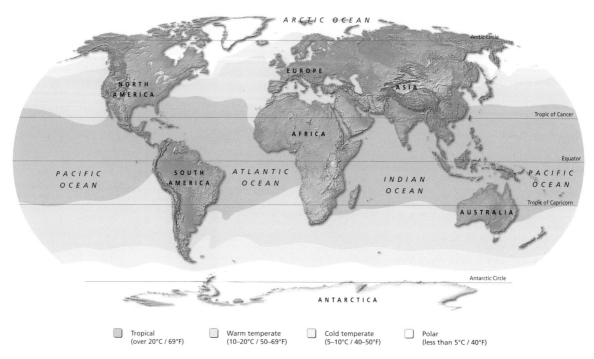

ARCTIC OCEAN

Arctic Circle

EUROPE

ASIA

NORTH
AMERICA

Tropic of Cancer

AFRICA

Equator

PACIFIC
OCEAN

SOUTH
AMERICA

ATLANTIC
OCEAN

INDIAN
OCEAN

PACIFIC
OCEAN

Tropic of Capricorn

AUSTRALIA

Antarctic Circle

ANTARCTICA

☐ Tropical
(over 20°C / 69°F)

☐ Warm temperate
(10–20°C / 50–69°F)

☐ Cold temperate
(5–10°C / 40–50°F)

☐ Polar
(less than 5°C / 40°F)

Ocean zones can be arranged by water temperature. Warm and cool currents can affect the boundaries of the zones, but they generally follow degrees north and south of the equator.

All the oceans are connected, so there is a "world ocean", and some of its inhabitants range widely through it. Most, however, stay within a particular part of the ocean. The oceans can be divided into geographical zones based on water temperature. A second set of zones is arranged by depth, based on the amount of light and nutrients. Each zone provides habitats for plants and animals. In some places on the ocean floor, hot water containing dissolved minerals spouts from the crust. Only very special life-forms can exist in these extreme habitats.

Tropical seas support coral reefs that are home to countless algae, fish and invertebrates.

Temperate seas have underwater seaweed forests not far from shore, with many fish, including seahorses.

Polar seas teem with life, despite the cold. They support marine mammals, including whales. These are belugas, or white whales.

# UNDER THE SEA

## UNDERWATER LANDSCAPES

Beyond the shore, the ocean floor slopes gently down the continental shelf until the water is about 150 metres (500 ft) deep. The angle gets steeper on the continental slope. At the bottom lies the abyssal plain, a vast expanse of the ocean floor, more than 2,000 metres (6,500 ft) below the surface. The ocean floor contains fracture zones, isolated hills called seamounts, mountains at the spreading ridges, and deep trenches.

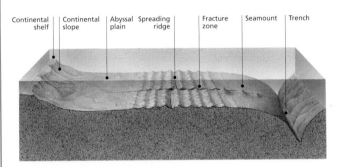

Continental shelf | Continental slope | Abyssal plain | Spreading ridge | Fracture zone | Seamount | Trench

## THE DARK ZONE

Light is made up of the colours of the spectrum, each one with a different wavelength. Water absorbs red—the longest wavelength—quickly, followed by the other colours. Green and blue travel deepest, but eventually there is no light at all.

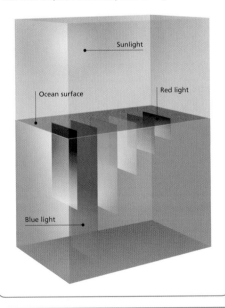

Sunlight

Ocean surface

Red light

Blue light

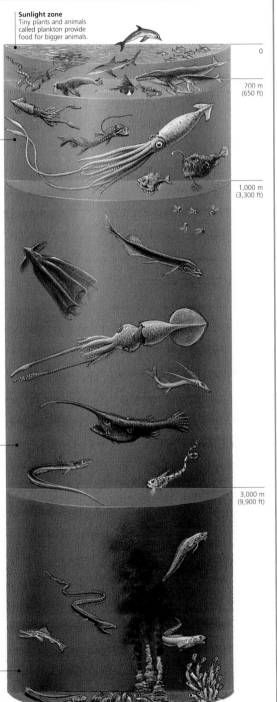

**Sunlight zone**
Tiny plants and animals called plankton provide food for bigger animals.

0

200 m (650 ft)

**Twilight zone**
Many fish carry bacteria that produce light. This may be for camouflage or for identifying species.

1,000 m (3,300 ft)

**Midnight zone**
Below 1,000 metres (3,300 ft) is total darkness. The water is cold, still and sparsely populated. Many animals produce their own light.

3,000 m (9,900 ft)

**Abyssal zone**
Covering 75 per cent of the ocean floor, this is a constant 4°C (39°F). Food particles rain down from above. Predators have lures and huge jaws for consuming prey larger than themselves.

# Coral reefs

Coral reefs cover up to 600,000 square kilometres (232,000 sq. mi) in tropical and subtropical seas. They grow best in brightly lit clear water at temperatures of 23–25°C (73–77°F). Coral polyps are small, soft-bodied animals that build an external skeleton called a corallite for protection. Reef-building polyps live side by side, and their corallites fuse together into a corallum. As

individual polyps die, others settle on top of the abandoned corallums. Little by little the structure grows into a coral reef. Algae grow on the outside of coral polyps. Together with waste products from the polyps, they form the basis of some of the world's richest ecosystems. Today, however, many coral reefs are fragile habitats.

Almond Point Reef, found near Bequia on the St Vincent and Grenadine Islands in the Caribbean, is teeming with life. Sea fans fringe the sides and base of two coral outcrops.

# CORAL REEFS OF THE WORLD

Coral reefs require clear water. Algae that live on the coral form a community that brings food to the polyps, and the algae need light to make their own food. Reefs rarely occur more than 60 metres (200 ft) deep. Corals are sensitive to temperature, so they grow only in warm tropical and subtropical waters.

 Warm ocean  Deep-water coral reefs   Warm-water coral reefs

## KINDS OF CORAL

A colony of bubble corals looks like cream-coloured grapes. The "bubbles" are filled with water.

Brain corals live in warm, shallow water. Their name refers to their appearance.

The tentacles of this soft coral look like the frilly petals of flowers, and the mouth looks like the stem.

Purple, or Californian, hydrocoral is a coastal species occasionally found in cold water.

### INSIDE A CORAL POLYP
A polyp consists of a hollow digestive chamber attached to a disc at the base. The mouth is at the top, surrounded by tentacles used to capture food. Zooxanthellae are single-celled creatures that live and feed inside the chamber.

## HABITAT WATCH

Crown-of-thorns starfish, seen here feeding on coral polyps, attack reefs throughout the world. They have caused considerable damage to Australia's Great Barrier Reef. Reefs also suffer from bleaching, caused by the loss of their algae due to pollution.

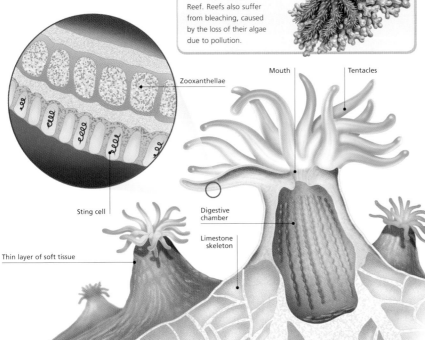

Zooxanthellae

Mouth

Tentacles

Sting cell

Digestive chamber

Limestone skeleton

Thin layer of soft tissue

# Along the coast

The coast is where land and sea meet and interact. What happens depends on the energy of the waves and the resistance of the land. Sea storms hurl water against the shore with great force. Waves erode even the hardest rocks, cutting into hills to create sea cliffs. If the coast is sheltered by a headland or offshore sandbar, the waves exert less force, and plants and animals thrive in rock pools. Tides erode sandy beaches, but also build them elsewhere. Winds can drive dry sand inland to build coastal dunes.

**A SANDY BEACH**
A beach has distinct zones. The berm is a hill of sediment piled up by waves. Currents sometimes create a buildup of sand called a sandbar. Most sand grains are made from eroded quartz, but white sand consists of finely ground seashells.

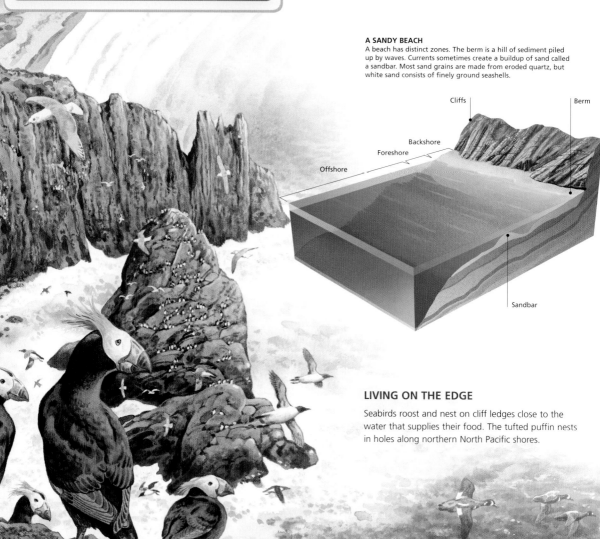

Cliffs

Berm

Backshore

Foreshore

Offshore

Sandbar

## LIVING ON THE EDGE

Seabirds roost and nest on cliff ledges close to the water that supplies their food. The tufted puffin nests in holes along northern North Pacific shores.

# BETWEEN THE TIDES

## IN A TIDAL ROCK POOL

Plants and animals living on the shore must cope with being dry and then exposed to salt water and rain. Rock pools in the zone between high and low tides are refreshed every time seawater flows in at high tide. Seaweeds grow in rock pools, and many animals live there permanently—among them sea anemones, hermit crabs, mussels and several kinds of fish.

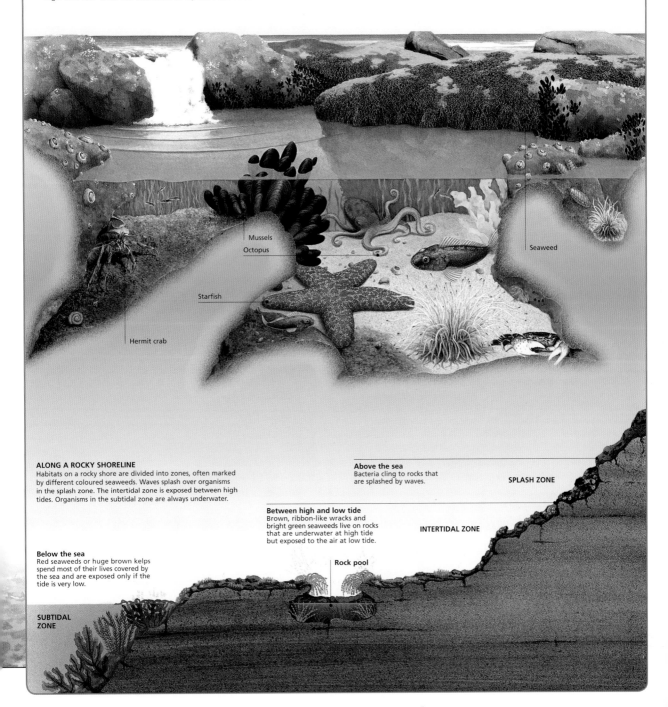

Mussels

Octopus

Starfish

Hermit crab

Seaweed

**ALONG A ROCKY SHORELINE**
Habitats on a rocky shore are divided into zones, often marked by different coloured seaweeds. Waves splash over organisms in the splash zone. The intertidal zone is exposed between high tides. Organisms in the subtidal zone are always underwater.

**Above the sea**
Bacteria cling to rocks that are splashed by waves.

**SPLASH ZONE**

**Between high and low tide**
Brown, ribbon-like wracks and bright green seaweeds live on rocks that are underwater at high tide but exposed to the air at low tide.

**INTERTIDAL ZONE**

**Below the sea**
Red seaweeds or huge brown kelps spend most of their lives covered by the sea and are exposed only if the tide is very low.

**Rock pool**

**SUBTIDAL ZONE**

# Into the deep

With increasing depth the ocean becomes darker and colder, and the pressure becomes much greater. Life is most abundant in the uppermost layer, where there is enough light for algae to make the sugars that provide their food. This is the sunlight zone above the continental shelves and extending to about 200 metres (650 ft). Many of the fish living in darkness below the sunlight zone are bioluminescent—they have glowing organs that beam out a deep-sea light show. They depend on food particles that sink from above and their bodies must withstand huge pressures. They cannot survive if they are brought to the surface.

## STUDYING THE DEEP

Scientists use submersibles—specially designed submarines—to study the deep ocean and its inhabitants. These vessels have bright lights and mechanical "arms" and "hands" to collect samples. The American *Alvin* can reach nearly 4,575 metres (15,000 ft) and the Russian *Mir* can reach 6,100 metres (20,000 ft).

The Japanese submersible *Shinkai* can descend to 6,527 metres (21,415 ft), the deepest of all.

## HABITAT WATCH

Fishing fleets have caught such large numbers of fish in the sunlight and twilight zones of the oceans that stocks are seriously depleted. Southern bluefin tuna has been hunted to the point where it is in danger of becoming extinct.

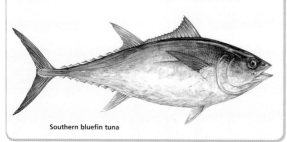

Southern bluefin tuna

1   Seaweed can grow only where there is light, so is rarely below 30 metres (100 ft).
2   Butterflyfish feed on coral polyps in shallow waters.
3   Anchovies dwell in waters above 300 metres (1,000 ft).
4   Bonito are fast-swimming fish above 200 metres (650 ft).
5   Marlin are one of the fastest species of fish in the open ocean; they live down to 900 metres (3,000 ft).
6   Jellyfish float in the surface layers, grazing on tiny plants and animals.
7   Requiem sharks prey on fish and turtles at depths up to 350 metres (1,100 ft).
8   Dolphins hunt small fish, squid and crustaceans. They live above 180 metres (600 ft).
9   Octopuses are stealth predators that live mostly in shallow coastal waters.
10  Sperm whales can dive to 3,000 metres (10,000 ft) to catch large deep-sea squid.
11  Animals become fewer with increasing depth. The width of the cone shows the numbers at each level.
12  Lanternfish live 300–

1,200 metres (1,000–4,000 ft) during the day, migrating upward at night to feed.

**13** Squid are found from the surface down to the depths.

**14** Hatchetfish live down to a depth of 1,500 metres (5,000 ft). At night, they feed on surface-living zooplankton.

**15** The mola mola has a distinctive body shape and can be up to 3 metres (10 ft) long.

**16** Deep-sea rays feed on the bottom of the sea, eating small molluscs, worms and crustaceans.

**17** Lanternfish, and many other fish of the deep sea, have large and sensitive eyes. These help them detect shapes and movement in the darkness.

**18** Viperfish live above 4,400 metres (14,500 ft). They are ambush predators of passing animals.

**19** Some anglerfish live in complete darkness. Their dark skin helps them to remain safely camouflaged.

**20** Ribbonfish reach up to 2.5 metres (8 ft) long, feed on smaller fish and squid, and live near the ocean floor.

**21** Filter-feeding sponges and soft corals are found from the edge of the sea down to 6,000 metres (20,000 ft).

**22** Grenadiers feed on dead and live material. They live between 200 and 2,000 metres (700 and 7,000 ft).

**23** Deep-sea eels are active predators and scavengers that are found down to 3,500 metres (11,500 ft).

**24** Giant squid are the largest invertebrates in the world. They can reach up to 20 metres (65 ft) in length.

**25** Anglerfish dangle a lure at the end of a long "fishing rod". Any fish trying to bite the lure will be trapped by the anglerfish's huge mouth, filled with sharp teeth.

**26** Mantas are related to sharks. They grow to 7 metres (25 ft) across and are the largest species of ray in the world.

**27** Tripodfish live between 250 and 5,700 metres (800 and 19,000 ft).

**28** Deep-sea isopods are found at all depths. Most species are found in the deepest parts of the ocean— between 1,000 and 5,000 metres (3,300 and 16,400 ft).

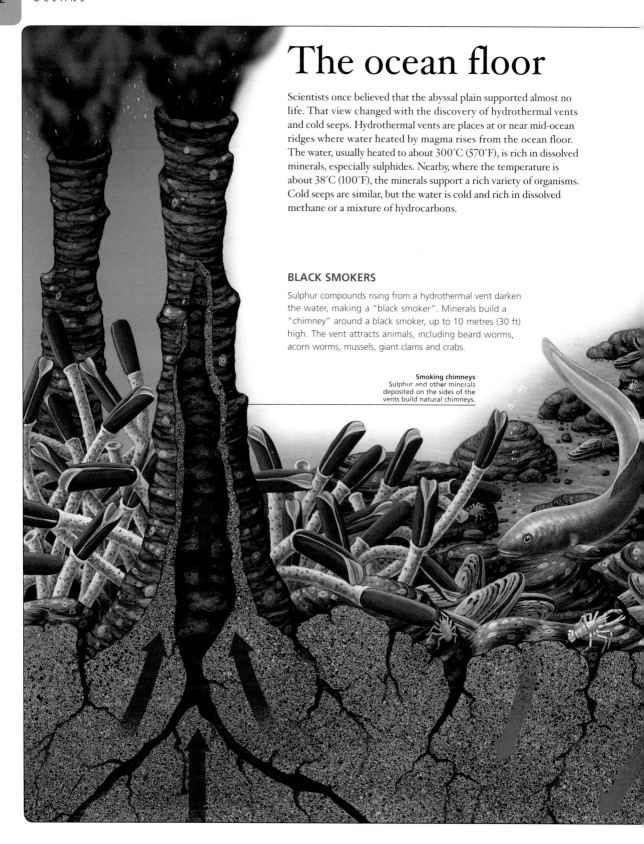

# The ocean floor

Scientists once believed that the abyssal plain supported almost no life. That view changed with the discovery of hydrothermal vents and cold seeps. Hydrothermal vents are places at or near mid-ocean ridges where water heated by magma rises from the ocean floor. The water, usually heated to about 300°C (570°F), is rich in dissolved minerals, especially sulphides. Nearby, where the temperature is about 38°C (100°F), the minerals support a rich variety of organisms. Cold seeps are similar, but the water is cold and rich in dissolved methane or a mixture of hydrocarbons.

## BLACK SMOKERS

Sulphur compounds rising from a hydrothermal vent darken the water, making a "black smoker". Minerals build a "chimney" around a black smoker, up to 10 metres (30 ft) high. The vent attracts animals, including beard worms, acorn worms, mussels, giant clams and crabs.

**Smoking chimneys**
Sulphur and other minerals deposited on the sides of the vents build natural chimneys.

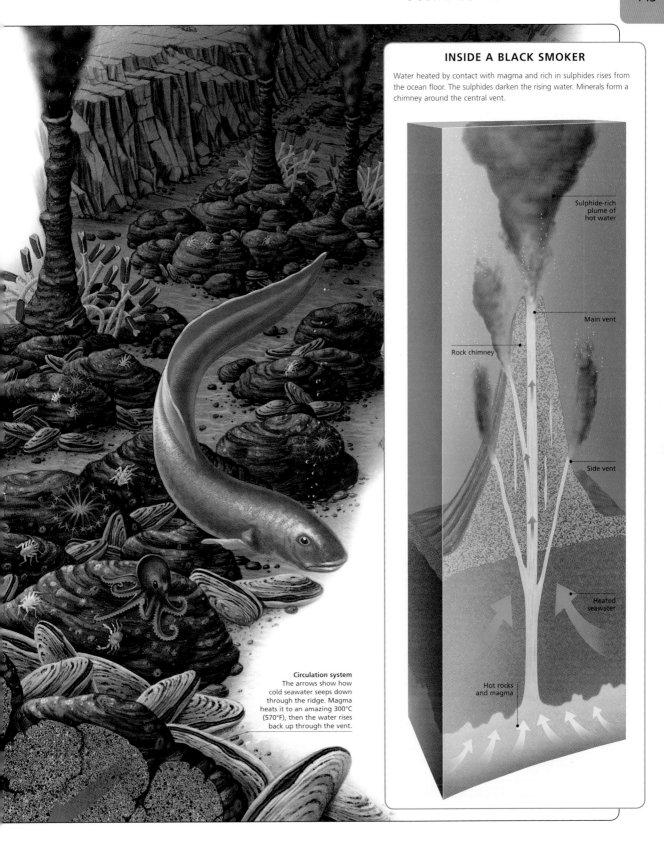

## INSIDE A BLACK SMOKER

Water heated by contact with magma and rich in sulphides rises from the ocean floor. The sulphides darken the rising water. Minerals form a chimney around the central vent.

Sulphide-rich plume of hot water

Main vent

Rock chimney

Side vent

Heated seawater

Hot rocks and magma

**Circulation system**
The arrows show how cold seawater seeps down through the ridge. Magma heats it to an amazing 300°C (570°F), then the water rises back up through the vent.

# THE OCEAN FOOD WEB

## A WEB OF SEA LIFE

Apart from the area around hydrothermal vents, all marine life, even in the deep ocean darkness, depends on photosynthesis, a process by which tiny plants—phytoplankton—turn the Sun's rays into food. Tiny animals—zooplankton—feed on phytoplankton, and larger animals feed on both types of plankton. The ocean food web shows that all marine organisms, as well as seabirds and mammals that spend time on land, are connected by the food they eat.

Sponges are clusters of specialized cells that feed on particles they filter from the water.

The Atlantic puffin has a beak with a saw-like edge that lets it carry several fish back to its young in the nest.

The Sun's energy drives the food web.

Seabirds feed on small fish.

Plants trap the energy of the Sun.

Phytoplankton trap the energy of the Sun.

Zooplankton graze on phytoplankton.

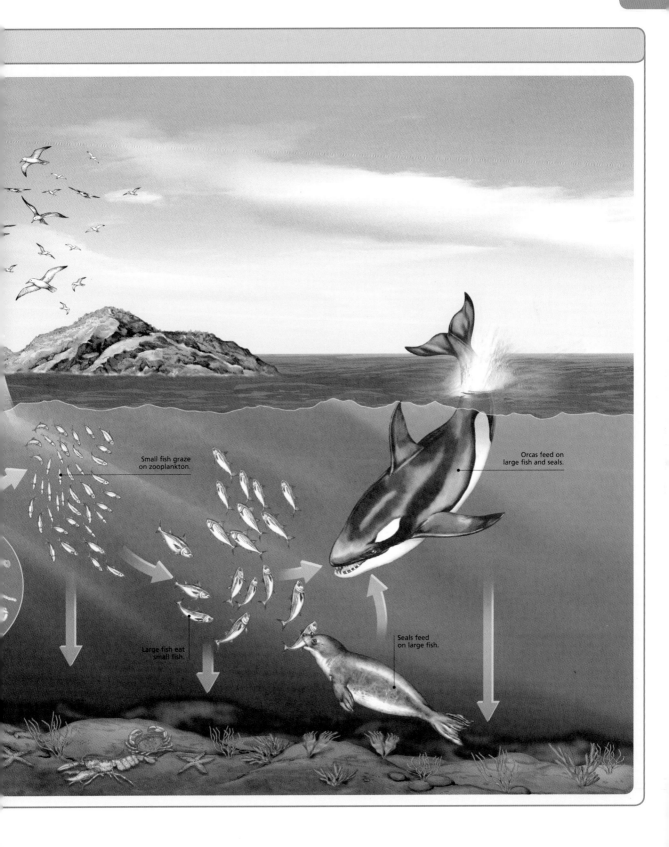

Small fish graze on zooplankton.

Orcas feed on large fish and seals.

Large fish eat small fish.

Seals feed on large fish.

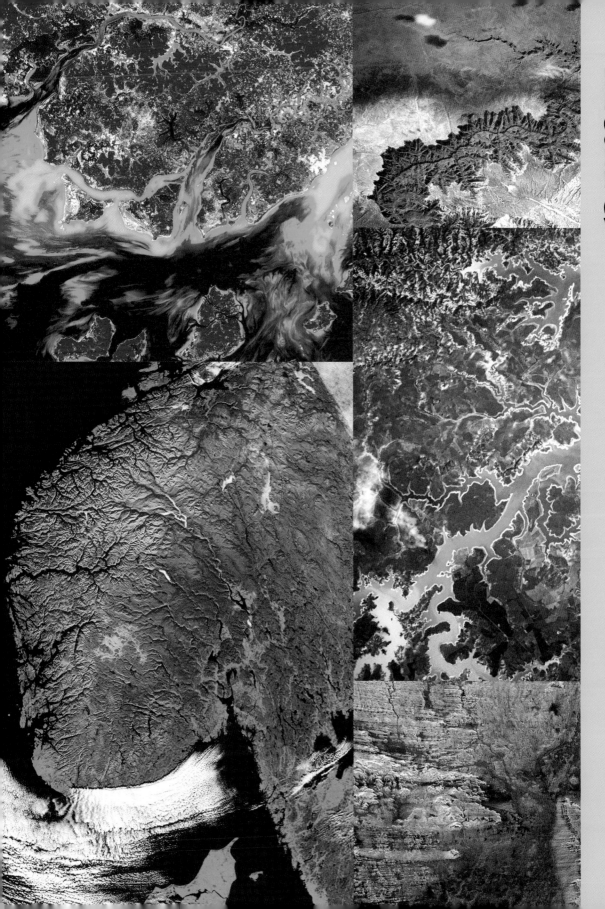

Land

# Mapping Earth

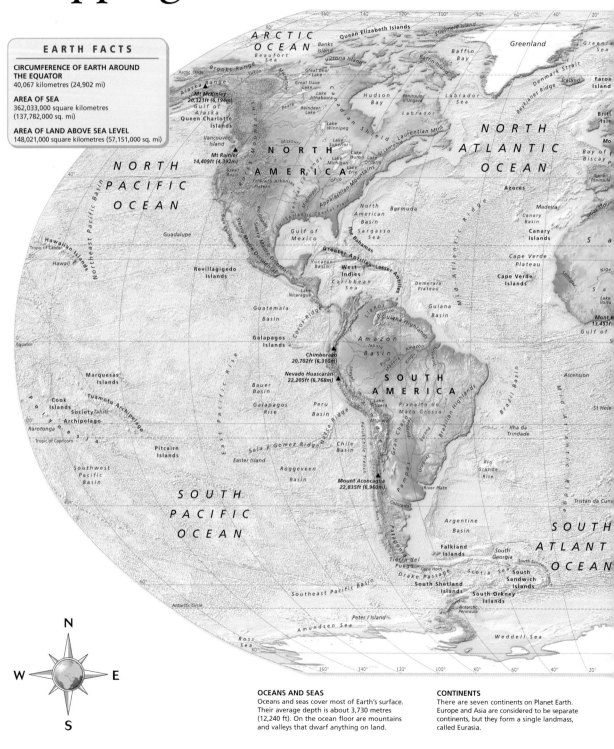

**OCEANS AND SEAS**
Oceans and seas cover most of Earth's surface.
Their average depth is about 3,730 metres
(12,240 ft). On the ocean floor are mountains
and valleys that dwarf anything on land.

**CONTINENTS**
There are seven continents on Planet Earth.
Europe and Asia are considered to be separate
continents, but they form a single landmass,
called Eurasia.

**NORTHERN HEMISPHERE**

**SOUTHERN HEMISPHERE**

**POLAR REGIONS**
Earth's polar regions have extremely low temperatures. The frozen continent of Antarctica lies in the south and the ice-laden Arctic Ocean in the north.

**HEMISPHERES**
Hemisphere, meaning "half ball", refers to a half of a planet's surface. More than two-thirds of Earth's land area is found in the Northern Hemisphere, north of the equator.

# Continents

Oceans and seas dominate the globe, covering 71 per cent of its surface. The land between these large bodies of water is traditionally divided into seven major continents: Europe, Asia, North America, South America, Africa, Australia and Antarctica. Europe and Asia form a single landmass, known as Eurasia, but are conventionally identified as separate continents because of their distinct peoples and histories. Though technically a continent in itself, Australia is usually considered part of the large region of Oceania, which includes other islands of the southwestern Pacific.

# North America

**AREA: 24,474,000** SQUARE KILOMETRES **(9,449,000 SQ. MI)**
**POPULATION: 520,000,000**

The continent of North America extends from just south of the North Pole to just north of the equator. It includes almost every kind of environment, from ice caps to forests, mountains, deserts and jungles. In the west, an almost unbroken chain of mountains stretches from Alaska to Costa Rica and includes the Rocky Mountains. The United States of America (the USA) and Canada are the largest of the continent's 23 countries.

0    1,000 miles

0    1,000 kilometres

## WORLD RECORDS

**WORLD'S LARGEST GORGE**
Grand Canyon, USA, 446 kilometres (277 mi) long, 16 kilometres (10 mi) wide, 1.6 kilometres (1 mi) deep

**WORLD'S LARGEST FRESHWATER LAKE**
Lake Superior, USA–Canada, 82,350 square kilometres (31,800 sq. mi)

**WORLD'S LONGEST CAVE SYSTEM**
Mammoth Caves, USA, 565 kilometres (351 mi)

**WORLD'S LARGEST ACTIVE VOLCANO**
Mauna Loa, Hawaii, USA, 4,170 metres (13,680 ft) high, 120 kilometres (75 mi) long, 50 kilometres (31 mi) wide

**WORLD'S LONGEST BORDER**
US–Canadian border, 6,416 kilometres (3,987 mi)

**WORLD'S TALLEST ACTIVE GEYSER**
Steamboat Geyser, Yellowstone National Park, USA, 115 metres (380 ft)

## NORTH AMERICAN MOUNTAINS AND RIVERS

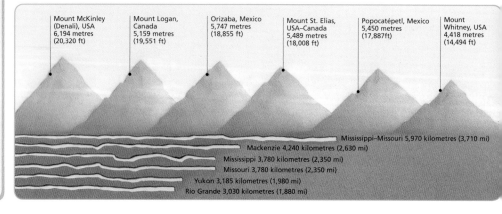

Mount McKinley (Denali), USA 6,194 metres (20,320 ft)

Mount Logan, Canada 5,159 metres (19,551 ft)

Orizaba, Mexico 5,747 metres (18,855 ft)

Mount St. Elias, USA–Canada 5,489 metres (18,008 ft)

Popocatépetl, Mexico 5,450 metres (17,887ft)

Mount Whitney, USA 4,418 metres (14,494 ft)

Mississippi–Missouri 5,970 kilometres (3,710 mi)

Mackenzie 4,240 kilometres (2,630 mi)

Mississippi 3,780 kilometres (2,350 mi)

Missouri 3,780 kilometres (2,350 mi)

Yukon 3,185 kilometres (1,980 mi)

Rio Grande 3,030 kilometres (1,880 mi)

# South America

**AREA:** 17,818,505 SQUARE KILOMETRES (6,877,943 SQ. MI)
**POPULATION:** 375,441,000

From its tropical north, South America stretches 7,240 kilometres (4,500 mi) to the chilly, storm-battered peninsula of Cape Horn, just 1,000 kilometres (600 mi) from Antarctica. The Andes run the entire length of the continent's west coast. In the north, the Amazon (the world's second longest river) snakes eastward from the Andes to the Atlantic Ocean, through vast rainforests that once covered more than one-third of the continent.

Rain falls in the Atacama Desert just once or twice a century, and in some parts of the desert, rain has never been recorded.

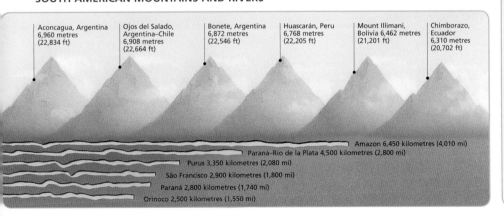

## SOUTH AMERICAN MOUNTAINS AND RIVERS

Aconcagua, Argentina 6,960 metres (22,834 ft)

Ojos del Salado, Argentina–Chile 6,908 metres (22,664 ft)

Bonete, Argentina 6,872 metres (22,546 ft)

Huascarán, Peru 6,768 metres (22,205 ft)

Mount Illimani, Bolivia 6,462 metres (21,201 ft)

Chimborazo, Ecuador 6,310 metres (20,702 ft)

Amazon 6,450 kilometres (4,010 mi)
Paraná–Rio de la Plata 4,500 kilometres (2,800 mi)
Purus 3,350 kilometres (2,080 mi)
São Francisco 2,900 kilometres (1,800 mi)
Paraná 2,800 kilometres (1,740 mi)
Orinoco 2,500 kilometres (1,550 mi)

---

### FAST FACT

Even though most South American countries have Spanish as their first language, more South Americans speak Portuguese. This is because Portuguese-speaking Brazil is the continent's largest country.

---

### WORLD RECORDS

**WORLD'S LONGEST MOUNTAIN CHAIN**
Andes, western South America, 7,600 kilometres (4,700 mi)

**WORLD'S DRIEST PLACE**
Atacama Desert, Chile, average annual rainfall less than 1.3 millimetres (0.05 in)

**WORLD'S HIGHEST WATERFALL**
Angel Falls, Venezuela, 979 metres (3,212 ft)

**WORLD'S HIGHEST CAPITAL CITY**
La Paz, Bolivia, 3,631 metres (11,913 ft)

**WORLD'S HIGHEST NAVIGABLE LAKE**
Lake Titicaca, Peru–Bolivia, 3,810 metres (12,506 ft)

**WORLD'S LARGEST RIVER BY VOLUME**
Amazon, Peru–Brazil, discharges 200,000 cubic metres per second (7,100,000 cu. ft/s) into Atlantic Ocean

**WORLD'S LARGEST RIVER BASIN**
Amazon Basin, northern South America, 7,045,000 square kilometres (2,720,000 sq. mi)

**WORLD'S LARGEST LAGOON**
Lagoa dos Patos, Brazil, 9,850 square kilometres (3,803 sq. mi)

# Europe

**AREA:** 10,354,636 SQUARE KILOMETRES (3,997,929 SQ. MI)

**POPULATION:** 689,546,932

Europe is not a self-contained continent, but the western part of Eurasia. Europe's boundaries are the Atlantic Ocean in the west, the Ural Mountains to the east, the Arctic Ocean in the north, and the Mediterranean Sea to the south. Southern Europe has mild winters and warm, dry summers, while the northern climate is temperate with distinct seasons.

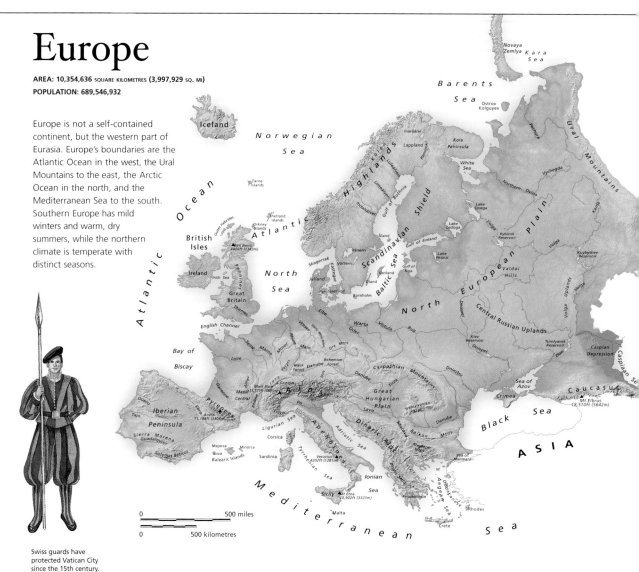

Swiss guards have protected Vatican City since the 15th century.

## EUROPEAN MOUNTAINS AND RIVERS

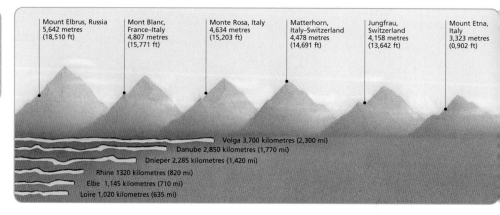

Mount Elbrus, Russia 5,642 metres (18,510 ft)

Mont Blanc, France–Italy 4,807 metres (15,771 ft)

Monte Rosa, Italy 4,634 metres (15,203 ft)

Matterhorn, Italy–Switzerland 4,478 metres (14,691 ft)

Jungfrau, Switzerland 4,158 metres (13,642 ft)

Mount Etna, Italy 3,323 metres (0,902 ft)

Volga 3,700 kilometres (2,300 mi)
Danube 2,850 kilometres (1,770 mi)
Dnieper 2,285 kilometres (1,420 mi)
Rhine 1320 kilometres (820 mi)
Elbe 1,145 kilometres (710 mi)
Loire 1,020 kilometres (635 mi)

# Africa

**AREA:** 30,354,852 SQUARE KILOMETRES (**11,716,972** SQ. MI)
**POPULATION:** 909,154,000

The world's second largest continent makes up almost one-fifth of Earth's land and stretches from the southern shores of the Mediterranean Sea to Cape Agulhas. It is separated from Europe by the Mediterranean Sea and from Asia by the Red Sea and Gulf of Aden. Africa contains the world's largest desert, the Sahara. Arab peoples form the majority of the population in the north. The south's population is made up of hundreds of native tribes, plus the descendants of European and Asian immigrants.

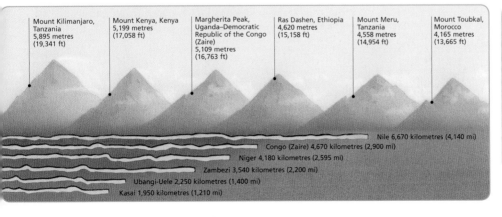

The Sahara, the world's largest desert, covers more than 9.2 million square kilometres (3.5 million sq. mi). Vast seas of sand fill depressions in the landscape. Elsewhere, the surface is rock or gravel.

## AFRICAN MOUNTAINS AND RIVERS

| Mount Kilimanjaro, Tanzania 5,895 metres (19,341 ft) | Mount Kenya, Kenya 5,199 metres (17,058 ft) | Margherita Peak, Uganda–Democratic Republic of the Congo (Zaire) 5,109 metres (16,763 ft) | Ras Dashen, Ethiopia 4,620 metres (15,158 ft) | Mount Meru, Tanzania 4,558 metres (14,954 ft) | Mount Toubkal, Morocco 4,165 metres (13,665 ft) |

Nile 6,670 kilometres (4,140 mi)
Congo (Zaire) 4,670 kilometres (2,900 mi)
Niger 4,180 kilometres (2,595 mi)
Zambezi 3,540 kilometres (2,200 mi)
Ubangi-Uele 2,250 kilometres (1,400 mi)
Kasai 1,950 kilometres (1,210 mi)

### WORLD RECORDS

**WORLD'S LARGEST DESERT**
Sahara, northern Africa, 9,270,000 square kilometres (3,579,000 sq. mi)

**WORLD'S LONGEST RIVER**
Nile, northern Africa, 6,670 kilometres (4,140 mi)

**WORLD'S LARGEST ARTIFICIAL LAKE**
Lake Volta, Ghana, 8,482 square kilometres (3,275 sq. mi)

**WORLD'S HIGHEST TEMPERATURE**
El-Azizia, Libya, shade temperature of 57.3°C (136°F) recorded on September 13, 1922

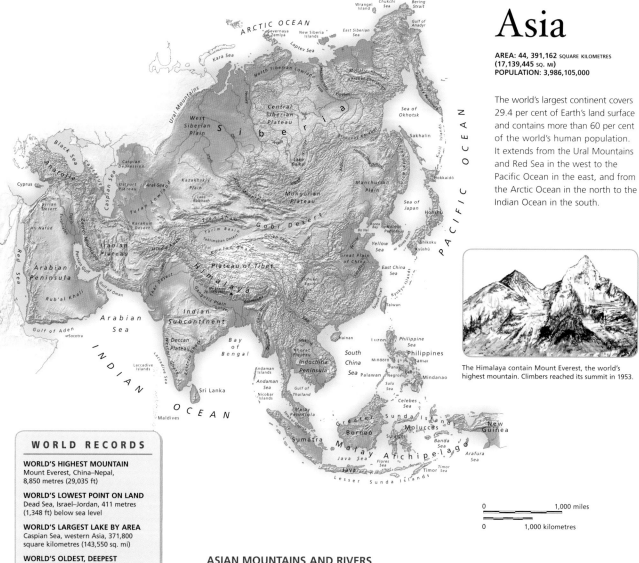

# Asia

**AREA: 44, 391,162** SQUARE KILOMETRES
**(17,139,445** SQ. MI)
**POPULATION: 3,986,105,000**

The world's largest continent covers
29.4 per cent of Earth's land surface
and contains more than 60 per cent
of the world's human population.
It extends from the Ural Mountains
and Red Sea in the west to the
Pacific Ocean in the east, and from
the Arctic Ocean in the north to the
Indian Ocean in the south.

The Himalaya contain Mount Everest, the world's
highest mountain. Climbers reached its summit in 1953.

## WORLD RECORDS

**WORLD'S HIGHEST MOUNTAIN**
Mount Everest, China–Nepal,
8,850 metres (29,035 ft),

**WORLD'S LOWEST POINT ON LAND**
Dead Sea, Israel–Jordan, 411 metres
(1,348 ft) below sea level

**WORLD'S LARGEST LAKE BY AREA**
Caspian Sea, western Asia, 371,800
square kilometres (143,550 sq. mi)

**WORLD'S OLDEST, DEEPEST
AND LARGEST (BY VOLUME) LAKE**
Lake Baikal, Russia, 25 million years old;
1,637 metres (5,371 ft) deep; 23,000
cubic kilometres (5,500 cu. mi) of water.

**WORLD'S LARGEST
COUNTRY BY AREA**
Russia, 17,075,383 square kilometres
(6,592,812 sq. mi)

**WORLD'S LARGEST COUNTRY
BY POPULATION**
China, population 1,313,974,000

**WORLD'S LARGEST CITY
BY POPULATION**
Tokyo, Japan, population 35,197,000

**WORLD'S LONGEST WALL**
Great Wall of China, 3,460 kilometres
(2,150 mi)

**WORLD'S LONGEST RAILWAY LINE**
Trans-Siberian, Russia, 9,297 kilometres
(5,777 mi)

## ASIAN MOUNTAINS AND RIVERS

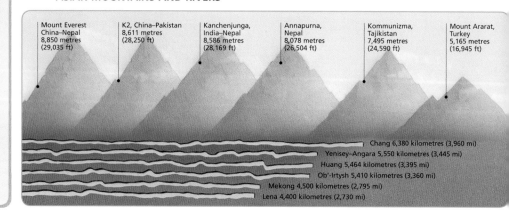

Mount Everest
China–Nepal
8,850 metres
(29,035 ft)

K2, China–Pakistan
8,611 metres
(28,250 ft)

Kanchenjunga,
India–Nepal
8,586 metres
(28,169 ft)

Annapurna,
Nepal
8,078 metres
(26,504 ft)

Kommunizma,
Tajikistan
7,495 metres
(24,590 ft)

Mount Ararat,
Turkey
5,165 metres
(16,945 ft)

Chang 6,380 kilometres (3,960 mi)
Yenisey–Angara 5,550 kilometres (3,445 mi)
Huang 5,464 kilometres (3,395 mi)
Ob'-Irtysh 5,410 kilometres (3,360 mi)
Mekong 4,500 kilometres (2,795 mi)
Lena 4,400 kilometres (2,730 mi)

# Oceania

**AREA: 8,507,753** SQUARE KILOMETRES **(3,283,993** SQ. MI)
**POPULATION: 32,289,000**

Oceania is a region in the South Pacific that consists of Australia, New Zealand, New Guinea, the islands of Melanesia (including Fiji, Papua New Guinea, Vanuatu and Indonesia), Micronesia and Polynesia. It stretches from the tropics to the remote subantarctic Macquarie Island. Australia, New Zealand, Christmas Island, Norfolk Island and the Cocos Islands make up a region called Australasia.

Uluru, the world's largest rock, is in Australia's Northern Territory. It is a sacred place for Australia's Aboriginal people.

## OCEANIAN MOUNTAINS AND RIVERS

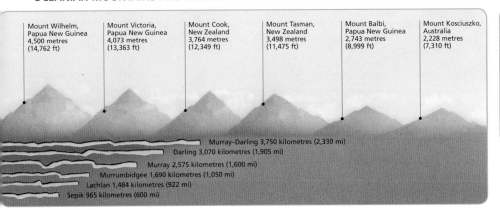

Mount Wilhelm, Papua New Guinea 4,500 metres (14,762 ft)

Mount Victoria, Papua New Guinea 4,073 metres (13,363 ft)

Mount Cook, New Zealand 3,764 metres (12,349 ft)

Mount Tasman, New Zealand 3,498 metres (11,475 ft)

Mount Balbi, Papua New Guinea 2,743 metres (8,999 ft)

Mount Kosciuszko, Australia 2,228 metres (7,310 ft)

Murray–Darling 3,750 kilometres (2,330 mi)
Darling 3,070 kilometres (1,905 mi)
Murray 2,575 kilometres (1,600 mi)
Murrumbidgee 1,690 kilometres (1,050 mi)
Lachlan 1,484 kilometres (922 mi)
Sepik 965 kilometres (600 mi)

## WORLD RECORDS

**WORLD'S LONGEST CORAL REEF**
Great Barrier Reef, Australia,
2,025 kilometres (1,260 mi)

**WORLD'S LARGEST ROCK**
Uluru, Australia, 348 metres (1,142 ft)
high; 2.5 kilometres (1.5 mi) long;
1.6 kilometres (1 mi) wide

**WORLD'S LARGEST SAND ISLAND**
Fraser Island, Australia, 120 kilometres
(74 mi) long

# Islands

Ireland, part of the British Isles, is a continental island off the coast of Europe. Its lush green hills are the result of a mild climate and moist air coming in from the Atlantic Ocean.

An island is an area of land completely surrounded by water. They are found in every ocean and sea—from huge Greenland to tiny dots on the map. There are two kinds of islands: continental and oceanic. A continental island consists of high ground that rises above sea level from a continental shelf. Oceanic islands are not on continental shelves; they are active or extinct volcanoes that rise above sea level from the ocean floor. Because they are isolated from other landmasses, islands are "laboratories of life" that are home to unique plants and animals.

## HOW CONTINENTAL ISLANDS ARE FORMED

When the sea level rises, water flows across low-lying coastal plains. If there is high ground between the plains and the sea, some land may remain above water as an island on the continental shelf.

**BEFORE THE ISLANDS ARE FORMED**

Mountain

Sea level is low.

Mountain

Continental shelf

Coastal plain

**AFTER THE ISLANDS ARE FORMED**

Continental island

Reef

Sea level is high.

Continental island

Continental shelf

# THE FIVE LARGEST ISLANDS

## GREENLAND
Geographically, the world's largest island is part of North America, but historically it is linked to Scandinavia, in Europe. Today, it is a Danish territory.

2,175,600 square kilometres
(840,004 sq. mi)

An iceberg forms a dramatic icy arch over water in the seas off Greenland's central ice sheet.

## NEW GUINEA
This continental island separated from Australia when rising sea levels formed the Torres Strait about 5,000 years ago. Its wildlife is similar to Australia's.

808,510 square kilometres
(312,167 sq. mi)

Buildings in New Guinea are made from local resources; palm trees are used for timber and roof thatch.

## BORNEO
Borneo is part of Asia. It has about 15,000 species of flowering plants, 221 species of mammals and 420 species of birds.

745,561 square kilometres
(287,863 sq. mi)

The high mountains and coral coasts of Borneo are home to more than 30 ethnic groups of people.

## MADAGASCAR
There are highlands in the east, volcanic mountains in the north, plains in the west, and a high, partly desert plateau in the southwest.

587,040 square kilometres
(226,657 sq. mi)

Lemurs are found only in Madagascar. They are part of the island's unique wildlife.

## BAFFIN ISLAND
An ice cap covers the centre of this Canadian Arctic island. Elsewhere the terrain is mountainous. The Norse called the island *Helluland*.

507,451 square kilometres
(195,927 sq. mi)

The Arctic Circle crosses Baffin Island. Midsummer days are 24 hours long, but winters are dark.

Mauritius is an oceanic island that was once an ancient hot-spot volcano. It lies in the Indian Ocean east of Madagascar.

## HABITAT WATCH

Some island species may depend so completely on their environment they cannot tolerate disturbance. The dodo flourished on the African island of Mauritius until the island was discovered in 1507. It was flightless and easy to kill and had been hunted to extinction by 1680.

Dodo

# Atolls

An atoll is a coral reef, usually circular, that projects above the surface of the sea and wholly or partly encloses an area of sea called a lagoon. There may be islands in the lagoon. Atolls begin to form when an underwater volcano rises above the surface. Corals build a fringing reef around the sides. When the rocks beneath the volcano cool and contract, the volcano sinks, but the corals continue to build upward at the same rate. When most of the volcano has sunk below the surface, water fills the area enclosed by the reef to form the lagoon.

## HABITAT WATCH

The coral atolls and islands of the Maldives, found in the Indian Ocean, make up the flattest country on Earth. The highest natural point is only 2.3 metres (7½ ft) above sea level. This means that the Maldives are at great risk from even small rises in sea levels.

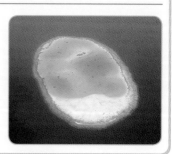

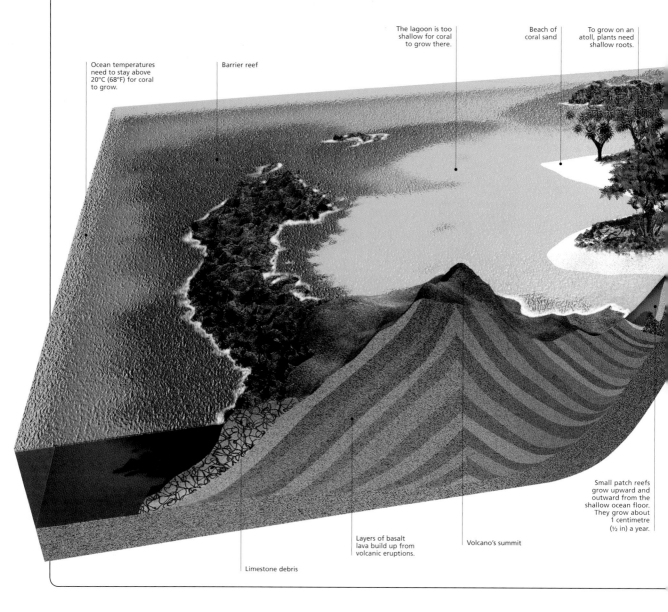

Ocean temperatures need to stay above 20°C (68°F) for coral to grow.

Barrier reef

The lagoon is too shallow for coral to grow there.

Beach of coral sand

To grow on an atoll, plants need shallow roots.

Limestone debris

Layers of basalt lava build up from volcanic eruptions.

Volcano's summit

Small patch reefs grow upward and outward from the shallow ocean floor. They grow about 1 centimetre (½ in) a year.

Bora Bora in Polynesia is a volcanic atoll surrounded by a lagoon and barrier reef.

The Cocos (Keeling) Islands consist of two main atolls and many smaller coral islets.

## HOW ATOLLS FORM

An atoll is a coral reef that grows around the sides of an extinct volcano. As the volcano sinks, the coral grows and encloses a lagoon.

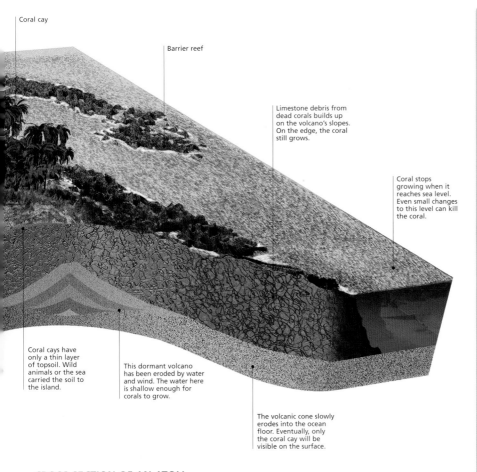

Coral cay

Barrier reef

Limestone debris from dead corals builds up on the volcano's slopes. On the edge, the coral still grows.

Coral stops growing when it reaches sea level. Even small changes to this level can kill the coral.

Coral cays have only a thin layer of topsoil. Wild animals or the sea carried the soil to the island.

This dormant volcano has been eroded by water and wind. The water here is shallow enough for corals to grow.

The volcanic cone slowly erodes into the ocean floor. Eventually, only the coral cay will be visible on the surface.

**Active volcano** A volcano rises above the sea, fed by magma from beneath the ocean floor.

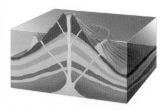

**Fringing reef** A reef forms as corals grow on the sides of the volcano just below sea level.

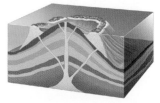

**Lagoon** The volcano sinks and erodes into the ocean floor, leaving the reef to enclose a lagoon.

## CROSS SECTION OF AN ATOLL

Coral on the sides of an extinct volcano grows upward as the volcano sinks. Birds drop seeds that germinate on the coral, which helps to form a shallow soil.

# Ecosystems

Almost every part of our planet is inhabited by an amazing variety of living things. There may be between 10 and 100 million kinds—or species—of plants and animals on Earth. All living things exist in the biosphere, which is made up of the land, oceans and atmosphere. Within the biosphere, there are many kinds of environments. Over millions of years, living things have gradually altered their bodies and behaviour to suit their environments. This process is called adaptation. Together, an environment and its inhabitants form an ecosystem. Members of an ecosystem depend on each other for food and resources.

## THE LIVING WORLD

Each of Earth's environments has its own community of plants and animals. This illustration shows how ecosystems change between the tropical rainforests (far left) and the polar ice caps (far right).

**OCEANS**
Water covers almost 71 per cent of Earth's surface. Marine environments vary, depending on latitude and depth, and animals travel extensively.

**TROPICAL FORESTS**
Tropical forests require year-round warmth and abundant rain. Rainforests need rain all year. Seasonal forests are dry for part of the year.

**SUBTROPICAL GRASSLANDS**
Grasses tolerate a climate that is too dry for forests. Subtropical grasslands, called savannah, border tropical forests. They have both dry and rainy seasons.

**DESERTS**
A desert occurs where more water evaporates than falls as rain. Deserts occur in the subtropics and on the west coast and interior of continents.

# WORLD ECOSYSTEMS

**KEY**

- Tropical forests
- Temperate and coniferous forests
- Grasslands
- Tundra
- Deserts
- Mountains
- Polar regions

**MOUNTAINS**
The higher the land, the fewer plants there are and the colder and windier it gets. Thick fur coats keep many mountain animals warm.

**TUNDRA AND POLAR REGIONS**
No plants can survive on ice caps, where snow and ice persist throughout the year. Tundra vegetation occurs where the ground surface thaws in summer.

**TEMPERATE GRASSLANDS**
...mperate grasslands—prairie, pampa, ...eppe and veld—occur where winters ...e cool and rainfall is light. Scattered ...oups of shrubs and trees thrive.

**TEMPERATE FORESTS**
Trees grow well in wet temperate regions. In areas with cold winters, most of the trees are deciduous. Some animals migrate in winter.

**CONIFEROUS FORESTS**
Coniferous forests form a wide belt around the Northern Hemisphere where winters are long and the ground is frozen.

# Tropical forests

Lowland regions near the equator that lie along river valleys and near coasts have a warm, wet climate. Rain falls fairly evenly through the year. This is the climate that supports tropical rainforest. In these steamy jungles, the air is always humid. Plant growth is dense, with tall trees covered in vines and smaller plants—epiphytes—growing on their trunks and branches. Tropical rainforests are home to more species than any other environment on Earth. Large areas of the tropics have distinct wet and dry seasons. There the forests are more open and a greater number of trees shed their leaves.

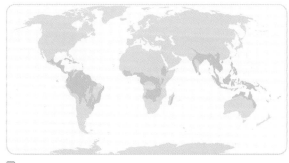

Tropical forests

## LIFE IN A BROMELIAD

The tank bromeliad grows on host trees high in the rainforest and produces food in its leaves. The leaves also collect water, which attracts many animals. They, in turn, deposit droppings, which provide nourishment for the bromeliad and help it to produce more food.

## SHALLOW ROOTS

Many tropical forests grow in poor soil. Tree roots are shallow and remain near the surface.

Velvet worms have been discovered in bromeliads, far above their usual home on the forest floor.

A female poison-dart frog deposits tadpoles into the water-filled bromeliad.

A mouse opossum eats a damsel fly larva from the bromeliad pool.

An alligator lizard drinks from the pool.

Beetle larvae prey on tadpoles.

A variety of land snails forage and hide between the leaves.

Predatory and scavenging ants patrol the area for anything they can find.

The roots take the nutrients before they are lost at deeper levels.

Root tips attach themselves to fallen leaves.

Harpy eagle

Red howler
monkeys

Silky (pygmy)
anteater

Linne's
two-toed
sloth

Kinkajou

Geoffroy's
spider monkey

Tree porcupine

Toco toucans

Zebra butterfly

Emerald
tree boa

Tamandua

Tree frog

Anole lizard

Jaguar

**SOUTH AMERICAN SCENE**
This scene shows many typical
rainforest features: tall trees
with straight trunks and high
crowns; buttress roots, vines,
and other creepers; bromeliads
and other epiphytes; forest
floor fungi and a diverse
range of creatures.

Brazilian
tapir

Cock of
the rock

Anaconda

Bushmaster
snake

Capybara

Giant armadillo

Reticulated
poison-dart frog

Hoatzin

# Tropical forests

A tropical rainforest is thick with vegetation and teeming with animal life. The year-round warm, moist climate means there is no seasonal slowing of plant growth, and organic material lying on the ground decomposes rapidly. The tallest trees compete for sunlight—some are more than 30 metres (100 ft) tall. Below them there are three layers of trees and shrubs that grow to different heights. Smaller plants—and many animals—flourish on the cool, damp and dark rainforest floor.

Bwindi Impenetrable Forest is an ancient rainforest in the East African country of Uganda. Half of the world's population of mountain gorillas live in its midst.

## ON THE FOREST FLOOR

When a tree sheds a branch or falls to the ground, it starts to decompose. Fungi and beetles feed on the rotting wood, and bacteria feed on their waste. Mosses, ferns and small plants grow on the fallen branch or tree. Their roots obtain nutrients from pockets of soil trapped in hollows and crevices.

Birds find food among the leaf litter.

Spiders and insects find food among the rotting wood.

## HABITAT WATCH

The Amazon basin holds the world's largest tropical rainforest, but about 23,310 square kilometres (9,000 sq. mi) is cleared each year. Efforts are being made to reduce the destruction.

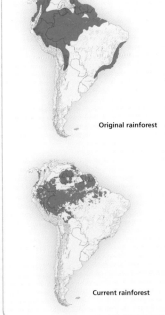

Original rainforest

Current rainforest

## USING THE FOREST

Tropical forests cover large areas of land that would support more people if it were converted to farmland. Many tropical trees yield valuable hardwood timber. Illegal logging opens up forest areas, providing many opportunities for exploitation.

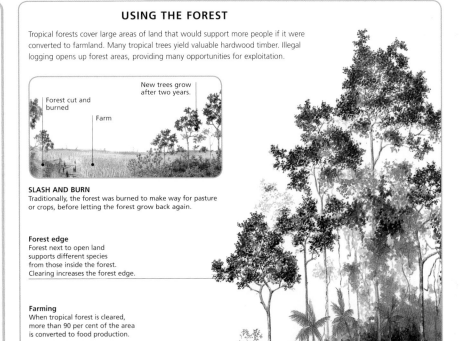

New trees grow after two years.

Forest cut and burned

Farm

**SLASH AND BURN**
Traditionally, the forest was burned to make way for pasture or crops, before letting the forest grow back again.

**Forest edge**
Forest next to open land supports different species from those inside the forest. Clearing increases the forest edge.

**Farming**
When tropical forest is cleared, more than 90 per cent of the area is converted to food production.

Termites eat large amounts of plant litter, especially bark and wood.

# Temperate and coniferous forests

Forests in Canada or Russia are different from the forests in France, India, Indonesia or Australia. Climate and soil influence the kind of trees that grow in a forest, and the trees determine what grows on the forest floor beneath them. In cold, northern latitudes, evergreen conifers grow in coniferous, or boreal, forests (named after Boreas, the Greek god of the north wind), but few plants grow on these dark forest floors. In temperate regions of the world, spring flowers grow on the floor of deciduous forests, where the trees shed their leaves in winter. Mixed temperate forests of different kinds of conifers and flowering trees grow in some parts of the world.

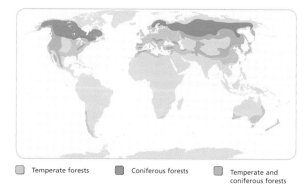

☐ Temperate forests    ■ Coniferous forests    ☐ Temperate and coniferous forests

## LIFE IN THE FOREST

The forest provides seeds, nuts, fruit and leaves for food, along with herbs and grasses in clearings, and holds nesting sites for many species. Plant eaters are prey for carnivores.

Brown bear

Squirrel

Moose

Lynx

Crossbills

Wolverine

**COLOUR BLAZE**
A mixed forest in autumn is ablaze with the green leaves of evergreen trees and the brown, yellow, orange and red leaves of deciduous trees.

**Burst of yellow dust**
In spring, the male pine cone releases millions of pollen grains. A few days later, the male cone drops off the tree. Its job is finished.

**THE CONIFER CYCLE**
Conifers do not need water to reproduce. They rely on wind to carry pollen from the male cone to seeds in the female cone.

**Sticky cone**
The pollen lands on a sticky female cone. A pollen tube starts to grow and, up to a year later, the seeds are fertilized.

**Germination**
If the seed finds a spot with enough warmth, moisture and light, it germinates and a new conifer grows.

**Swelling cone**
The female cone grows to four times its size as the seeds grow inside. Two years later when the seeds are mature, the cone opens to release them.

**Spreading seeds**
Each seed has a wing and can take off in the wind. It also has food for germination inside a tough, outer casing.

Owl

Grouse

## HABITAT WATCH

About 8,000 years ago, forests covered about 70 per cent of Europe. Many were cleared to provide fuel, farmland and building materials.

Now they are being replanted by governments and private industry. The forested area of Europe is increasing by about 0.1 per cent a year.

Original forest cover

Current forest cover

# Grasslands

Grasslands occur in areas that get more rain than deserts but not as much as forests. They have few trees, and some have no trees at all. Grasses are hardier than trees and lose less water in dry winds than taller plants. Grasslands have different names in different parts of the world. The North American prairie once extended over much of the continent. When Spanish explorers first saw the South American pampa, they had to stand on the backs of their horses to see across the grass. Eurasia's grasslands, or steppes, extend from Hungary to China. Tropical grasslands, called savannahs, grow on all continents, but are most famous in Africa. African savannah supports elephants, giraffes, zebras and lions.

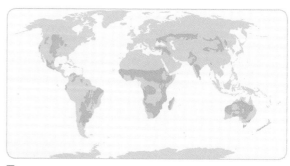

Grasslands

## HABITAT WATCH

During the 19th and early 20th centuries, much of the North American prairie was plowed to grow grain. Little of the original prairie survived, but some is now returning.

Original prairie cover

Current prairie cover

Bison, the native cattle of North America, were hunted almost to extinction. Now they are recovering. This herd is grazing on grassland in Grand Teton National Park, Wyoming.

## GRASSLANDS AROUND THE WORLD

Grasses are the main plants in all grasslands, but the species are different on each continent, as are the other plants growing with them. They provide abundant food for herds of grazing mammals. Most temperate grasslands are used to raise livestock or grow crops. African savannah is unsuitable for farming.

A herd of antelope grazes beneath a stormy sky on the African savannah.

Flowering plants beneath a clear blue sky bring colour to the Kazakhstan steppe.

Much of the pampas in Argentina is used to graze sheep and cattle.

Western grey kangaroos live in the western and southern grasslands of Australia.

Giraffes

Elephants

Zebras

Wading bird

Cheetah

Gazelle

Vultures

Hyenas

Lions

## AFRICAN SAVANNAH

Open tropical grassland, with
scattered thorn trees, supports
herds of grazing mammals and
the predators that hunt them, as
well as birds and reptiles. Much
of the savannah is now protected
to conserve wildlife. However,
poaching remains a problem.

# Tundra

Tundra exists beyond the limit of coniferous forest, where the climate is too cold and the gales too drying for forest trees to survive. A little way below the surface, a layer of soil remains permanently frozen—this is called permafrost. Tree roots cannot penetrate the rock-solid frozen soil, so the trees that do grow, such as birch and juniper, are only about 90 centimetres (3 ft) tall. In summer, the surface thaws and sedges grow in pools and marshy areas. Lichens and mosses grow among the rocks. Grasses grow in the drier places and everywhere there are plants that flower and go to seed before the ice returns.

Tundra

Flowering plants that emerged when the ice began to thaw on the slopes of Mount Marathon in Alaska, USA, are now releasing seeds that will germinate next summer.

## HABITAT WATCH

Polar bears live in the Arctic tundra and hunt seals on the pack ice offshore. As Arctic temperatures rise, coniferous forest expands northward into the tundra, and the pack ice starts to melt. This reduces the polar bears' range.

Glacier ice recedes from the tundra on South Georgia Island, off the coast of Cape Horn.

## ARCTIC TUNDRA

At the tree line, the trees are bare on the windblown side. Low-growing flowering plants, grasses, mosses and lichens survive better near ground level, where the temperature is warmer and the wind less chilling. In summer there is water and warmth for a short growing season.

### COPING WITH THE COLD

The glacier buttercup has adapted to bitter cold and a short growing season.

White petals reflect sunlight to the centre of the flower.

Flowers move slowly around to trap sunlight throughout the day.

Dark flower centre absorbs heat to warm the flower.

Strong roots anchor the plant firmly in the soil.

# Deserts

Deserts cover one-seventh of Earth's land surface. They are dry regions that on average receive less than 100 millimetres (4 in) of rain per year. Because there are no clouds, the days are very hot. But when the Sun sets, the temperature drops quickly and the nights can be freezing cold. Only about a quarter of the world's deserts are made up of sand; most are rugged, rocky landscapes. The main subtropical deserts of the Northern Hemisphere are the Sahara, Arabian and the Thar deserts, and the deserts of southwestern United States and Mexico. In the Southern Hemisphere, the major deserts are the Namib and Kalahari in Africa, the Atacama in South America, and the deserts of central Australia.

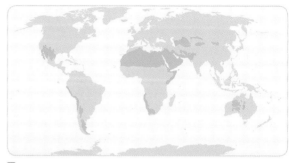

 Deserts

The sand dunes of the Sahara cover such a vast area they are called seas of sand. Like ocean waves, the dunes are constantly shifting.

## HABITAT WATCH

From time to time, prolonged drought allows deserts to expand. When the rains return, plants appear and the land recovers. If livestock farmers are forced into smaller pastures, overgrazing may destroy the plant cover, making recovery difficult. This is called desertification. The map shows areas under threat in Africa.

☐ Desert
■ Low risk
■ At risk

A poisonous gila monster suns itself beneath a prickly pear cactus in the Arizona Desert, USA.

**ASIAN DESERT**
The Thar Desert in northwestern India and Pakistan is covered by rolling sand dunes, with some rocky outcrops.

**AUSTRALIAN DESERT**
The Pinnacles Desert in Western Australia is covered in limestone formations, which are the eroded remains of ancient sea shells.

**NORTH AMERICAN DESERT**
Saguaro cactus grow in the Sonoran Desert, Arizona, USA. This slow-growing plant stores food in its tall green stem.

## HOT AND COLD

Rock and sand absorb heat quickly. During the day they can grow very hot. From late afternoon, as the Sun sinks lower in the sky, the desert surface loses heat by radiation faster than it absorbs it. Nights are cold.

By day the desert surface absorbs warmth rapidly, and by noon it is very hot.

At night the surface loses the heat it absorbed by day, and the temperature falls.

## WHY DESERTS ARE DRY

Cool, moist air approaches a mountain range and drops over the mountains as rain. The air that reaches the other side is dry and sinks to the ground, where it heats up and becomes even drier.

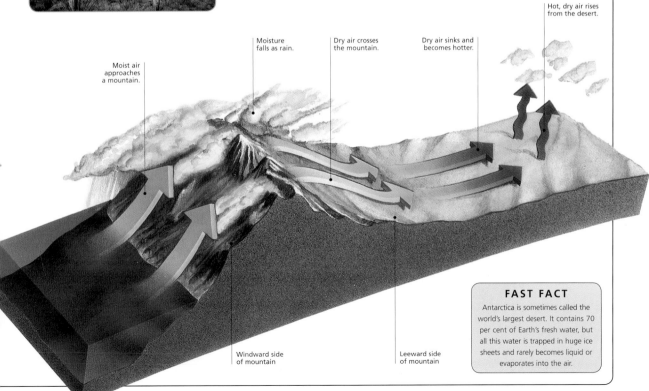

Moist air approaches a mountain.

Moisture falls as rain.

Dry air crosses the mountain.

Dry air sinks and becomes hotter.

Hot, dry air rises from the desert.

Windward side of mountain

Leeward side of mountain

**FAST FACT**
Antarctica is sometimes called the world's largest desert. It contains 70 per cent of Earth's fresh water, but all this water is trapped in huge ice sheets and rarely becomes liquid or evaporates into the air.

# Deserts

In some deserts, rain may not fall for many years. Then, quite suddenly, a storm will break and there is a huge downpour that lasts just a few hours. The absence of moisture in the air means that clouds are rare and the skies are clear for most of the year. When the land is heated by the Sun, daytime temperatures can soar above 40°C (100°F). Plants and animals survive only if they adapt to the extreme heat and dryness and make the most of the little rain that does fall. But, although they are dry and windy, not all deserts are hot. The cold winds that blow across the Gobi Desert of central Asia produce freezing conditions, but it is still considered a desert because it has very little rain.

**GROWTH SPURTS**
Saguaro cacti grow very slowly, with spurts during the summer rainy season. They flower and produce fruit after about 30 years and live 150 to 200 years.

| 10 years | 50 years | 75 years | 100 years | 150–200 years |

## LIFE AMONG THE SPINIFEX

Spinifex is a kind of hummock grass found in the desert areas of Australia. Each plant has a centre of dead, matted leaves, with green leaves covering the outside. Most are less than 90 centimetres (3 ft) tall, but they support many kinds of wildlife.

 The jewelled gecko feeds on termites that live in the spinifex.

 Small cockroaches find food and shelter in the spinifex.

 The crimson chat visits spinifex to find insects such as cockroaches.

 A legless lizard preys on smaller lizards and geckos.

 The desert skink eats termites and other small creatures.

 A tiny ninguai wriggles through spinifex to find insects.

**WATER STORAGE**
The succulent leaves and the soft fibre inside the trunk of the quiver tree store water. The white-powdered branches and pale trunk reflect the Sun's rays and stop the tree from overheating.

White-winged doves feed on the flowers and the moist, energy-rich ripening saguaro fruit.

# THE DESERT AT NIGHT

The saguaro cactus produces flowers, fruit and seeds that attract animals. It also provides nesting sites for birds. Its flowers open mainly at night.

Saguaro flowers close during the midday heat to save water. They usually open at night.

The cactus wren builds its nest in the saguaro's branches.

The Sonoran whipsnake steals eggs and chicks from a bird's nest fixed to the saguaro.

The antelope ground-squirrel obtains most of its water from the seeds, fruit and nectar.

The gila woodpecker builds its nest in a hole that it digs in the saguaro.

Lesser long-nosed bats feed at night, using their long tongues to obtain nectar from flowers.

Saguaro flowers, with large yellow centres, appear in May and June.

# Mountains

Mountains make up about one-fifth of the land surface of Earth and are home to about a tenth of the human population. Most mountains form part of a chain or range. These may be linked to form a mountain belt, or cordillera (from the Spanish for "little rope"), and in turn may form part of a global mountain system. There are two main mountain systems. One circles the Pacific Ocean and includes the Andes of South America, the mountains of the American west, the icy mountains of Alaska and the mountains of Indonesia, Japan, New Guinea and New Zealand. The second includes the European Alps and the Himalaya Mountains in Asia.

 Mountains

The Matterhorn is one of Europe's highest mountains, with a distinctive, steep-sided shape. Its name comes from the German words *matt*, meaning valley, and *horn*, meaning peak.

## HABITAT WATCH

Mount Everest in the Himalaya attracts many climbers and some have discarded used packaging and equipment rather than carry it, leaving large amounts of rubbish. Volunteers are clearing it, and the Nepalese government now restricts access to the mountain.

The Himalaya are still rising, as the Indian tectonic plate moves northward. They are the world's highest mountains and are growing by about 0.5 centimetres (0.2 in) a year.

# HOW THE HIMALAYA FORMED

About 71 million years ago, India broke away from the southern supercontinent of Gondwana and began moving northward. The Indian Plate made contact with the Eurasian Plate about 30 million years ago, and the mountains began to rise. The main episode of mountain building occurred 20 million years ago.

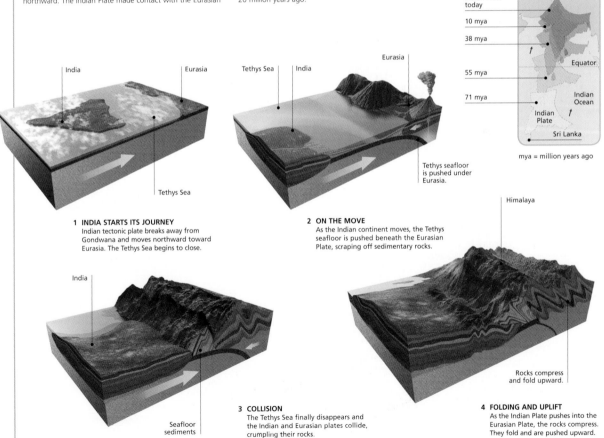

Eurasian Plate

Indian Plate today

10 mya

38 mya

55 mya

Equator

71 mya

Indian Ocean

Indian Plate

Sri Lanka

mya = million years ago

**1  INDIA STARTS ITS JOURNEY**
Indian tectonic plate breaks away from Gondwana and moves northward toward Eurasia. The Tethys Sea begins to close.

India            Eurasia

Tethys Sea

**2  ON THE MOVE**
As the Indian continent moves, the Tethys seafloor is pushed beneath the Eurasian Plate, scraping off sedimentary rocks.

Tethys Sea   India                     Eurasia

Tethys seafloor is pushed under Eurasia.

**3  COLLISION**
The Tethys Sea finally disappears and the Indian and Eurasian plates collide, crumpling their rocks.

India

Seafloor sediments

**4  FOLDING AND UPLIFT**
As the Indian Plate pushes into the Eurasian Plate, the rocks compress. They fold and are pushed upward.

Himalaya

Rocks compress and fold upward.

# Mountains

The rugged terrain, steep slopes and harsh climates of mountain regions make them hostile places for people to live permanently. Mountains are wild places, where only plants and animals that have adapted to the severe conditions can live and thrive. Above the tree line, the soil is thin and winds are strong, which restricts plant growth. This limits the food supply for animals. Wild sheep and llamas live in small flocks, but mountain pastures cannot support large groups of animals. Instead, small numbers of many species, all with different needs, share the resources but do not compete for food.

**North American Rockies** These pikas live in the Rockies, part of a parallel chain of ranges that extends from New Mexico to British Columbia.

**South American Andes** The Andes run the length of South America. They are home to wild guinea pigs and these llamas, a kind of camel.

**European Alps** Occupying a large area in central Europe, the Alps are accessible to grazing animals such as the goat-like chamois.

**African Atlas Mountains** This forested and snow-capped range extends 2,400 kilometres (1,500 mi) parallel to the Mediterranean coast.

**Asian Tien Shan Mountains** Between Russia and China, Asia's Tien Shan have snow-covered peaks rising to more than 6,100 metres (20,000 ft).

## ANIMALS OF THE MOUNTAINS

Many mountain animals are closely related to species found in the lowlands. Others, such as sure-footed mountain sheep, are found only among cliffs and narrow shelves where birds of prey and wildcats cannot reach them.

### MOUNTAIN CREATURES

1　Rock hyrax
2　Golden eagle
3　Mountain goat
4　Puma
5　Poison-dart frog
6　Grasshopper
7　White-tailed jackrabbit

**Transantarctic Mountains** Extending 4,827 kilometres (3,000 mi) across Antarctica, the mountains' bare rock peaks rise above the ice sheet.

**New Zealand Southern Alps** Rising more than 3,660 metres (12,000 ft), this eroded range occupies the centre of New Zealand's South Island.

# Rivers

Rivers carry fresh water across the land and into the sea. Many begin their journey high in the mountains. They start as small streams that tumble over the rocks, growing larger as other streams join them. They can be quite large by the time they reach the lowlands. Other rivers start on lower ground, emerging as springs at places where groundwater rises to the surface. As rivers flow across plains and wide valleys, they slow down and widen, often meandering from side to side. Water draining into rivers from the surrounding land carries nutrients that allow aquatic plants to grow. These provide food for insects and fish, which in turn are hunted by larger fish and birds.

On level ground a river slows, widens and meanders. River meanders move slowly forward as the river erodes one bank while depositing material on the other.

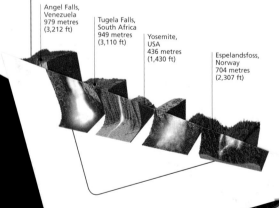

Angel Falls, Venezuela 979 metres (3,212 ft)

Tugela Falls, South Africa 949 metres (3,110 ft)

Yosemite, USA 436 metres (1,430 ft)

Espelandsfoss, Norway 704 metres (2,307 ft)

## WATERFALLS

A sharp, vertical drop in a river, usually produced by a fault in the underlying rocks, sends water tumbling down to the lower level and forms a waterfall. Angel Falls is the world's highest. Iguazú Falls, on the Brazil–Argentina border, is the widest at 2.7 kilometres (1.7 mi).

Iguazú Falls contains 270 individual waterfalls that form a horseshoe around Devil's Throat (above).

# DELTAS

## FROM RIVER TO SEA

When large rivers cross a level plain before reaching the coast, they lose speed. The slow-moving river divides to pass obstacles and deposits the silt it has carried from upstream, which forms new obstacles. Eventually, a complex, often fan-shaped network of channels is formed. This is a delta.

### HOW A DELTA GROWS

A river slows as it enters the sea. This causes it to drop its load of sediment. A major river will constantly deposit new sediment on top of earlier deposits, so its delta builds steadily outward into the sea.

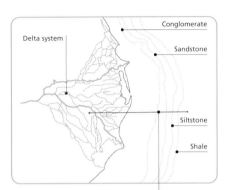

Delta system

Conglomerate

Sandstone

Siltstone

Shale

Area of illustration

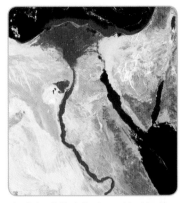

The Nile is probably the best known delta. It begins near Cairo in Egypt. It is about 160 kilometres (100 mi) long and 240 kilometres (150 mi) wide at the coast.

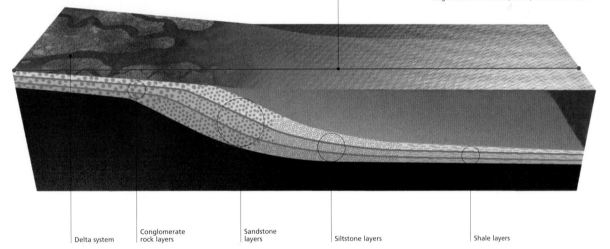

Delta system

Conglomerate rock layers

Sandstone layers

Siltstone layers

Shale layers

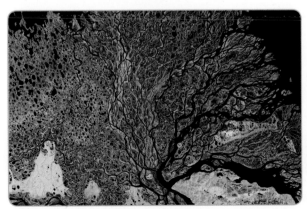

**Braided delta** Rivers such as the Lena, in Russia that carry large sediment pieces deposit them as they slow, blocking their channels. The water flows in a braided pattern around the pieces.

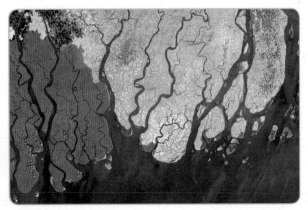

**Meandering delta** Rivers such as the Ganges, in India, that carry fine sand or silt but few large pieces of sediment do not block their channels. They follow slowly changing meandering paths.

# Estuaries

An estuary occurs where the fresh water of a river meets the salt water of the sea. As the river enters the sea, it slows until it can no longer carry the material it has picked up along its journey. It deposits sand and coarser sediment, which form sandbars. Where fresh and salt water meet, reactions between them cause fine particles to clump together and settle, creating mud flats. Many estuaries are tidal. Where the tide is large, the fresh and salt water can form separate, parallel channels. Where the tide is small, the salt water may flow beneath the fresh water. The constantly changing conditions of an estuary attract many different kinds of life.

## HABITAT WATCH

Large-scale shrimp farming is big business in Asia. Shrimp are grown in the mangrove swamps of Asia's estuaries, and most of these estuaries are now under threat. Malaysia alone lost 2,350 square kilometres (910 sq. mi) of mangroves between 1980 and 1990 to shrimp farming and agriculture.

## LIFE IN AN ESTUARY

Waterbirds, insects, worms, shellfish, crabs, fish and plants share the safe environment of an estuary, where there is always plenty of food.

A great white egret stalks the waters for fish.

A tributary of the river flows into the estuary.

Sea

The estuary is where river and sea meet.

Mangroves can grow in fresh or salt water.

River

**VIEW FROM ABOVE**
Fresh water from a river flows into a sheltered estuary, where it mixes with salt water from the sea. Mangroves grow on both sides of this estuary, with only a narrow channel between them.

Bluefish live in both fresh and salt water.

Blue crabs bury themselves into the mud for the winter.

Avocets sweep their upturned beaks through the water for fish.

Buried ghost nippers nip attackers with their claws.

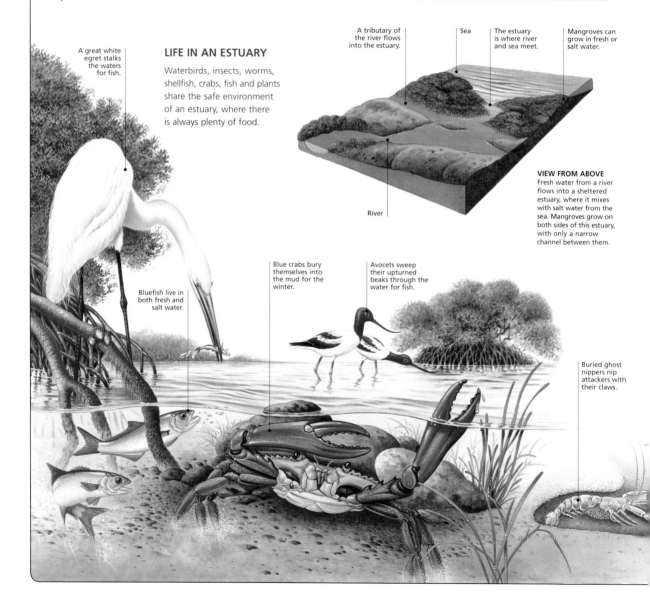

As the Maroochy River flows into the sea in Queensland, Australia, the shifting sandbars of the estuary are clearly seen.

## KINDS OF ESTUARIES

Although a river empties into it, an estuary is really an inlet of the sea. There are four ways such an inlet can form.

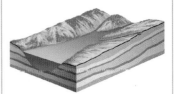

**Drowned river valley** This forms where a rise in sea level has flooded an existing river valley.

**Fjord** This is a deep, steep-sided valley carved by a now-melted glacier, which carries a small river.

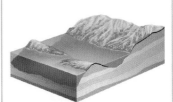

**Bar-built estuary** Sediment from a river creates a sandbar across its mouth with a lagoon behind.

**Tectonic estuary** This occurs where rock faults cause a section of coast to sink below sea level.

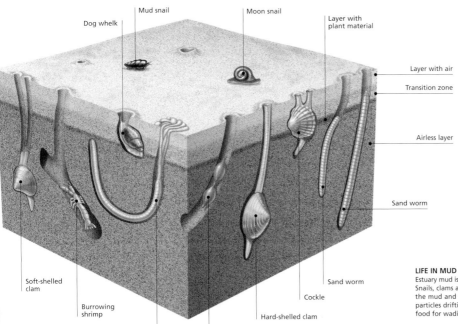

Dog whelk · Mud snail · Moon snail · Layer with plant material · Layer with air · Transition zone · Airless layer · Sand worm · Soft-shelled clam · Burrowing shrimp · Lugworm · Peanut worm · Hard-shelled clam · Cockle · Sand worm

**LIFE IN MUD**
Estuary mud is waterlogged and airless. Snails, clams and worms burrow into the mud and feed at high tide on particles drifting past. They are then food for wading birds.

# Wetlands

A wetland is any area of land that is wholly or partly covered by shallow water. The water can be fresh or salty. Swamps, marshes, bogs, lakes, rivers and estuaries are all wetlands. Wetlands offer many habitats for plants and animals that cannot survive in deep water or on dry land. They are a haven for birds, providing a wealth of fish, plants and insects for food, as well as reeds and rushes for nesting. As rivers continually deposit sediment and plants grow in the mud, wetlands are slowly changing all the time. Many wetlands are threatened, however, because they can be drained and used for farming, forestry or building. Others have been drained to control insect pests, such as mosquitoes.

## HABITAT WATCH

The Pantanal in Brazil is the world's largest wetland. In summer, the rivers overflow their banks to form swamps and marshes that are home to thousands of plants and animals. However, 99 per cent of the Pantanal is privately owned by cattle ranchers. Grazing cattle threaten the delicate ecosystem.

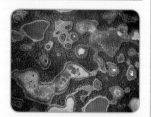

The American alligator inhabits swamps, marshes, lakes and rivers across the southeastern USA. There are about 1 million alligators in the Florida Everglades.

**FROM LAKE TO SWAMP**
When sediment builds up in a lake, the lake bed is raised and the water becomes shallower. Plants root in the mud and slowly creep out from the shore until the lake disappears.

**Lake** A lake is an inland body of water with plants growing in the shallow water around the edges.

**Marsh** As sediment builds up, plants advance further into the lake. This makes a marsh around the edges.

**Swamp** The lake disappears. Plants gradually cover almost the entire area, forming a swamp.

## LIFE IN THE WETLANDS

Tall reeds and rushes growing close
to a lake provide cover for nesting
waterbirds and sheltered water where
they can feed. Diving birds swim in
the open water.

Terns fly overhead.

Reeds provide safe
places for nesting
and roosting.

Spoonbills gather
food while wading in
shallow water.

Curlew

Teals

Some birds, such as
sandpipers, forage for
food in the mud flats.

Grebes

# Arctic regions

Around the shores of the Arctic Ocean, in the far north of North America and Europe, there is a short summer when the snow melts and flowers bloom. This is the tundra. North of the tundra lies the permanent ice that extends from the coasts. It covers much of the ocean in summer and all of it in winter. This is the high Arctic, home to polar bears that feed mainly on seals they catch when the seals surface to breathe. The seals feed on fish, which prey on tiny animals called krill. In the brief Arctic summer, the days are long and at least one night a year the Sun does not set. In the long, cold winter, the days are short and there is one day when the Sun does not rise above the horizon.

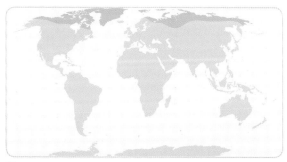

Arctic regions

The snowcapped mountains and glaciers of the island of Spitzbergen, in Norway's far north, are seen from the air. The name "Spitzbergen" means "jagged peaks".

## HABITAT WATCH

Climate change specialists see the Arctic as an early warning system. Rising ocean temperatures are already reducing pack ice in summer. This will affect the Inuit people of Greenland and Canada, who hunt on the ice. Their way of life may disappear if the ice continues to shrink.

Photographs taken at intervals through one summer night show that the "midnight sun" travels around the horizon. It never sinks below it, but remains low in the sky.

**INUIT HUNTER**
The Inuit were once nomadic people who used dogsleds for transport. Today they are more likely to use snowmobiles and live in towns.

**ICE FISHING**
Inuit fishermen cut holes through the ice and use baited lines to catch the fish swimming in the icy waters below.

**ARCTIC RESEARCH**
Scientists travel to study the Arctic in icebreakers—special ships that are designed to travel through icy waters.

## FIGHTING THE FREEZE

Arctic animals are well protected against the bitter cold. To prepare for winter, land mammals grow a thick layer of body fat to insulate them from the cold and give them energy. They have waterproof coats that trap a layer of warm air next to their skin and small ears to reduce heat loss.

**CARIBOU**
Caribou, or reindeer, have dense fur and a thick layer of body fat to keep them warm.

**ARCTIC TERN**
This migrating bird spends its summers in the Arctic and northern winters in the Antarctic.

**POLAR BEAR CUBS**
Cubs are born in the middle of winter, but are nursed by their mother in a snow den until spring.

**WALRUS**
It uses its two long tusks to anchor itself to the ice or to keep fishing holes open.

**HARP SEAL**
Like all seals, it has a thick insulating layer of blubber for warmth in the icy waters.

# Antarctic regions

Isolated from all other continents by the vast and stormy ocean, Antarctica is the coldest place on Earth. It has dry valleys where lichens and mosses survive, with a few species of insects and mites. The continent provides no food for larger animals. Birds visit, and penguins breed on the ice, but they feed at sea, where life is abundant. Algae growing on the underside of the floating ice shelves provide food for shrimp-like krill. Fish, seals and whales feed on the krill; penguins feed on fish; and fast, fearsome leopard seals hunt penguins and smaller seals. The land is permanently covered with ice and snow, which melt in summer only in a narrow coastal area. The ocean freezes each winter.

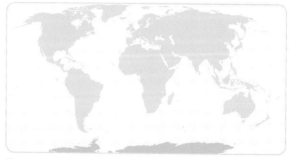

 Antarctic regions

Emperor penguins, the continent's most famous inhabitants, are clumsy until they dive into the sea. Then they manoeuvre effortlessly through the water.

## UNDER THE SURFACE

Ice floats because frozen water is less dense than liquid water. When most icebergs float, about 85 per cent of their volume is below the water's surface.

The part of the iceberg above the water is made up of compressed snow.

The cold core of ice has a constant temperature of about –15° to –20°C (5° to –4°F).

## TRAVELLING TO THE ANTARCTIC

Antarctica has become a tourist destination. Visitors land on the Antarctic Peninsula so they can say they have set foot on the continent. They cannot travel overland. Their numbers are controlled to protect the environment.

More than 15,000 tourists visit Antarctica each year, for its scenery and wildlife.

### HABITAT WATCH

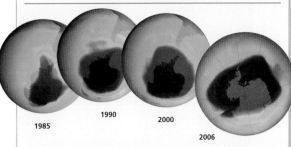

1985     1990     2000     2006

Earth's ozone layer absorbs harmful ultraviolet rays from the Sun. Over Antarctica the ozone thins naturally each spring, but in 1985 scientists observed a much larger loss, nicknamed the "ozone hole". This was caused by gases, called CFCs, used in aerosol cans. The largest hole yet was recorded in 2006.

### KINDS OF ICEBERGS

**Tabular** Broken-off pieces of ice shelves are large, wide and flat-topped.

**Dry dock** An iceberg this shape is called a dry dock. The centre lies below the waterline.

**Pinnacle** A pinnacle iceberg has sharp spires that project high above the water's surface.

# Agricultural areas

Rye was first cultivated in southwest Asia about 13,000 years ago. This was the beginning of one of the most important changes in human history: from finding food by hunting animals and gathering plants to producing it by tending livestock and growing plants. Farmers cleared away the existing plants, ploughed the land to destroy weeds and sowed seeds of crop plants. This was the most radical change to the natural environment humans have ever made. European farmers replaced their forests with crop fields and pasture. In central North America, farmers cleared the prairie grasses for cereal crops. Today, when tropical forests are cleared it is almost always to provide land for farming.

Although the first farms were usually small, modern farms in some countries can be huge and mechanized. Farmers use tractors to haul heavy machinery for harvesting grain.

## TERRACED HILLS

Farmers in Asia learned long ago that the best way to cultivate a hillside is to plough around the slope (not up and down) and to build level terraces for their crops. Unfortunately, clearing plants from hillsides can speed up soil erosion.

American midwestern farms are vast and need irrigation. Here, water is supplied in a circular pattern from automatic sprinklers. This field is also sown in circles.

European farms, like this one in England, often contain many small fields enclosed by hedges. This region was once forested.

# Urban areas

When people began to farm the land, they also began to settle in one place. They built villages that grew into towns and cities. In cities, not everyone was needed to produce food, so other activities could flourish. Cities produced craft workers of all kinds, as well as teachers, priests, artists, musicians, inventors and scholars. More and more people moved to the cities in search of work and access to services such as health care and education. Today, more than half of the entire human population are city dwellers. In many developing countries, cities are growing too quickly for there to be enough basic services, such as clean drinking water and electricity. As a result, millions of people live in extreme poverty and unhealthy conditions.

### HABITAT WATCH

City dwellers burn large quantites of fuel and generate a lot of waste, as seen here at a dump in Pennsylvania, USA. Both cause pollution unless they are managed. Air pollution from traffic fumes is a health hazard in many cities. Separating trash from recycling can ease the waste disposal problem.

## MODERN CITIES

The skyscrapers of New York, USA, let more than 8 million people live in a small area.

Kolkata, India, has 4.6 million inhabitants. One-third of the people live in slums.

### ÇATALHÜYÜK

Around 6000 BC, several thousand people lived in Çatalhüyük, one of the first villages, in what is now Turkey. Their houses were so tightly packed that people entered through doors in the roof.

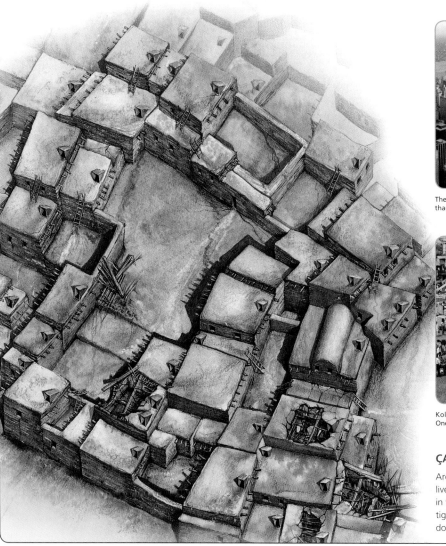

# A CROWDED WORLD

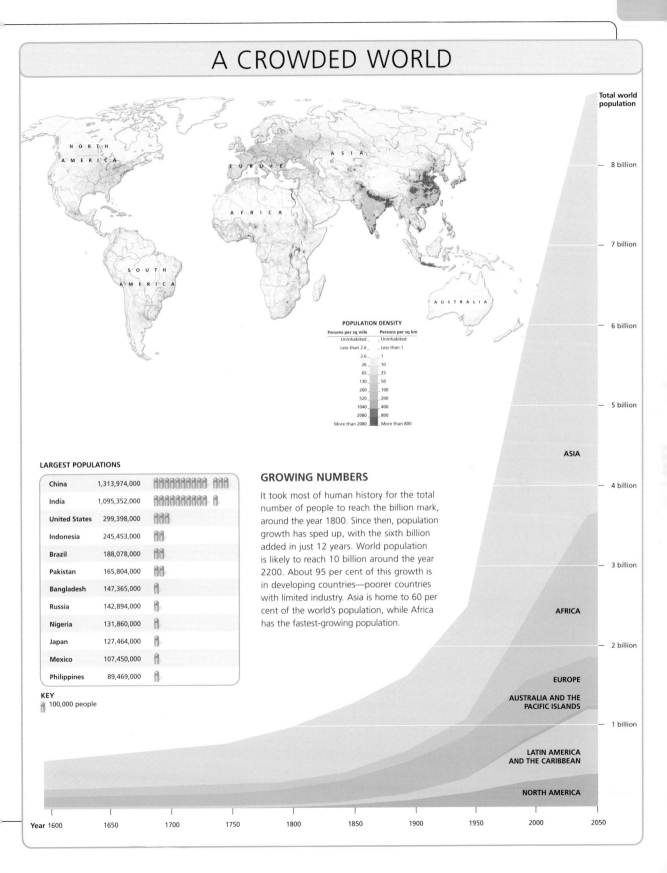

**POPULATION DENSITY**

| Persons per sq mile | Persons per sq km |
|---|---|
| Uninhabited | Uninhabited |
| Less than 2.6 | Less than 1 |
| 2.6 | 1 |
| 26 | 10 |
| 65 | 25 |
| 130 | 50 |
| 260 | 100 |
| 520 | 200 |
| 1040 | 400 |
| 2080 | 800 |
| More than 2080 | More than 800 |

**LARGEST POPULATIONS**

| | | |
|---|---|---|
| China | 1,313,974,000 | |
| India | 1,095,352,000 | |
| United States | 299,398,000 | |
| Indonesia | 245,453,000 | |
| Brazil | 188,078,000 | |
| Pakistan | 165,804,000 | |
| Bangladesh | 147,365,000 | |
| Russia | 142,894,000 | |
| Nigeria | 131,860,000 | |
| Japan | 127,464,000 | |
| Mexico | 107,450,000 | |
| Philippines | 89,469,000 | |

**KEY**
100,000 people

## GROWING NUMBERS

It took most of human history for the total number of people to reach the billion mark, around the year 1800. Since then, population growth has sped up, with the sixth billion added in just 12 years. World population is likely to reach 10 billion around the year 2200. About 95 per cent of this growth is in developing countries—poorer countries with limited industry. Asia is home to 60 per cent of the world's population, while Africa has the fastest-growing population.

**Total world population**

— 8 billion
— 7 billion
— 6 billion
— 5 billion

ASIA

— 4 billion
— 3 billion

AFRICA

— 2 billion

EUROPE

AUSTRALIA AND THE PACIFIC ISLANDS

— 1 billion

LATIN AMERICA AND THE CARIBBEAN

NORTH AMERICA

Year 1600    1650    1700    1750    1800    1850    1900    1950    2000    2050

# Biodiversity

The Daintree, in Australia's northeast, is one of the oldest rainforests on Earth. Offshore lies the Great Barrier Reef, the largest structure made by living organisms.

Biodiversity is short for "biological diversity". It refers to the incredible variety of living things that exist on Earth, where they live and how they interact. It is not just how many species live in one area, but how varied a particular species is and how complex an ecosystem, or community, is. Rainforests are the most diverse ecosystems in the world. Pollution makes life difficult for some animals and plants, which reduces their biodiversity in the affected area. Changing the use of land, by clearing forests for farmland, for example, may reduce or increase biodiversity, depending on the circumstances. Scientists agree that we should preserve as much biodiversity as possible.

## WORLD VIEW

This map shows the biodiversity of different countries, as researched by their governments. Biodiversity is greater in countries with warm climates than countries with cold ones. It is lowest in extreme habitats, such as deserts and polar regions.

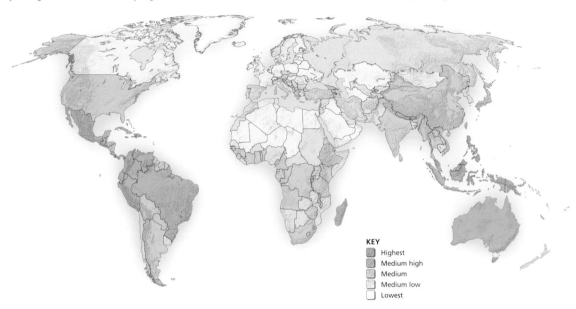

**KEY**
- Highest
- Medium high
- Medium
- Medium low
- Lowest

## LIFE IN DANGER

The World Conservation Union publishes a Red List of endangered animals and plants. It currently lists more than 16,000 species at risk.

**Number of species assessed**

| | |
|---|---|
| Mammals | 4,856 |
| Birds | 9,934 |
| Reptiles | 664 |
| Amphibians | 5,918 |
| Fish | 2,914 |
| Insects | 1,192 |
| Molluscs | 2,163 |
| Crustaceans | 537 |
| Plants | 11,901 |

■ Extinct  ■ Critically endangered  □ Threatened  □ Assessed species

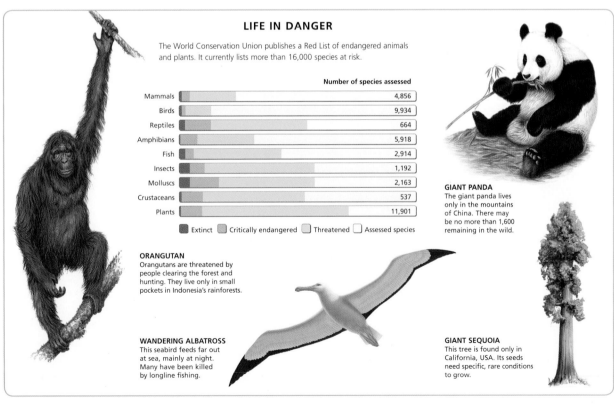

**GIANT PANDA**
The giant panda lives only in the mountains of China. There may be no more than 1,600 remaining in the wild.

**ORANGUTAN**
Orangutans are threatened by people clearing the forest and hunting. They live only in small pockets in Indonesia's rainforests.

**WANDERING ALBATROSS**
This seabird feeds far out at sea, mainly at night. Many have been killed by longline fishing.

**GIANT SEQUOIA**
This tree is found only in California, USA. Its seeds need specific, rare conditions to grow.

# Global Environment

There are now so many people in the world—and the industries supplying our needs are so large—that we are having a significant effect on the natural environment, including the global climate. Traffic fumes reduce air quality in many cities. In some places, factories pollute both air and water. Gases emitted by many factories and power stations make rain more acid, which damages lakes and rivers. Poor land management erodes the soil and can allow nearby deserts to expand. None of these problems is irreversible, but to solve them all, we need to improve the way we look after our planet.

Only 26 per cent of forests in Tasmania, Australia, remain after years of logging.

### PLANET IN PERIL

Industry and development can cause serious environmental damage, such as pollution of the air, land and sea. The problems of industrialized countries are now reappearing in developing regions.

**HOLDING BACK THE DESERT**
Deserts expand and contract naturally. Careful livestock and crop management along the edge can provide permanent plant cover that gradually forces the desert to retreat.

**SAVING THE FORESTS**
Temperate forests are expanding, but tropical forests are disappearing. This can sometimes be reduced if local people are allowed to profit from the standing forest.

**REDUCING AIR POLLUTION**
Older industrialized countries now set strict limits on factory and vehicle emissions. The limits are becoming tighter and are being introduced worldwide.

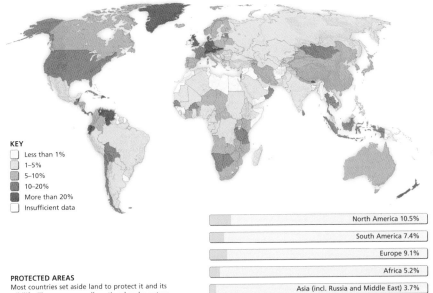

## KEY
- Less than 1%
- 1–5%
- 5–10%
- 10–20%
- More than 20%
- Insufficient data

## PROTECTED AREAS
Most countries set aside land to protect it and its wildlife. These are generally national parks, nature reserves and other protected areas. The amount of protected land varies greatly from region to region.

North America 10.5%
South America 7.4%
Europe 9.1%
Africa 5.2%
Asia (incl. Russia and Middle East) 3.7%
Oceania 7.1%
**WORLD** 6.4%

Area protected    Total area

Overgrazing destroys plant life. In regions such as Rajasthan, India, it can allow land to become desert.

When forests are cleared from hillsides, the soil erodes. It washes downhill into rivers, killing fish.

### ELIMINATING ACID RAIN
Acid rain, caused by factories, power stations and vehicles, has been brought under control in many countries, although its effects are slow to disappear.

### SAVING THE OZONE LAYER
Scientists discovered that gases, called CFCs, used in aerosol cans created a hole in the ozone layer. CFCs are now banned and the ozone layer may recover.

### KEEPING OUR WATER CLEAN
Most governments no longer allow waste to be dumped in rivers or the sea. International agreements aim to reduce and prevent water pollution.

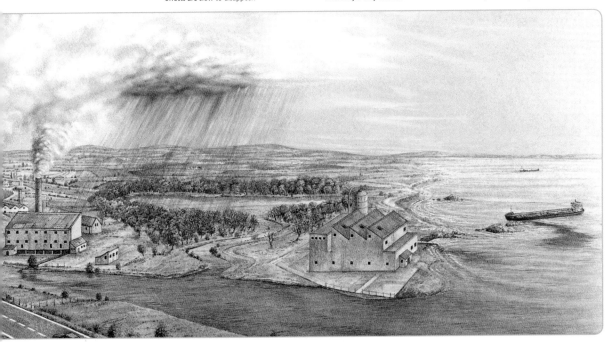

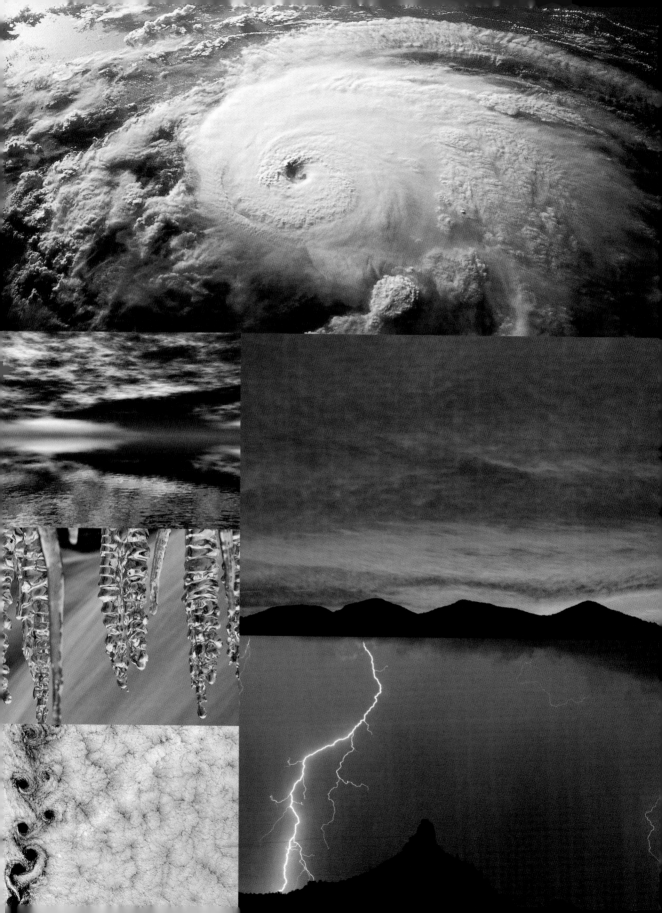

Weather

# World Weather

It is likely, wherever you live, that one of the first things you do each day is check the weather. Weather affects our lives in many ways, from what we wear and how we feel to what we grow in our gardens. But what makes weather? Weather is, simply, air that moves over Earth's surface. Images from satellites in space show how air swirls over landmasses, bringing wind and clouds, rain and snow, storms and hurricanes. Generally, people in a particular region experience similar weather from year to year. This regular pattern of weather over an extended period of time is called a region's climate.

Hurricanes are huge storms. This picture clearly shows Hurricane Fran's anticlockwise, spiral wind pattern as it approached the Florida coast in 1996.

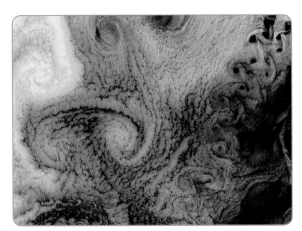

Winds do not blow over obstacles but try to find ways around them. This creates a complex pattern of swirling eddies, which can be seen from above in a cloudy sky.

Cold air moving across Antarctica and the surrounding oceans causes large areas of ice and snow to form over parts of the Weddell Sea to the northwest of the continent.

# Climate Zones

Different regions of the world have different climate patterns, and smaller areas within those regions also have their own kinds of climate. We call these regions and areas climate zones. Near the equator are tropical zones; they have hot and wet climates. At the other extreme are the north and south poles, which are extremely cold and dry. In between are warm subtropical zones; dry desert, or arid, zones, where days are hot and nights cold; high mountain zones, with cold, snowy winters; and temperate zones, where conditions are generally moderate year-round.

## ADAPTING TO CLIMATE

Plants and animals are found in most places on Earth, even in locations where weather patterns are extreme. Over time, living things have developed ways of dealing with, or adapting to, the climate in which they live.

**PLANTS**
Cactus plants grow in some arid desert regions. They have few or no leaves, grow an extensive root system, and store the little water they get in fleshy green stems.

Fleshy green stem

Extensive, shallow root system

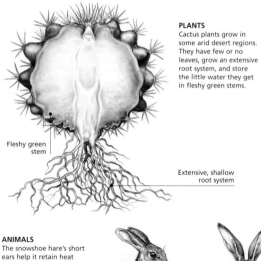

**ANIMALS**
The snowshoe hare's short ears help it retain heat in snowy environments. Long ears allow the desert-dwelling antelope jackrabbit to lose excess heat in hot weather.

Snowshoe hare          Antelope jackrabbit

**Most snow in one year**
31,102 mm (1,224 in)
on Mt. Rainier, Washington, USA, 1971–72

**Greatest temperature change in a day**
56°C (100°F), from 6.7°C (44°F) to −49°C (−56°F), at Browning, Montana, USA, 1916

**Strongest measured wind gust**
372 km/h (231 mph)
on Mt. Washington, New Hampshire, USA, 1934

**NORTH AMERICA**

**SOUTH AMERICA**

## HOT AND COLD, WET AND DRY

This map shows the world's eight main climate zones. Even within the same region, there can be more than one kind of climate.

**Driest place**
0.5 mm (0.02 in) per year
in Quillagua, Atacama Desert, Chile, 1964–2001

Mountain zones may be cold, wet and windy.

Polar zones are very cold all year round.

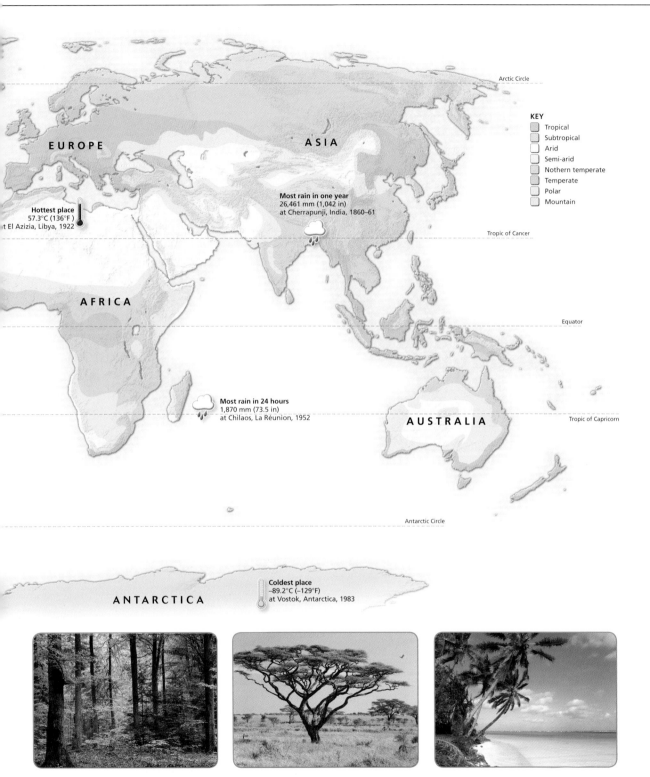

**KEY**
- Tropical
- Subtropical
- Arid
- Semi-arid
- Nothern temperate
- Temperate
- Polar
- Mountain

Arctic Circle

EUROPE

ASIA

**Most rain in one year**
26,461 mm (1,042 in)
at Cherrapunji, India, 1860–61

**Hottest place**
57.3°C (136°F)
t El Azizia, Libya, 1922

Tropic of Cancer

AFRICA

Equator

**Most rain in 24 hours**
1,870 mm (73.5 in)
at Chilaos, La Réunion, 1952

AUSTRALIA

Tropic of Capricorn

Antarctic Circle

**Coldest place**
−89.2°C (−129°F)
at Vostok, Antarctica, 1983

ANTARCTICA

Temperate zones have cold winters and cool summers.

Semi-arid zones are hot and dry throughout the year.

Tropical zones are warm and wet all through the year.

# Weather Engine

The Sun fuels our weather. Earth's surface is warmed by sunlight. The tropics on either side of the equator receive the most intense heat, while the poles receive the least. Earth's surface absorbs half the available energy from the Sun; the atmosphere absorbs the rest or reflects it back into space. Bright white snow, which reflects most of the Sun's energy, retains very little heat. Dark green tropical rainforests absorb much more. Temperatures on land vary more than those in the oceans. These differences generate winds. Winds set in motion the vast circulation of the atmosphere, which produces the world's weather.

**THE LAYERS OF THE ATMOSPHERE**

**Thermosphere**
Above 80 kilometres (50 mi)
This is the atmosphere's outer layer. Gases here are very thin.

**Mesosphere**
50–80 kilometres (30–50 mi)
The mesosphere is much colder than the stratosphere.

**Stratosphere**
15–50 kilometres (9–30 mi)
The stratosphere has dry, warm air.

**Troposphere**
0–15 kilometres (0–9 mi)
The air here contains lots of water vapour and dust. Most of the world's weather occurs here.

## THE SUN AND THE SEASONS

Because Earth's axis is tilted at an angle of 23.5 degrees, the amount of solar energy that reaches different parts of the globe varies as the planet orbits the Sun. These variations create our seasons, which are opposite in the Northern and Southern hemispheres.

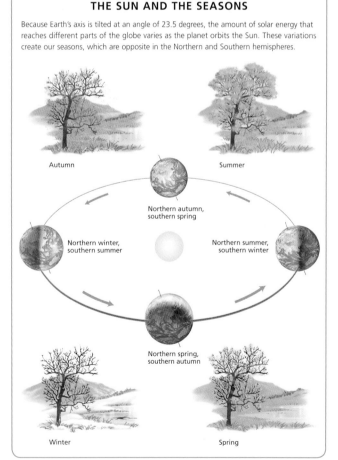

Autumn

Summer

Northern autumn, southern spring

Northern winter, southern summer

Northern summer, southern winter

Northern spring, southern autumn

Winter

Spring

## HEAT FROM THE SUN

Air is warmed more at the equator than at the poles. Near the equator, the Sun hits directly. At the poles, however, the rays hit Earth at an angle and are spread over a wider area, which weakens them.

☐ Light travelling to equator
☐ Light travelling to poles

### EARTH'S CLIMATE

At the equator, the Sun's rays hit Earth almost directly all year long. This is the hottest zone on Earth. Further away from the equator, the rays hit at more of an angle and the climate is cooler.

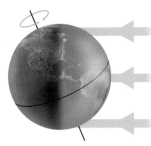

This diagram shows how the Sun's rays hit Earth during the northern winter (southern summer).

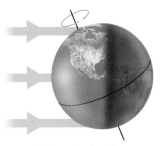

This diagram shows how the Sun's rays hit Earth during the northern summer (southern winter).

### SEASONAL CHANGES

The Sun's path creates the seasons, which change the appearance of the land, from the new growth of spring to the bare trees of winter.

Spring

Summer

Autumn

Winter

# World winds

The Sun heats the tropics year-round, which causes the air at the equator to rise. It then spreads out, cools and sinks to the surface around 30° north and south of the equator. From there, some air flows back towards the equator at ground level. This completes a circular pattern of airflow, called a cell. Similar cells exist between 30° and 60° and between 60° and the poles. The movement of air at ground level within these cells creates Earth's major wind patterns. As the winds move north and south, they are deflected by the planet's rotation: to the right in the Northern Hemisphere, to the left in the Southern Hemisphere. This is known as the Coriolis effect.

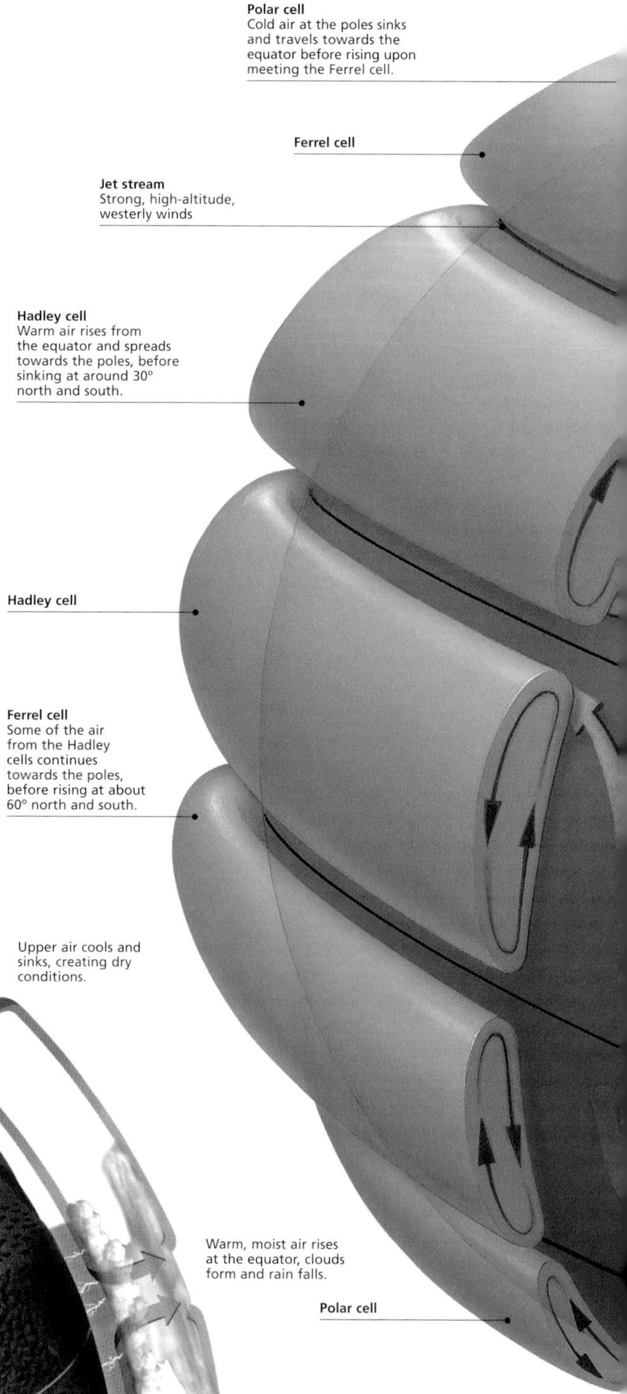

## WIND CELLS

Wind cells nearest to the equator are called Hadley cells, after the English scientist George Hadley, who described them in 1753. Ferrel cells are named after American scientist William Ferrel, who first noted them in 1856.

### WIND PATTERNS

Because hot air rises and cold air sinks, the Sun's uneven heating of Earth's surface causes air to circulate as shown in the diagram below. Winds are important influences on climate.

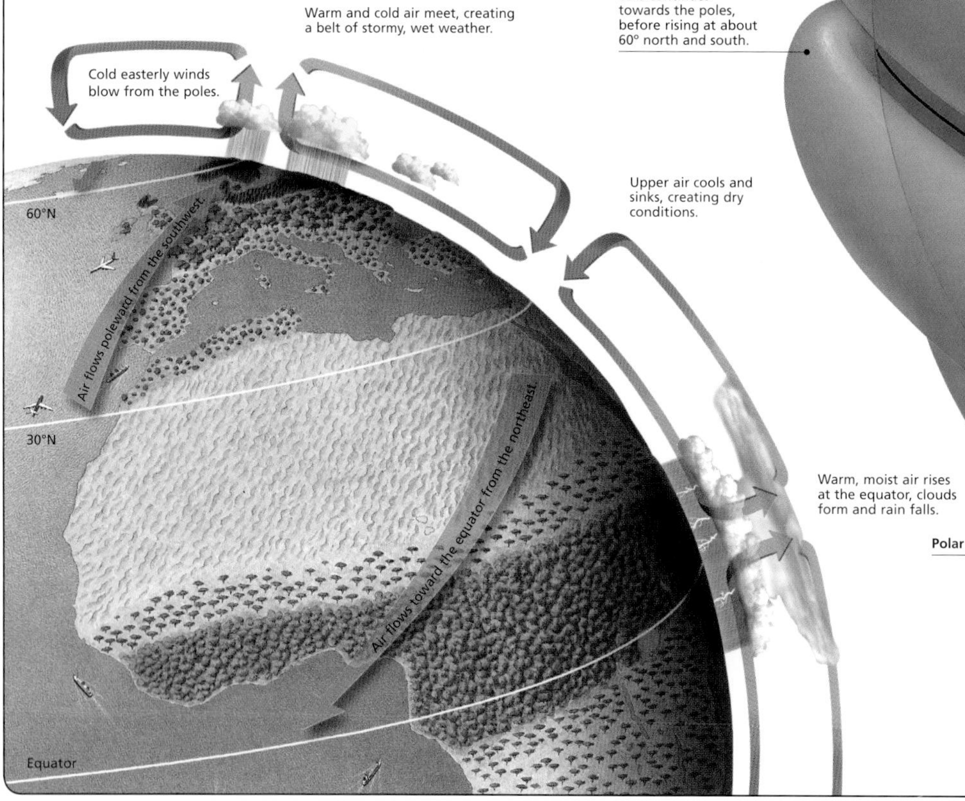

Warm and cold air meet, creating a belt of stormy, wet weather.

Cold easterly winds blow from the poles.

60°N

Air flows poleward from the southwest.

30°N

Air flows toward the equator from the northeast.

Equator

**Polar cell**
Cold air at the poles sinks and travels towards the equator before rising upon meeting the Ferrel cell.

**Ferrel cell**

**Jet stream**
Strong, high-altitude, westerly winds

**Hadley cell**
Warm air rises from the equator and spreads towards the poles, before sinking at around 30° north and south.

**Hadley cell**

**Ferrel cell**
Some of the air from the Hadley cells continues towards the poles, before rising at about 60° north and south.

Upper air cools and sinks, creating dry conditions.

Warm, moist air rises at the equator, clouds form and rain falls.

**Polar cell**

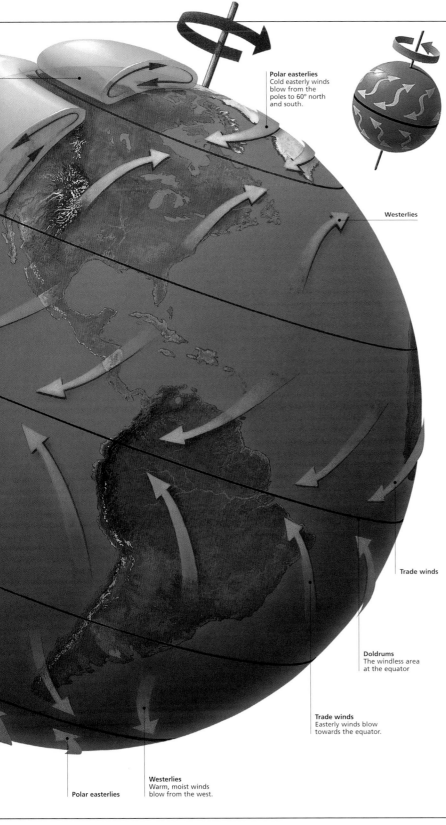

**Polar easterlies**
Cold easterly winds blow from the poles to 60° north and south.

**Westerlies**

**Trade winds**

**Doldrums**
The windless area at the equator

**Trade winds**
Easterly winds blow towards the equator.

**Westerlies**
Warm, moist winds blow from the west.

**Polar easterlies**

**CORIOLIS EFFECT**
In the Northern Hemisphere, the Coriolis effect causes air to move clockwise and down around high pressure, and anticlockwise and up around low pressure. It is the opposite in the Southern Hemisphere.

# THE MONSOON

Patterns of global airflow influence local winds such as the monsoon. This seasonal wind brings heavy rain to many subtropical parts of the world, especially India and Bangladesh.

People who live in India and Bangladesh have to cope with heavy monsoon rain.

**Dry season** In winter, high pressure creates winds that push moist air away from India and Bangladesh.

**Wet season** In summer, inland low pressure draws moist air in from the ocean, bringing torrential rain.

# The water cycle

The way water moves between the atmosphere, land and sea creates a cycle of moisture that shapes our weather and provides us with a continuous supply of fresh water. When the Sun heats the oceans, lakes and rivers, some of that water turns into water vapour, which is released into the atmosphere. Water contained in plants is also released as part of photosynthesis. The release of water from all these sources is known as evaporation. This water vapour forms clouds, which in turn produce rain. Some rain is absorbed by soil and plants, while the rest flows back to the sea in rivers and underground channels.

Heavy clouds bring rain and mist to rainforests in Colombia, South America.

## FROM THE SEA AND BACK AGAIN

Water that evaporates from oceans and other sources condenses as clouds. Winds carry the clouds inland, rain then falls on the land, and the water makes its way back to the sea. This completes the cycle.

Clouds build up over land.

Water evaporates and forms clouds.

Rain falls
from clouds.

Rain forms when separate drops of water fall from
water-laden clouds down to Earth.

Water drains
into lakes, rivers
and underground
channels and flows
back to the sea.

The dark blue areas in this satellite photo show the parts of the world that have the greatest concentration
of water vapour in the atmosphere. These are the areas where most rain falls.

# Clouds

Clouds are masses of water droplets and ice crystals that float in the sky. They are formed by a process that begins when warm, moist air rises. As the warm air cools, it is unable to hold water vapour. Some of the water vapour condenses around dust particles and forms minute water droplets. These tiny drops make up clouds. The sky can be covered with a blanket of cloud that is formed when a mass of warm air rises above cooler air and causes the water vapour to condense. Clouds also form when warm air is forced to rise over mountains, or when warm air blows over a colder surface such as cool water. On hot days, storm clouds appear when warm, moist air rises and then cools rapidly.

## THE COLOURS OF CLOUDS

Water droplets in clouds scatter all the colours in white sunlight equally, so clouds appear white, except when they are in shadow or blocking out the light.

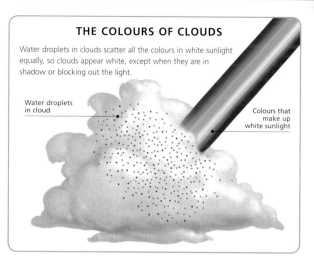

Water droplets in cloud

Colours that make up white sunlight

Thick cumulonimbus clouds will soon bring a storm with heavy rain over Lake Poopo in Bolivia.

## HOW CLOUDS FORM

Clouds usually form as a result of warm air that rises from the ground. When the warm air meets colder air higher in the atmosphere, the water vapour in the rising air condenses to form clouds. This happens in three main ways: by convection currents, over mountains and through frontal activity.

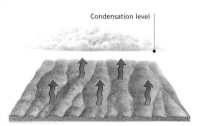

Condensation level

**Convection** Heating of the ground warms air near the surface, causing an air mass to rise.

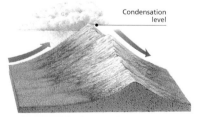

Condensation level

**Over mountains** If air meets a mountain range, it is forced upward, and clouds form over the mountaintops.

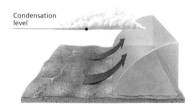

Condensation level

**Frontal activity** When two air masses meet, the warmer air rises and forms clouds.

Cumulonimbus

Cirrocumulus

## A SKY OF CLOUDS

Clouds are named
according to their height
and shape, by combining
the Latin names *alto* (high),
*stratus* (flat), *cirrus* (wispy),
*cumulus* (puffy) and
*nimbus* (rain-bearing).
Rain clouds, depending
on shape, are known
as *nimbostratus* or
*cumulonimbus*.

5,000 metres (16,500 ft)

Altostratus

Altocumulus

2,000 metres (6,500 ft)

Cumulus

Stratocumulus

Stratus

Sea level

# Kinds of clouds

No two clouds are exactly the same. They are usually grouped according to how high they are above the ground. Although they vary in shape and size, they can be divided broadly into two kinds: heaped, fluffy clouds and layered clouds. Heaped clouds are formed when pockets of warm air drift upward, while layered clouds are created by moist air moving horizontally between cooler layers. It is important to identify kinds of clouds because they give us information about the weather. White, puffy cumulus clouds are associated with warm sunny days. Cirrus clouds may be followed by lower altostratus clouds and low stratus rain clouds, which cover the entire sky in a solid gray sheet.

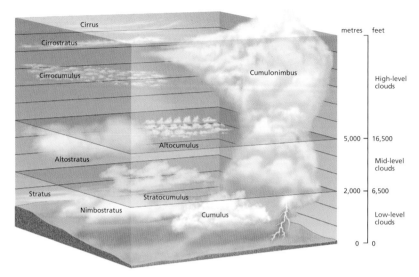

Cirrus

Cirrostratus

Cirrocumulus

Cumulonimbus

Altocumulus

Altostratus

Stratus

Stratocumulus

Nimbostratus

Cumulus

metres    feet

High-level clouds

5,000   16,500

Mid-level clouds

2,000   6,500

Low-level clouds

0     0

## HIGH CLOUDS

**CIRRUS**
Streaky cirrus clouds, blown by strong winds, can signal an approaching storm.

**SUPERB CIRRUS**
Large cirrus clouds form when upper-level winds are weak and the clouds are not dispersed.

**CIRROCUMULUS**
Cirrocumulus clouds consist of ice crystals, and the clouds have a cellular appearance.

## MIDDLE CLOUDS

### ALTOCUMULUS
Altocumulus clouds form when there is a lot of moisture but only light winds are blowing.

### ALTOSTRATUS
Near the polar regions, thick layers of cloud can cover the sky and bring snow.

## LOW CLOUDS

### STRATOCUMULUS
In subtropical coastal places, sheets of stratocumulus move inland from the moist oceans.

### STRATUS
This mountain slope is covered with a thick layer of stratus cloud as cold air moves across the region.

### SHALLOW CUMULUS
Flat-topped shallow cumulus clouds like these are a common sight on a fine day.

# Local winds

Air begins to move when the Sun heats the land and warms the atmosphere. Molecules in the air move faster when they are heated and the air starts to expand. Like a huge, invisible bubble, warm air rises through the surrounding cooler air. At the same time, cooler, heavier air is drawn in to replace the rising air. This circulation of air is called convection. Wind speed depends on air pressure. Wind blows from areas of high pressure to areas of low pressure. Meteorologists use the Beaufort scale to measure the force of wind, ranging from 0 (calm) to 12 (strong winds associated with hurricanes).

Jet streams are fast-moving ribbons of air blowing high above Earth. This photograph from space shows a jet stream above Egypt.

| THE BEAUFORT SCALE | | | | |
|---|---|---|---|---|
| FORCE | SPEED (PER HOUR) | | DESCRIPTION | EFFECT |
| | KM | MI | | |
| 0 | 1 | 1 | Calm | Smoke moves straight up |
| 1 | 5 | 3 | Light air | Smoke slightly bent |
| 2 | 11 | 7 | Light breeze | Leaves rustle |
| 3 | 18 | 11 | Gentle breeze | Leaves move |
| 4 | 30 | 19 | Moderate breeze | Small branches move |
| 5 | 39 | 24 | Fresh breeze | Small trees sway |
| 6 | 50 | 31 | Strong breeze | Large branches move |
| 7 | 61 | 38 | Moderate gale | Whole trees sway |
| 8 | 74 | 46 | Fresh gale | Twigs break off |
| 9 | 87 | 54 | Strong gale | Roofs damaged |
| 10 | 102 | 63 | Gale | Trees uprooted |
| 11 | 117 | 73 | Storm | Widespread damage |
| 12 | 120+ | 74+ | Hurricane | Widespread destruction |

**Going down**
Air sinks over cool areas, such as the sea.

**From the sea**
Wind blows from the sea as cool air flows towards the city to replace the rising warm air.

**LAND AND SEA BREEZES**
Coastal winds blow in from the sea during the afternoon. These create cooling sea breezes, which are strongest in the late afternoon. At night, the winds blow in the opposite direction, from the land and out to sea.

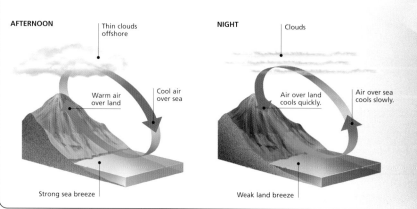

**AFTERNOON**
Thin clouds offshore
Warm air over land
Cool air over sea
Strong sea breeze

**NIGHT**
Clouds
Air over land cools quickly.
Air over sea cools slowly.
Weak land breeze

## MOUNTAIN WINDS

Cool winds enter mountain valleys both during the day and at night, but in different ways. In the daytime, the wind descends into the centre of the mountain valley. At night, it flows down the sides of the mountains.

When the Sun heats the mountain slopes, warm air rises. The air then cools and falls into the valley to replace the rising air.

At night, warm mountain air loses its heat and flows down the mountain slopes into the valley to create a cool wind.

## DAY BREEZES

On warm, sunny days, sea breezes blow on the coast. These onshore breezes are caused by differences in temperature between the hot land and the cooler water.

**On the move**
Warm air spreads
out at high altitudes.

**Moving up**
The air over the land,
particulary city areas,
warms during the day.
This warm air rises
into the atmosphere.

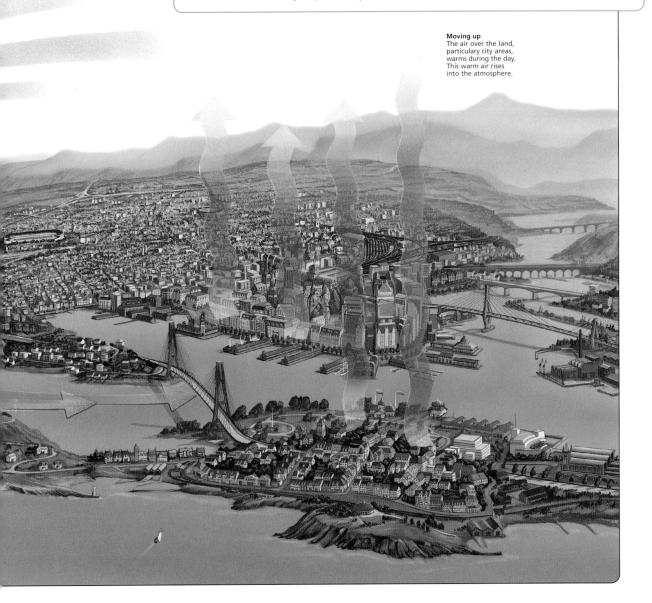

# Rain, hail and snow

Water or ice that falls from clouds is called precipitation. It may be in the form of rain, drizzle, sleet, snow or hail. The conditions within a cloud, and the temperature outside it, control the kind of precipitation that falls. Water droplets in a cloud can turn into ice if the cloud is at a height that is called the freezing level. This can be as low as 300 metres (1,000 ft) or as high as 5,000 metres (16,500 ft) above the ground. Snow falls from very cold, low clouds when the air temperature is around freezing; this allows the ice crystals to reach the ground without melting.

**SNOWFLAKES**
Snowflakes are loose clusters of ice crystals. They are usually six-sided (hexagonal), but their exact shape depends on the temperature of the air.

**RAIN**
Rain forms when water droplets collect around ice crystals until they are heavy enough to fall.

**HAIL**
As strong air currents circulate and cause layers of ice to build up around small ice crystals, they become larger and form hail.

**SNOW**
Snow forms in low-level clouds, where ice crystals do not melt before they hit the ground.

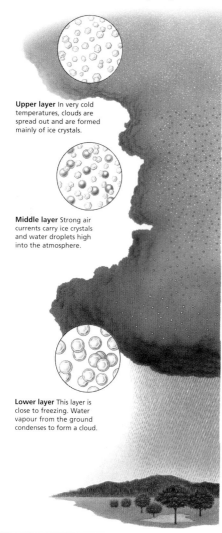

**Upper layer** In very cold temperatures, clouds are spread out and are formed mainly of ice crystals.

**Middle layer** Strong air currents carry ice crystals and water droplets high into the atmosphere.

**Lower layer** This layer is close to freezing. Water vapour from the ground condenses to form a cloud.

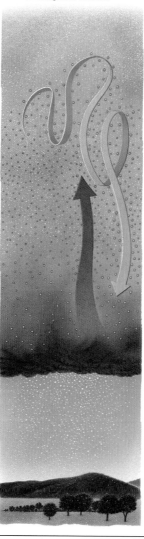

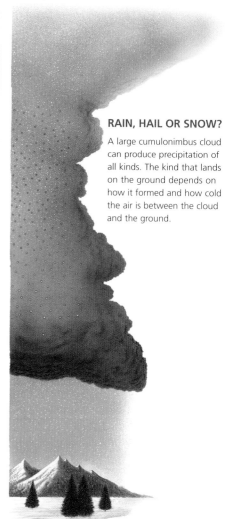

## RAIN, HAIL OR SNOW?

A large cumulonimbus cloud can produce precipitation of all kinds. The kind that lands on the ground depends on how it formed and how cold the air is between the cloud and the ground.

# FLOODS

## CAUSE AND EFFECT

Rivers can flood when so much rain falls over a prolonged period that they overflow their banks. A severe flood occurred in northeastern Italy in October 2000, when torrential rain caused huge streams of water to engulf houses. Roadways turned into fast-flowing rivers. Dams designed to trap floodwaters collapsed as water levels reached their highest point in more than 30 years.

## PREVENTING FLOODS

For thousands of years, humans have tried to reduce the risks of flooding by building structures to block and channel rising waters and the flow of rivers and oceans.

**Levees** Banks of earth built up beside rivers are called levees. Erosion, earthquakes or high rainfall can cause levees to fail.

**Tidal barriers** These are large walls built in low-lying areas, to control tidal flooding and block large waves.

**Dams** Concrete walls built to block rivers are called dams. They are strong to hold back the water that builds up behind them.

**CHANG IN FLOOD**

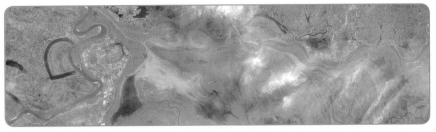

This satellite photo shows the pinkish ribbons of China's Chang River before a flood surged down it in August 2002.

In this photo, taken after the 2002 flood, the extent to which the floodwaters spread across the land can be clearly seen.

# Storms

Storms are created when warm, rising air currents and water vapour combine with colder air at middle and upper levels of the atmosphere. As rising moist air cools, the water vapour turns into a cloud. This cloud will continue to grow into a cumulonimbus, or thundercloud, if strong, warm updraughts meet cold air at middle and upper levels. The cold air in the upper part of the thundercloud starts to sink, creating downward air currents called down draughts. The combination of updraughts and down draughts causes water droplets and ice crystals to grow and form rain and hail. It also creates the electrical charges that cause lightning.

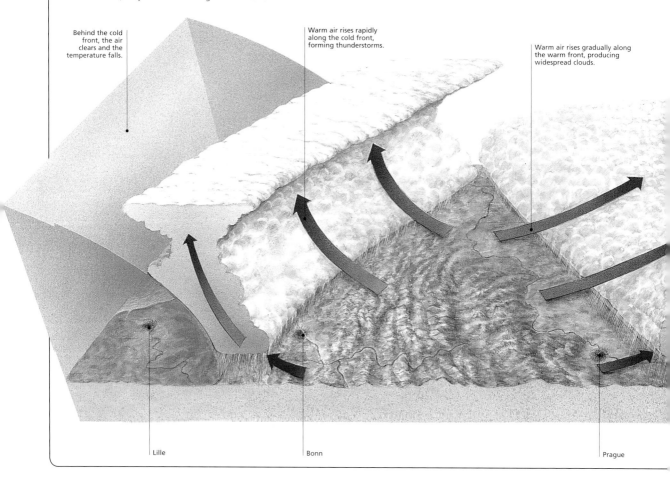

Warm front     Cold front     • City / town

## CHANGING WEATHER

This diagram shows a low-pressure system over northern Europe. Its precise location is shown in the map above right. The cold front is creating stormy conditions over western Europe. Further east, a warm front is bringing light rain to much of Poland. As the fronts move eastward, they can either strengthen or weaken.

Behind the cold front, the air clears and the temperature falls.

Warm air rises rapidly along the cold front, forming thunderstorms.

Warm air rises gradually along the warm front, producing widespread clouds.

Lille

Bonn

Prague

## THE STORM CYCLE

There are usually three main stages in the progress of a thunderstorm. They involve the formation of cumulus clouds and then the opposing updraughts and down draughts of air currents. The entire cycle may last for only about 15 minutes or it could last for several hours.

Updraught

**Building up** Rising air currents cause water vapour to condense and form cumulus clouds.

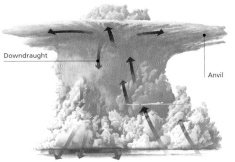

Downdraught

Anvil

**At its peak** The cumulonimbus cloud forms an anvil, or flat top. Air begins to sink, creating down draughts.

**On the wane** Down draughts outnumber updraughts. The storm's supply of warm, rising air is finally cut off.

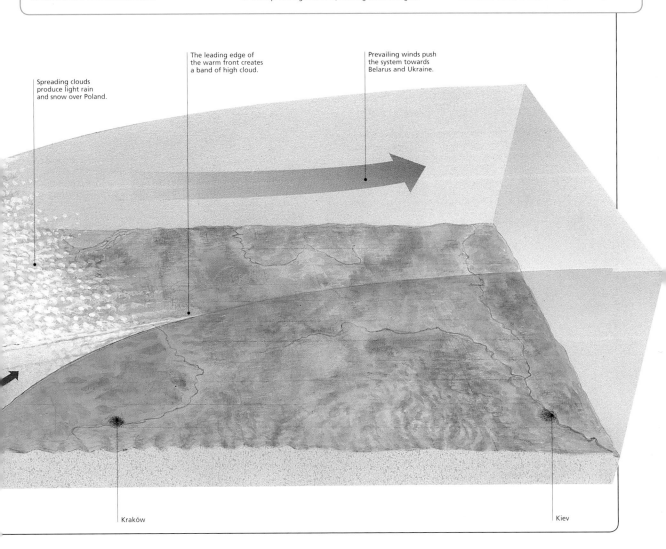

Spreading clouds produce light rain and snow over Poland.

The leading edge of the warm front creates a band of high cloud.

Prevailing winds push the system towards Belarus and Ukraine.

Kraków

Kiev

# Tornadoes

A tornado—also called a twister or a whirlwind—is one of the most powerful forces on Earth. Hot and humid conditions are ideal for a tornado, which starts with an enormous thundercloud. From its dense, black base, a spinning, funnel like form snakes down to the ground. When it touches, it gathers up a huge, billowing cloud of dust and debris. This can measure up to 1.6 kilometres (1 mi) across, move at up to 105 kilometres per hour (65 mph), and generate winds of up to 480 kilometres per hour (300 mph). It can be powerful enough to flatten buildings and lift cars, trees and people high into the air.

**WHERE AND WHEN**
This United States map shows where and when tornadoes are likely. It indicates the number of tornadoes per year that normally occur in different areas.

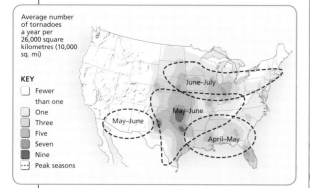

Average number of tornadoes a year per 26,000 square kilometres (10,000 sq. mi)

**KEY**
- Fewer than one
- One
- Three
- Five
- Seven
- Nine
- Peak seasons

June–July

May–June

May–June

April–May

## FORMATION OF A TORNADO

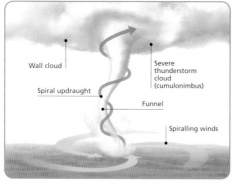

- Wall cloud
- Severe thunderstorm cloud (cumulonimbus)
- Spiral updraught
- Funnel
- Spiralling winds

Tornadoes typically look like an elephant's trunk or a funnel hanging from the base of a storm cloud. Very low air pressure inside this funnel causes moisture in the atmosphere to condense, making it visible. The bulge at the base of the thunderstorm is known as the wall cloud. Severe weather conditions may produce a line of storms that result in a series of tornadoes.

As this tornado sweeps through Pampa in Texas, USA, debris is thrown in all directions, extending well outside the funnel. The colour of a tornado's funnel depends on the dust and debris it gathers up.

# Hurricanes

A hurricane is a huge, spinning storm system that begins as a cluster of thunderstorms over the tropics. If the cluster drifts beyond 5° north or south of the equator, it starts rotating. As it moves further away from the equator, the hurricane spins faster and becomes more powerful. Hurricanes can measure up to 800 kilometres (500 mi) across and can produce torrential rain, winds up to 300 kilometres per hour (190 mph) and an enormous high tide called a storm surge. The calmest place in a hurricane is its centre, or eye, which is free of clouds and strong winds.

Hurricane Katrina hit the U.S. Gulf Coast in 2005. As it passed low-lying New Orleans, the city's protective levees broke, flooding most of the city for several weeks.

## INSIDE A HURRICANE

Hurricanes start life as small thunderstorms over warm water.

Eye of the storm

As the hurricane rotates, it continues to draw in moist air from the ocean, gaining energy all the time.

Warm water heats the air and creates a rising current of moist air.

Cool air is pulled in to replace the rising current.

Huge banks of cumulonimbus clouds build up.

## HURRICANE LIFE CYCLE

**Day 1**
A storm cluster forms.

**Day 2**
The storm begins to spin.

**Day 3**
A spiral shape develops.

**Day 6**
The eye of the storm emerges.

**Day 12**
The storm begins to fade.

**WILD WINDS**
Strong winds are a feature of all hurricanes. A hurricane can cover thousands of kilometres.

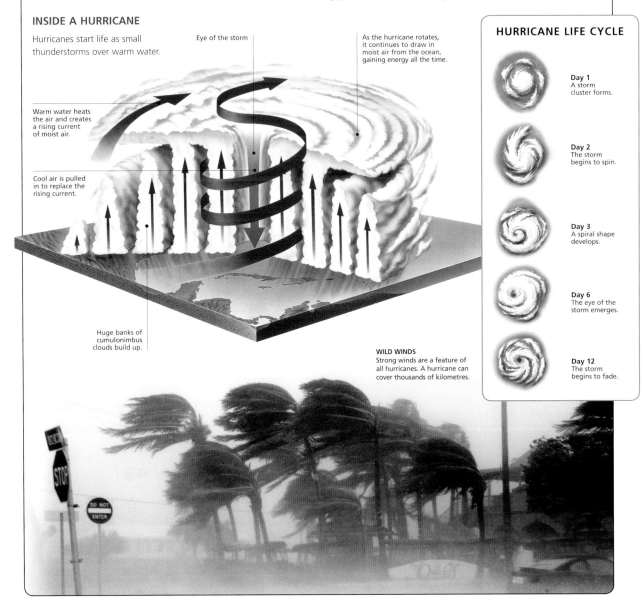

# Lightning

Lightning is probably the most dramatic feature of a thunderstorm. We still do not know exactly what causes lightning, but we do know that it involves an increase of positive and negative electrical charges inside a thundercloud. It is likely that the updraughts in a storm carry positive charges to the top of the cloud, and down draughts pull negative charges to the bottom. These opposite charges are attracted to each other. The attraction grows stronger until, eventually, the electricity leaps, or discharges, from one area to the other. We see this as a lightning bolt.

## CLOUD-TO-CLOUD LIGHTNING

Most lightning occurs between or within clouds. Often, the positive charge in one cloud is attracted to the negative charge in another. Lightning leaps between them. Lightning can also occur in a single cloud.

Positive charge in upper cloud

Negative charge at base of cloud

## CLOUD-TO-AIR LIGHTNING

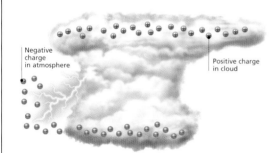

Negative charge in atmosphere

Positive charge in cloud

A positive charge that builds up at the top of the cloud is close to a negative charge in the atmosphere next to the cloud. Lightning eventually jumps between them.

Most lightning bolts discharge about 100 million volts of electricity. A strike in a city, such as this one in Istanbul, Turkey, can cause sudden power surges that may disrupt power supplies.

## CLOUD-TO-GROUND LIGHTNING

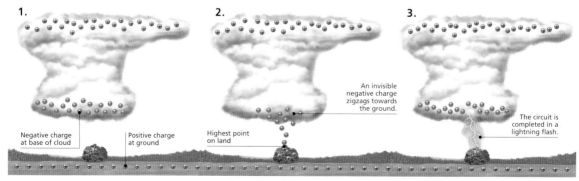

**1.**

Negative charge at base of cloud

Positive charge at ground

**2.**

Highest point on land

An invisible negative charge zigzags towards the ground.

**3.**

The circuit is completed in a lightning flash.

Sometimes the strong negative charges along the bottom of cumulonimbus clouds can cause equally strong positive charges on the ground below. The two charges eventually meet in the form of lightning. This may strike open ground or tall objects such as trees.

# COLOURS IN THE SKY

**HOW RAINBOWS FORM**
When sunlight passes through glass or water, it bends slightly, or refracts, and breaks up into the separate colours that make up white light. A rainbow forms when sunlight is refracted as it enters raindrops, is reflected from the rear of the drop, and is refracted a second time as it leaves.

## WHY THE SKY IS BLUE

Sunlight is a mixture of all the colours of the spectrum: red, orange, yellow, green, blue, indigo and violet. Particles in the atmosphere scatter these colours one by one, beginning with violet. When the Sun is high in the sky, only violet, indigo, blue and a little green are scattered—so the sky looks blue.

Yellows and reds are reflected in the water in this glowing sunset scene.

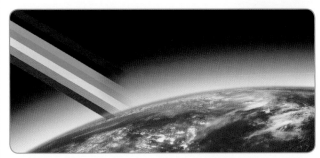

At about noon, the Sun is high in the sky and only bluish colours in the spectrum are scattered.

Towards sunset, sunlight travels further through the atmosphere. Red and yellow are scattered.

Sunrise can produce reddish skies near the horizon and blue skies higher up.

# Global Freezing

Earth's climate has changed many times in the last few million years. During periods of severe cold, known as ice ages or glacials, ice crept across the land. It gouged out hollows as it pushed soil and rocks ahead of it. Sea levels dropped greatly as much of the water froze. During the warmer periods between the ice ages—called interglacials—the ice melted and the huge hollows filled with water to become lakes. Evidence of past climates comes largely from animal and plant fossils found in sediments from ocean beds.

St Pauls Cathedral

## THE LITTLE ICE AGE

Between 1450 and 1850 northern Europe experienced a "Little Ice Age". The River Thames in London, England, froze over in winter. From 1607 to 1814, people held events called frost fairs on the ice, with food stalls, games and dancing. Nowadays, the Thames never freezes over.

**ICE AGE ANIMALS**
One ice age, called the Würm Ice Age, lasted from 120,000 to 20,000 BC. During this time, huge elephant-like mammoths lived on the cold plains of what is now Siberia.

**A CLIMATE TIMELINE**
This timeline shows the major climate changes that have occurred during Earth's 4.6-billion-year history. The wavy line on the chart indicates the temperature relative to today's average, which is marked by the straight horizontal line.

**3.7 bya** Climate 10°C (18°F) warmer than today

**330 mya** Start of long ice age

**2.7–1.8 bya** Ice sheets widespread

**450 mya** Brief ice age

**245 mya** Climate warms; dinosaurs appear.

Present average temperature     bya = billion years ago     mya = million years ago     ya = years ago

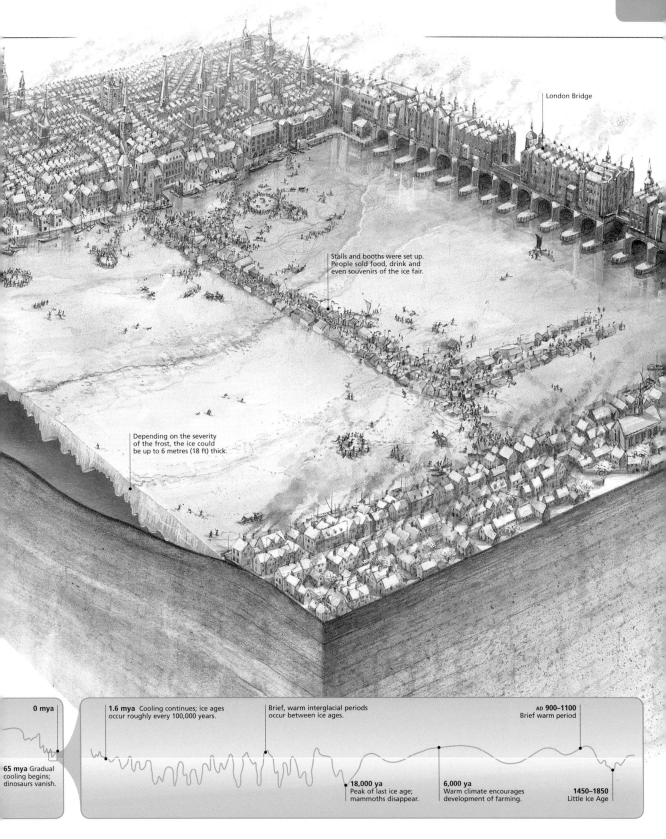

London Bridge

Stalls and booths were set up.
People sold food, drink and
even souvenirs of the ice fair.

Depending on the severity
of the frost, the ice could
be up to 6 metres (18 ft) thick.

0 mya

65 mya Gradual
cooling begins;
dinosaurs vanish.

1.6 mya  Cooling continues; ice ages
occur roughly every 100,000 years.

Brief, warm interglacial periods
occur between ice ages.

AD 900–1100
Brief warm period

18,000 ya
Peak of last ice age;
mammoths disappear.

6,000 ya
Warm climate encourages
development of farming.

1450–1850
Little Ice Age

# Global Warming

Earth's climate is now changing as a result of human activity. Earth has steadily been getting warmer since the end of the "Little Ice Age" in the 1800s. Last century, global temperatures rose by 0.6°C (1°F). This increase is called global warming and it is caused by greenhouse gases. Greenhouse gases—such as water vapour and carbon dioxide—occur naturally in the atmosphere and keep our planet warm by trapping heat from the Sun. However, when fuels such as coal and oil are burned to create electricity and power cars, extra carbon dioxide forms. More carbon dioxide means more heat is trapped in the atmosphere, and Earth heats up.

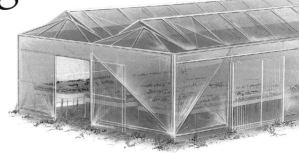

**INSIDE A GREENHOUSE**
Greenhouses are made of glass and have slanted roofs to allow the maximum amount of sunlight to enter. The Sun's heat is trapped inside, which raises the temperature inside the greenhouse and helps the plants to grow.

## THE GREENHOUSE EFFECT

Greenhouse gases absorb heat from the Sun and warm the planet. However, some greenhouse gases, such as carbon dioxide and methane, have built up in the atmosphere. As a result, the natural "greenhouse" has become warmer.

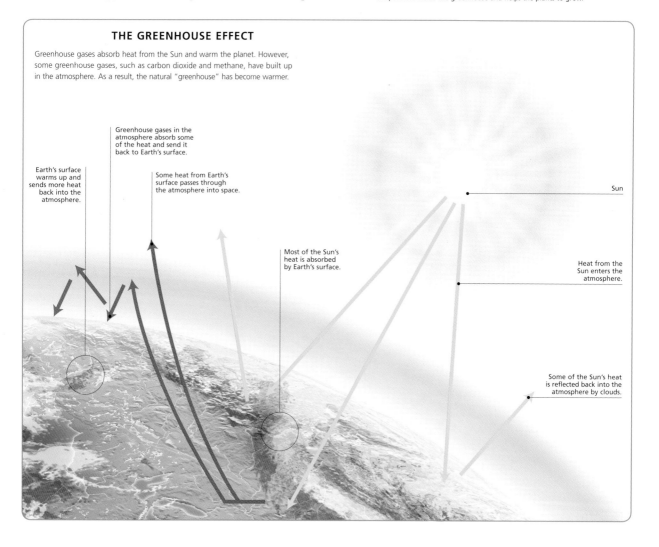

Greenhouse gases in the atmosphere absorb some of the heat and send it back to Earth's surface.

Earth's surface warms up and sends more heat back into the atmosphere.

Some heat from Earth's surface passes through the atmosphere into space.

Most of the Sun's heat is absorbed by Earth's surface.

Sun

Heat from the Sun enters the atmosphere.

Some of the Sun's heat is reflected back into the atmosphere by clouds.

# CARBON DIOXIDE EMISSIONS

The United States, with less than 5 per cent of the world's population, is responsible for more than a quarter of human greenhouse gas emissions. This graph shows the total carbon dioxide gas emissions divided by the population of a number of countries. Each American emits more than 20 tonnes (22 t) each year. Australians are the next worst offenders.

**Carbon dioxide emissions per person**

- 20 tonnes (22 t)
- 15 tonnes (16.5 t)
- 10 tonnes (11 t)
- 5 tonnes (5.5 t)
- 0

Global average

Kenya · India · Indonesia · Egypt · Brazil · China · Turkey · Mexico · Malaysia · Sweden · Venezuela · France · South Africa · UK · Japan · Germany · Russia · Saudi Arabia · Australia · USA

## CHANGING TEMPERATURE

This graph shows average yearly global temperatures since 1850. The 1990s were the warmest decade on record. Temperatures are expected to keep rising, with an increase of between 1°C and 4°C (2°F and 7°F) by the end of this century.

—— Measured global temperature
– – – Predicted global temperature

**Temperature**

- 15.5°C (60°F)
- 15°C (59°F)
- 14.5°C (58°F)
- 14°C (57°F)
- 13.5°C (56°F)
- 13°C (55°F)

Average global temperature 1961–1990 (14°C / 57.2°F)

Year 1860 1870 1880 1890 1900 1910 1920 1930 1940 1950 1960 1970 1980 1990 2000 2010 2020 2030 2040 2050

Cars and trucks are big contributors to greenhouse gas emissions. Heavy traffic is common in industrialized countries, and more people are buying vehicles in the developing world.

Coal-fired power stations, such as this one in the UK, are one of the biggest emitters of carbon dioxide and other polluting chemicals into the atmosphere.

# Effects of global warming

Earth has heated and cooled naturally in cycles for millions of years. What is different about the heating cycle we are currently experiencing is that experts now agree that humans are the cause. Most societies in the world are dependent on burning coal for electricity. The increased amounts of greenhouse gases that result are causing the atmosphere to overheat. If this trend continues, the effects could be devastating. As ice sheets and glaciers melt, sea levels will rise and flood islands and coastal regions. Rainfall patterns may change, causing drought in Africa and India. To slow down this climate change, most industrialized countries signed the Kyoto Protocol in 1997 and agreed to reduce greenhouse gas emissions.

Jökulsárlón is the largest glacial lake in Iceland. It appeared in 1934 and has steadily increased in size as the glaciers that feed it have melted.

**HOT SPOTS OF GLOBAL WARMING**
Scientists have noted many changes in Earth's climate. These include changes in Arctic temperatures and ice, patterns of floods and droughts, the saltiness of the oceans, wind patterns, and extreme weather such as heat waves, wildfires and hurricanes.

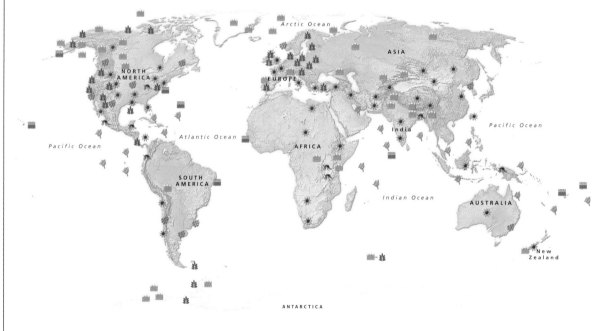

**KEY**

- Melting glaciers and ice
- Rising sea levels
- Heat waves, droughts and fires
- Storms and flooding
- Coral reef bleaching
- Plants and animals affected by warmer temperatures
- Spread of mosquito-borne diseases

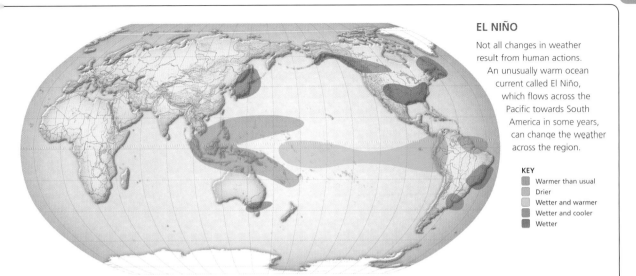

## EL NIÑO

Not all changes in weather result from human actions. An unusually warm ocean current called El Niño, which flows across the Pacific towards South America in some years, can change the weather across the region.

**KEY**

- Warmer than usual
- Drier
- Wetter and warmer
- Wetter and cooler
- Wetter

This fishing boat was once moored by the shores of the Aral Sea, Kazakhstan. Now it lies kilometres from the shrinking sea.

The Arctic ice caps have been getting smaller, because more ice is melting than is being replaced by snowfalls.

Changing rainfall patterns may cause droughts in some regions. These parched conditions increase the risk of wildfires.

## RETREATING GLACIERS

Glaciers supply essential water to people in parts of Asia, South America and Africa. If the glaciers melt and disappear, people in these regions will face serious water shortages.

**1917** The peak of Mount Kilimanjaro in Tanzania, Africa, was covered by glaciers.

**2007** More than 80 per cent of Mount Kilimanjaro's glaciers have melted away.

Scientists predict that the mountain's glaciers will disappear completely by the middle of this century.

Earth's Resources

# Earth's Riches

Earth provides us with the resources we need to live. If we manage them carefully, some of these resources—water, plants and animals—will never run out. These are renewable resources. Others, such as fossil fuels (coal, oil and gas), minerals and precious stones, are not renewable. Fossil fuels supply most of the energy we use to light and heat our homes and to fuel our cars. These fuels are "fossil" because they are the remains of animals and plants buried deep underground. Because some resources may run out soon, scientists are trying to find new ways to supply the energy we need.

**SUPPLY AND DEMAND**
The three fossil fuels—coal, oil and gas—are by far the most important sources of energy. The United States uses about a quarter of all the world's energy.

**SOURCES OF ENERGY**

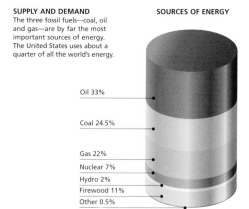

Oil 33%

Coal 24.5%

Gas 22%

Nuclear 7%

Hydro 2%

Firewood 11%

Other 0.5%

**USERS OF ENERGY**

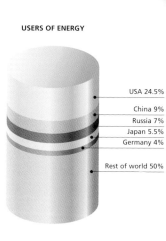

USA 24.5%

China 9%

Russia 7%

Japan 5.5%

Germany 4%

Rest of world 50%

## WHERE TO FIND RESOURCES

As supplies of coal, oil and gas decline, other energy sources, such as wind and solar power, become more important.

**Oil and gas**
Found together in rock layers in Earth's crust, oil and gas are extracted by drilling from land and sea.

**Coal**
Coal, the most plentiful fossil fuel, can be collected by digging at the surface or by mining deep underground.

**Nuclear power**
Certain elements, such as uranium, emit high-energy particles that are converted into electricity at nuclear power plants.

**Geothermal power**
In some regions, groundwater is heated by hot, volcanic rock to create steam that is used to generate power.

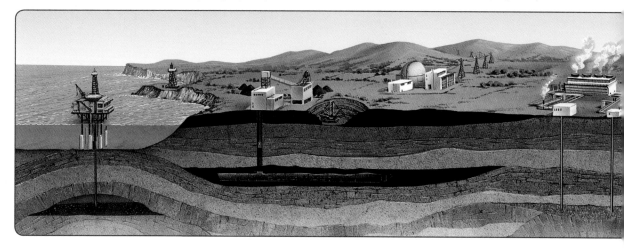

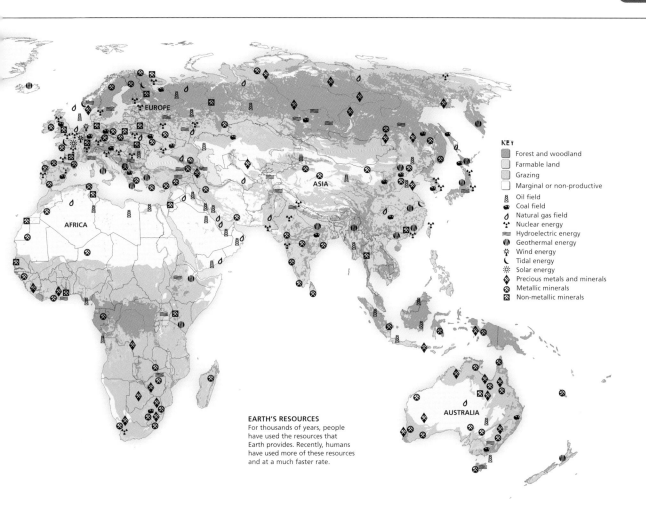

**KEY**

- Forest and woodland
- Farmable land
- Grazing
- Marginal or non-productive
- Oil field
- Coal field
- Natural gas field
- Nuclear energy
- Hydroelectric energy
- Geothermal energy
- Wind energy
- Tidal energy
- Solar energy
- Precious metals and minerals
- Metallic minerals
- Non-metallic minerals

**EARTH'S RESOURCES**
For thousands of years, people have used the resources that Earth provides. Recently, humans have used more of these resources and at a much faster rate.

**Hydroelectric power**
Hydroelectric power is created when water passes through electricity-generating turbines at the bottom of a dam.

**Wind power**
Wind turbines convert the power of the wind into electricity. The wind turns the turbine blades, which drive electrical generators.

**Solar power**
Clusters of mirror-like solar panels reflect the Sun's rays onto a solar furnace, where the intense heat is converted into electricity.

**Tidal power**
Water passing through narrow tunnels in a tidal barrage, which is like a dam, drives huge turbines that produce power.

# Oil and gas

The most sought-after resources are oil and natural gas. New fields are being searched for and found all the time. Countries that have large reserves of oil and gas under their land or in nearby seas sell to countries that need these resources. This trade affects the economy of the whole world. Modern industries, and the growing number of people on Earth, use an ever-increasing amount of oil and gas. However, as it takes millions of years for oil and gas to develop, there are only limited amounts remaining. When they are all used up, we will have to find other sources of energy, such as solar energy or the power of moving wind and water.

This huge machine, called a pump jack or nodding donkey, lifts oil through a bore hole from deep underground reserves in Alberta, Canada.

## LIMITED SUPPLY
The graph below shows the number of years that known supplies of fossil fuels are expected to last, if they continue to be used at the present rate.

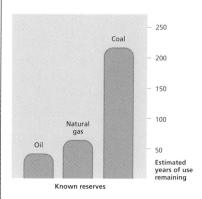

Known reserves

**Revolving crane**
Huge cranes reach out from the platform.

**Flare**
Excess gas is burned off when it reaches the surface.

## ON AN OIL RIG

An oil platform is like a huge steel and concrete hotel in the middle of the ocean. Several hundred workers can live there for weeks at a time. Most platforms stay in position for about 25 years.

**Well heads**
These transport oil and gas to the platform.

## FOSSIL FUEL RESERVES
The whole world relies on fossil fuels, but only a few countries produce and supply them. Most of the world's oil and gas comes from Middle Eastern countries.

### NATURAL GAS RESERVES

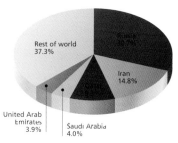

Rest of world 37.3%
Russia 30.7%
Iran 14.8%
United Arab Emirates 3.9%
Saudi Arabia 4.0%

### OIL RESERVES

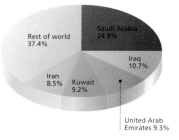

Rest of world 37.4%
Saudi Arabia 24.9%
Iraq 10.7%
Iran 8.5%
Kuwait 9.2%
United Arab Emirates 9.3%

### COAL RESERVES

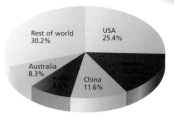

Rest of world 30.2%
USA 25.4%
Australia 8.3%
China 11.6%
India 8.6%

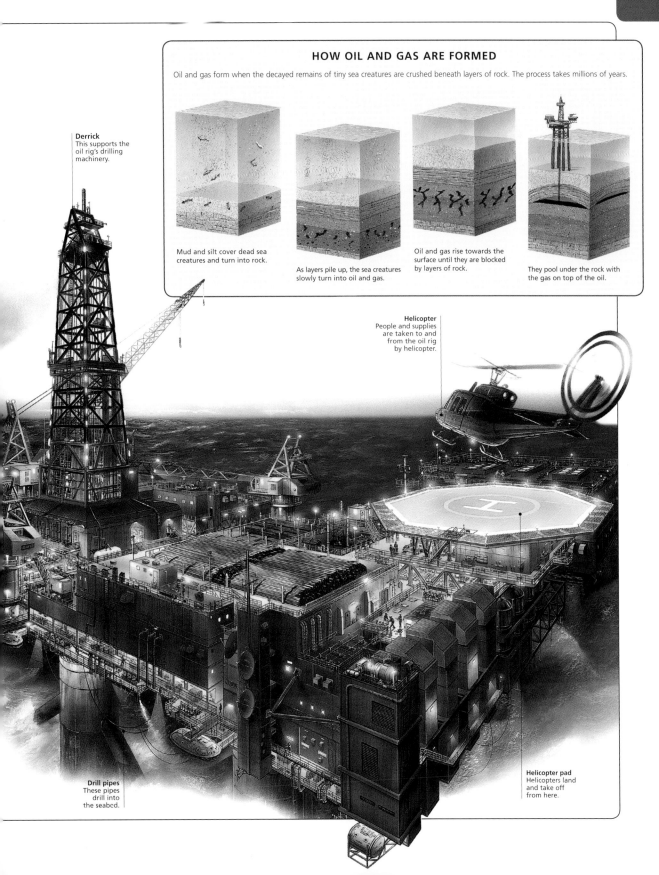

## HOW OIL AND GAS ARE FORMED

Oil and gas form when the decayed remains of tiny sea creatures are crushed beneath layers of rock. The process takes millions of years.

Mud and silt cover dead sea creatures and turn into rock.

As layers pile up, the sea creatures slowly turn into oil and gas.

Oil and gas rise towards the surface until they are blocked by layers of rock.

They pool under the rock with the gas on top of the oil.

**Derrick**
This supports the oil rig's drilling machinery.

**Helicopter**
People and supplies are taken to and from the oil rig by helicopter.

**Drill pipes**
These pipes drill into the seabed.

**Helicopter pad**
Helicopters land and take off from here.

# Coal

Coal is one of the most widely used fuels. It is burned for heat and energy. Coal consists of the remains of ancient swamp plants. As the plants decay in mud, they turn into a moist, spongy substance called peat. Sometimes, sedimentary rock forms on top of the peat and compresses it. The crushed peat then turns into a dark brown rock called lignite, or brown coal. As more layers of rock press down on it, lignite becomes bituminous coal. Under extreme pressure, bituminous coal changes into anthracite—a hard, shiny, black coal. The more coal is compressed, the harder it becomes and the more energy it releases when burned.

While most coal is mined deep underground, some is mined near the surface. Mines like this one in Germany are called open-pit mines.

**HOW COAL IS FORMED**
Over thousands of years, buried plant material can become compressed and lose most of its water, oxygen and other gases. During compression its carbon content gradually increases and it turns into coal.

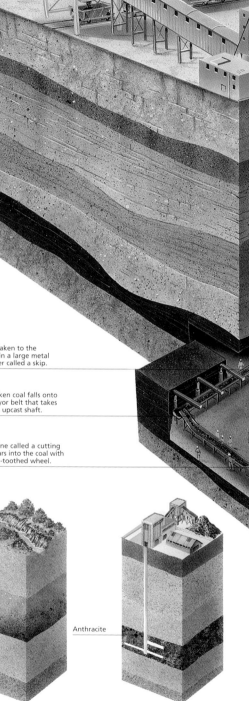

Upcast shaft and fan

6. Coal is taken to the surface in a large metal container called a skip.

5. The broken coal falls onto a conveyor belt that takes it to the upcast shaft.

4. A machine called a cutting head tears into the coal with its sharp-toothed wheel.

Peat

Decayed plants become peat. This material includes high levels of moisture and gases.

Lignite, or brown coal

Bituminous, or black, coal

Layers of sedimentary rock compress the peat, turning it into lignite, or brown coal.

Anthracite

Increased pressure turns lignite into bituminous, or black, coal.

Anthracite, the highest quality coal, is the most compressed, and contains little water or gas.

**7.** Coal is loaded onto rail cars for transportation.

**1.** Miners take the downcast shaft to reach the coal face. Fans supply them with air.

**3.** The miners dig tunnels through the rock. They use metal pillars to support the roof.

**2.** The miners descend to the coal face in a metal lift known as a cage.

## MINING COAL

Today, machines do most of the digging involved in mining coal. The method shown here, known as continuous mining, is used in most coal mines.

## MAKING STEEL

Steel is a mixture of iron and carbon, which combine when heated with coal. We use it to make many objects, tools, utensils, cars and trains.

### THE RAW INGREDIENTS

To make steel, iron must be removed from iron ore.

Coke—a type of heated coal—heats iron ore to extract molten iron.

Limestone removes impurities from the molten iron.

### THE PRODUCTION PROCESS

Coke and iron ore are heated together in a large furnace. When the molten iron sinks to the bottom, limestone is added.

In another furnace, oxygen is blasted into the iron to reduce the amount of carbon and turn it into steel.

The molten steel is tipped into a continuous casting system. Steel is shaped into long sections by being squeezed between rollers.

### THE END RESULT

Flexible wire is an important steel product.

Sheets of steel are used for many products.

Steel girders provide support in large buildings.

Many types of pipes are made of steel.

# Solar and wind energy

The Sun is a powerful source of energy. It could, in fact, supply the whole world's energy needs—Earth receives 20,000 times as much energy from the Sun as we currently use. Energy from the Sun—called solar energy—can be harnessed in many ways. Satellites in space have large panels covered with solar cells that turn sunlight into electrical power. Some buildings have glass-covered solar panels that use solar energy to heat water. They are painted black inside to absorb the heat. Solar energy is a clean fuel that will continue to reach Earth long after all the fossil fuels have been used up. Wind, too, is a source of energy, which can be harnessed by sails or blades. In the past, wind powered sailboats and windmills. Today, modern versions of windmills called turbines are used to generate electricity.

## MAKING SOLAR POWER

Solar cells convert light into electricity. The first layer in a solar cell is made from N-type silicon, which has many electrons. The second layer is P-type silicon, which has fewer electrons. Solar energy causes electrons to jump from the first layer to the second, producing an electric current.

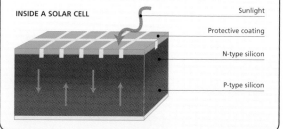

INSIDE A SOLAR CELL

Sunlight

Protective coating

N-type silicon

P-type silicon

Rows of solar panels are being installed for solar power stations in dry, sunny places, such as the southwestern U.S., the Australian desert, and parts of Spain and Germany.

## HARNESSING THE WIND

Wind turbines with large sails or
blades convert wind into energy.
Wind farms, as they are called,
are built in very windy locations.
As the wind turns the blades, the
spinning motion produces electricity.

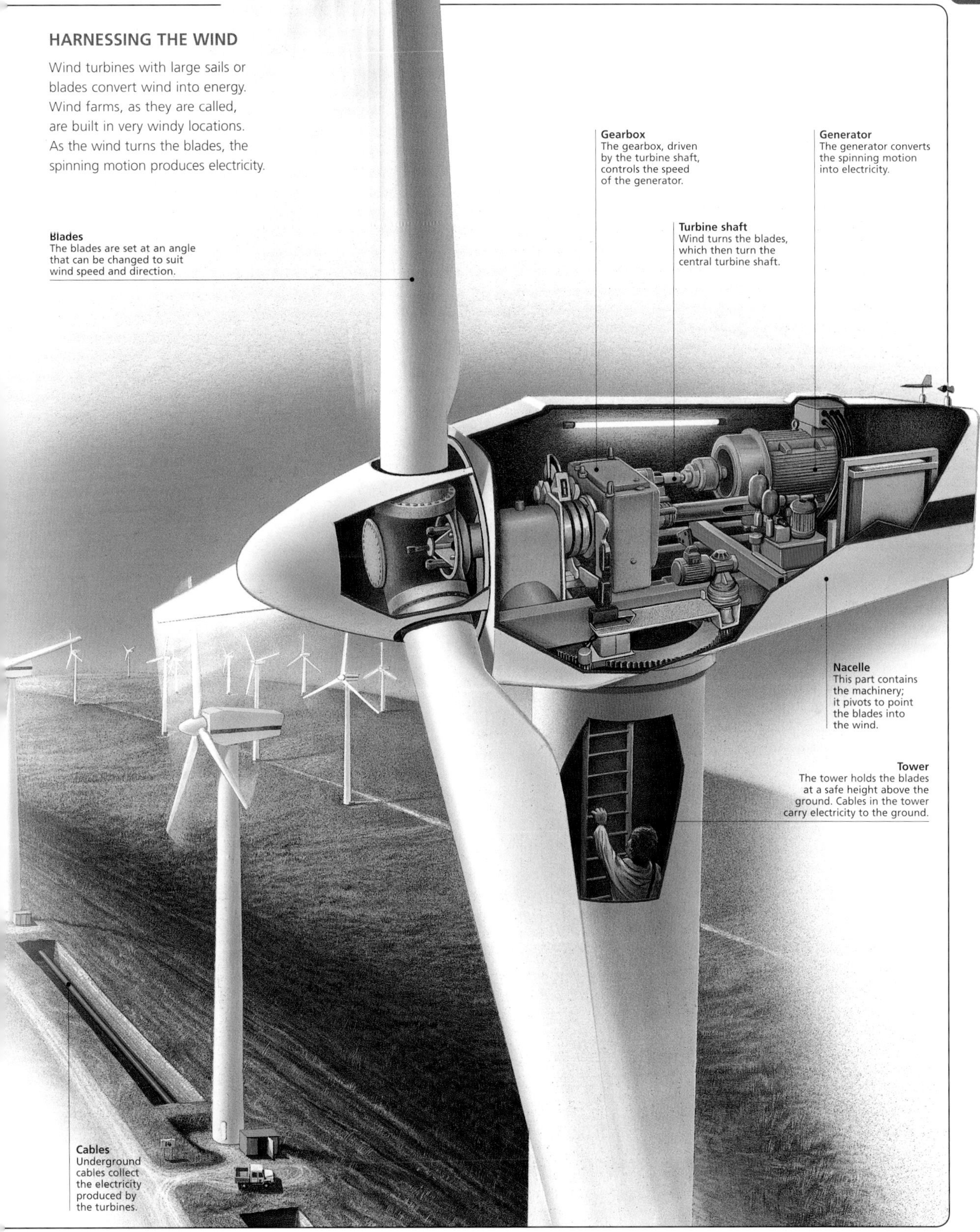

**Gearbox**
The gearbox, driven
by the turbine shaft,
controls the speed
of the generator.

**Generator**
The generator converts
the spinning motion
into electricity.

**Blades**
The blades are set at an angle
that can be changed to suit
wind speed and direction.

**Turbine shaft**
Wind turns the blades,
which then turn the
central turbine shaft.

**Nacelle**
This part contains
the machinery;
it pivots to point
the blades into
the wind.

**Tower**
The tower holds the blades
at a safe height above the
ground. Cables in the tower
carry electricity to the ground.

**Cables**
Underground
cables collect
the electricity
produced by
the turbines.

# Power from water and Earth's heat

Hydroelectric power stations use moving water to generate electricity. These enormous concrete structures are usually found in mountain regions that have high rainfall. Engineers build huge dams across steep-sided valleys. Turbines are placed in the path of the water that gushes forcefully through the dam. The blades of the turbines spin and extract enormous energy from the water. Geothermal energy makes use of heat from Earth's molten core to heat water sent in pipes below the surface. Steam from this heated water travels back to power stations on the surface, where its force spins turbines that produce electric power.

Hydroelectric dams have a major advantage over coal-burning power plants. They use a renewable resource—water—which is constantly being recycled in the environment.

The Svartsengi power plant in southwest Iceland is one of five major geothermal power stations that together generate about one-quarter of Iceland's electricity needs.

Since 1958, hot springs have provided a source of electricity generation at the Wairakei geothermal power station on New Zealand's North Island.

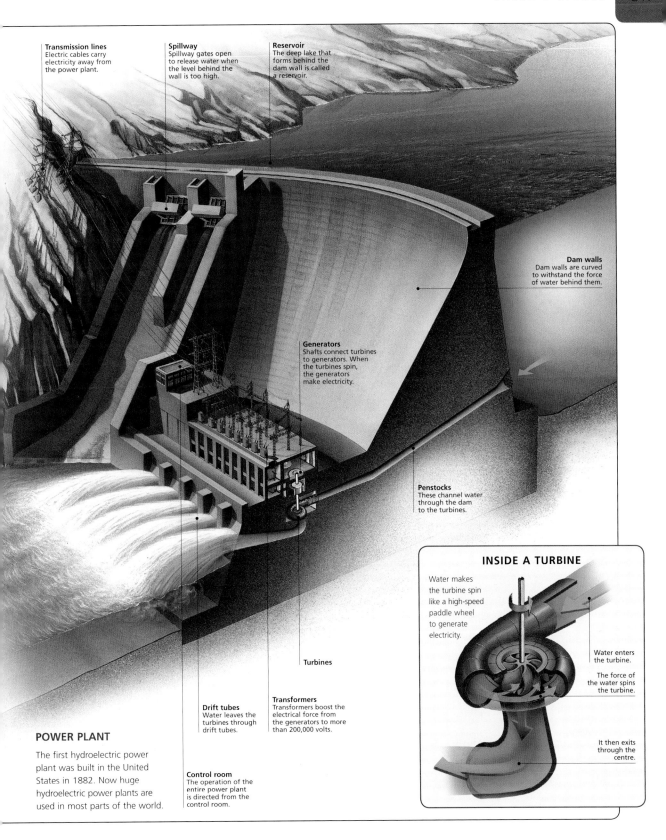

**Transmission lines**
Electric cables carry electricity away from the power plant.

**Spillway**
Spillway gates open to release water when the level behind the wall is too high.

**Reservoir**
The deep lake that forms behind the dam wall is called a reservoir.

**Dam walls**
Dam walls are curved to withstand the force of water behind them.

**Generators**
Shafts connect turbines to generators. When the turbines spin, the generators make electricity.

**Penstocks**
These channel water through the dam to the turbines.

**Turbines**

**Drift tubes**
Water leaves the turbines through drift tubes.

**Transformers**
Transformers boost the electrical force from the generators to more than 200,000 volts.

**Control room**
The operation of the entire power plant is directed from the control room.

## POWER PLANT

The first hydroelectric power plant was built in the United States in 1882. Now huge hydroelectric power plants are used in most parts of the world.

### INSIDE A TURBINE

Water makes the turbine spin like a high-speed paddle wheel to generate electricity.

Water enters the turbine.

The force of the water spins the turbine.

It then exits through the centre.

# Comparing Earth

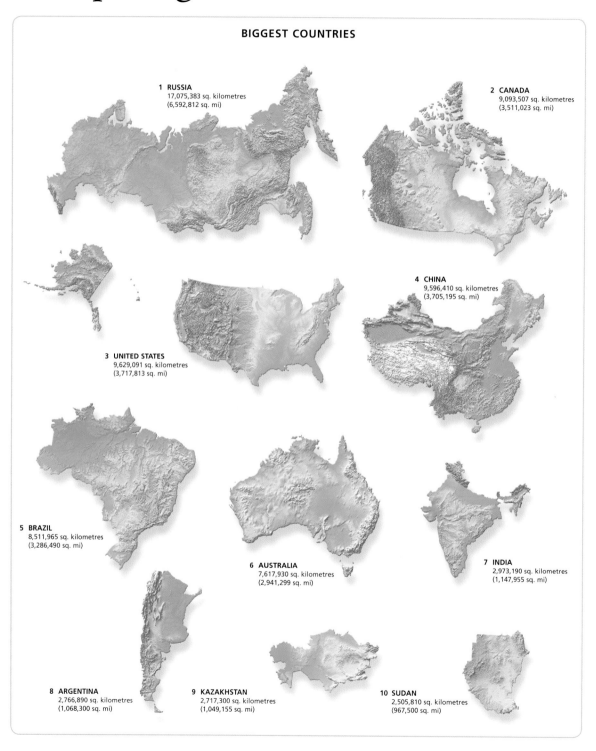

## BIGGEST COUNTRIES

**1  RUSSIA**
17,075,383 sq. kilometres
(6,592,812 sq. mi)

**2  CANADA**
9,093,507 sq. kilometres
(3,511,023 sq. mi)

**4  CHINA**
9,596,410 sq. kilometres
(3,705,195 sq. mi)

**3  UNITED STATES**
9,629,091 sq. kilometres
(3,717,813 sq. mi)

**5  BRAZIL**
8,511,965 sq. kilometres
(3,286,490 sq. mi)

**6  AUSTRALIA**
7,617,930 sq. kilometres
(2,941,299 sq. mi)

**7  INDIA**
2,973,190 sq. kilometres
(1,147,955 sq. mi)

**8  ARGENTINA**
2,766,890 sq. kilometres
(1,068,300 sq. mi)

**9  KAZAKHSTAN**
2,717,300 sq. kilometres
(1,049,155 sq. mi)

**10  SUDAN**
2,505,810 sq. kilometres
(967,500 sq. mi)

# LARGEST LAKES

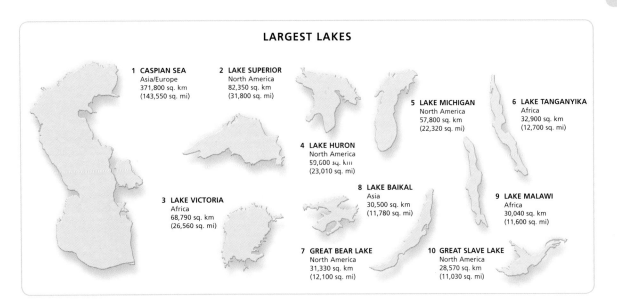

**1  CASPIAN SEA**
Asia/Europe
371,800 sq. km
(143,550 sq. mi)

**2  LAKE SUPERIOR**
North America
82,350 sq. km
(31,800 sq. mi)

**5  LAKE MICHIGAN**
North America
57,800 sq. km
(22,320 sq. mi)

**6  LAKE TANGANYIKA**
Africa
32,900 sq. km
(12,700 sq. mi)

**4  LAKE HURON**
North America
59,600 sq. km
(23,010 sq. mi)

**8  LAKE BAIKAL**
Asia
30,500 sq. km
(11,780 sq. mi)

**9  LAKE MALAWI**
Africa
30,040 sq. km
(11,600 sq. mi)

**3  LAKE VICTORIA**
Africa
68,790 sq. km
(26,560 sq. mi)

**7  GREAT BEAR LAKE**
North America
31,330 sq. km
(12,100 sq. mi)

**10  GREAT SLAVE LAKE**
North America
28,570 sq. km
(11,030 sq. mi)

# LONGEST RIVERS

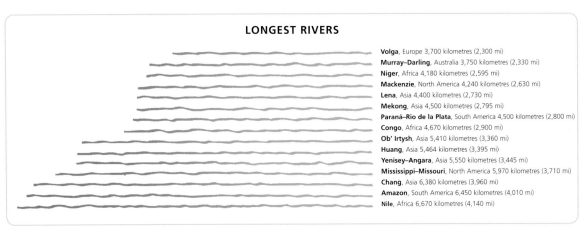

**Volga**, Europe 3,700 kilometres (2,300 mi)

**Murray–Darling**, Australia 3,750 kilometres (2,330 mi)

**Niger**, Africa 4,180 kilometres (2,595 mi)

**Mackenzie**, North America 4,240 kilometres (2,630 mi)

**Lena**, Asia 4,400 kilometres (2,730 mi)

**Mekong**, Asia 4,500 kilometres (2,795 mi)

**Paraná–Rio de la Plata**, South America 4,500 kilometres (2,800 mi)

**Congo**, Africa 4,670 kilometres (2,900 mi)

**Ob' Irtysh**, Asia 5,410 kilometres (3,360 mi)

**Huang**, Asia 5,464 kilometres (3,395 mi)

**Yenisey–Angara**, Asia 5,550 kilometres (3,445 mi)

**Mississippi–Missouri**, North America 5,970 kilometres (3,710 mi)

**Chang**, Asia 6,380 kilometres (3,960 mi)

**Amazon**, South America 6,450 kilometres (4,010 mi)

**Nile**, Africa 6,670 kilometres (4,140 mi)

# HIGHEST MOUNTAINS

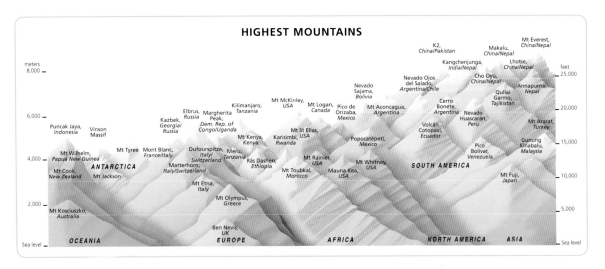

# Planet Earth

## EARTH THROUGH TIME

Earth's life can be divided into different units of time, called eras, periods and epochs. Different plants and animals lived at different times—for example, the dinosaurs lived only in the Mesozoic era.

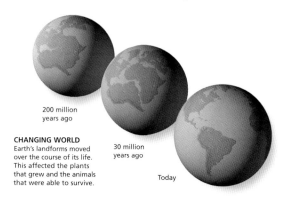

200 million years ago

30 million years ago

Today

**CHANGING WORLD**
Earth's landforms moved over the course of its life. This affected the plants that grew and the animals that were able to survive.

### ERAS AND PERIODS

| EON/Era | Period | Epoch | Began mya |
|---|---|---|---|
| **PHANEROZOIC EON** | | | |
| | Pleistogene | Holocene | 0.1 |
| | | Pleistocene | 1.8 |
| **Cenozoic Era** | Neogene | Pliocene | 5.3 |
| | | Miocene | 23 |
| | Paleogene | Oligocene | 34 |
| | | Eocene | 55 |
| | | Paleocene | 65.5 |
| **Mesozoic Era** | Cretaceous | Late | 100 |
| | | Early | 146 |
| | Jurassic | Late | 161 |
| | | Middle | 176 |
| | | Early | 200 |
| | Triassic | Late | 228 |
| | | Middle | 245 |
| | | Early | 251 |
| **Palaeozoic Era** | Permian | Late | 260 |
| | | Middle | 271 |
| | | Early | 299 |
| | Carboniferous | Pennsylvanian | 318 |
| | | Mississipian | 359 |
| | Devonian | Late | 385 |
| | | Middle | 398 |
| | | Early | 416 |
| | Silurian | Late | 423 |
| | | Early | 444 |
| | Ordovician | Late | 461 |
| | | Middle | 472 |
| | | Early | 488 |
| | Cambrian | Late | 501 |
| | | Middle | 513 |
| | | Early | 542 |
| **PROTEROZOIC EON** | | | 2,500 |
| **ARCHAEAN EON** | | | 3,800 |
| **HADEAN EON** | | | 4,600 |

## WHAT MAKES UP SOIL

Soil consists of broken pieces of bedrock combined with the remains of once-living plants and animals that are decomposing. Living creatures, such as worms, mix up the soil. Rainwater draining through the soil carries minerals with it, which causes older soils to form distinct layers.

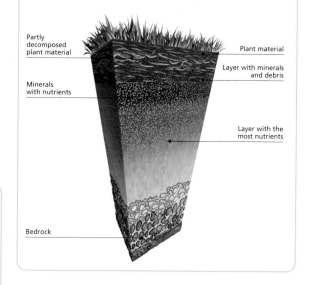

Partly decomposed plant material

Minerals with nutrients

Bedrock

Plant material

Layer with minerals and debris

Layer with the most nutrients

## GEMSTONES AND JEWELS

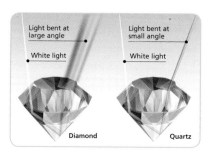

Light bent at large angle

White light

Diamond

Light bent at small angle

White light

Quartz

**WHY DIAMONDS SPARKLE**
When white light shines through a transparent crystal, it bends and breaks into its colours, or spectra. Light needs to bend at a larger angle for diamonds than other crystals, which is why they sparkle so brilliantly.

**WORLD'S LARGEST DIAMONDS**
The size of some famous diamonds is compared to a 1-carat ring.

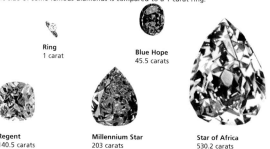

Ring
1 carat

Blue Hope
45.5 carats

Regent
140.5 carats

Millennium Star
203 carats

Star of Africa
530.2 carats

# Volcanoes

## DECADE VOLCANOES

There are 16 Decade Volcanoes—volcanoes that are internationally recognized as being important for constant study. They are generally large, have a long history of violent activity and are located close to towns or cities.

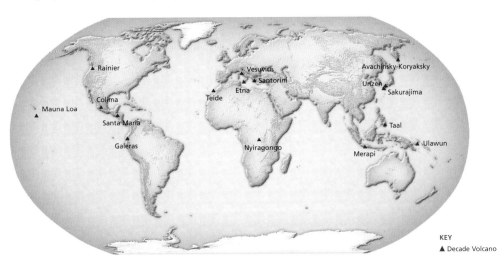

KEY
▲ Decade Volcano

## 10 WORST VOLCANIC ERUPTIONS

| Year | Volcano | Location | Fatalities | Cause of deaths |
|------|---------|----------|-----------|-----------------|
| 1815 | Tambora | Indonesia | 92,000 | Ash, tsunami, disease, starvation |
| 1883 | Krakatau | Indonesia | 36,400 | Tsunami, ash |
| 1902 | Mt. Pelee | Martinique | 26,000 | Ashflows |
| 1985 | Nevado del Ruiz | Colombia | 23,000 | Mudflows |
| 79 | Vesuvius | Italy | 16,000 | Ash, ashflows |
| 1792 | Unzen | Japan | 14,500 | Volcano collapse, tsunami |
| 1586 | Kelut | Indonesia | 10,000 | Unknown |
| 1783 | Laki | Iceland | 9,350 | Disease, starvation |
| 1919 | Kelut | Indonesia | 5,000 | Mudflows |
| 1631 | Vesuvius | Italy | 4,000 | Mudflows, lava flows |

## OUT OF THIS WORLD

Volcanoes are not restricted to Earth. They appear in a number of places in our Solar System. Volcanoes have played a part in shaping the surface of all four inner rocky planets (Mercury, Venus, Earth and Mars) as well as some of the moons of the outer gas giants.

**NEPTUNE'S TRITON**
Triton is the largest moon of Neptune. Its volcanoes do not expel lava but throw out freezing plumes of liquid nitrogen, rather like geysers. This material rises about 8 kilometres (5 mi) above the surface, before raining down as nitrogen frost.

**The Moon**
The dark patches on its surface are dried lava lakes.

**Venus**
Sulphur from its volcanoes formed its thick atmosphere.

**Mars**
The volcanoes on Mars dwarf those on our planet.

**Jupiter's moon Io**
This moon spews sulphur dioxide from its surface.

**Neptune's moon Triton**
Not all volcanoes are hot; Triton's geysers are freezing.

# Earthquakes

## EARTHQUAKE RISK

The chances of being shaken up by an earthquake depend on where on Earth you are. In many places you could live a whole lifetime and never feel the ground move. In other places, tremors are a regular occurrence and the risk of a destructive earthquake is always present.

**KEY**
- ☐ Low risk
- ☐ Medium risk
- ☐ High risk
- ☐ Very high risk

---

## EARTHQUAKE THEORIES

As long as people have felt the ground shake, they have sought to explain the frightening phenomenon of earthquakes. But it is only very recently that we have worked out what is happening beneath our feet.

**MYTHICAL EXPLANATIONS**
According to an ancient Hindu myth, Earth is carried on the back of an elephant, which stands on a turtle that is balanced on a cobra. Whenever one moves, Earth trembles and shakes.

A Hindu cosmos

**EARLY MODERN EUROPE**
In the 1660s the French philosopher René Descartes suggested that Earth was once as hot as the Sun and that it is still cooling and shrinking. These contractions created the mountains and caused earthquakes.

Cross section of Earth's interior from 1665

**MODERN TIMES**
Plate tectonic theory had its beginnings in 1915, when German scientist Alfred Wegener suggested that all the continents were once joined together and had subsequently drifted apart. This theory has proved to be a convincing explanation for earthquakes and other geological phenomena.

Seismograph

---

## 10 WORST EARTHQUAKES

| Year | Location | Fatalities |
|------|----------|-----------|
| 1201 | Egypt–Syria | 1,100,000 |
| 1556 | Shanxi, China | 830,000 |
| 1139 | Caucasus | 300,000 |
| 1662 | China | 300,000 |
| 1737 | Calcutta, India | 300,000 |
| 2004 | Sumatra–Andaman | 283,000 |
| 115 | Antioch, Turkey | 260,000 |
| 1976 | Tangshan, China | 240,000 |
| 1139 | Aleppo, Syria | 230,000 |
| 1876 | Andaman Islands | 215,000 |

## 5 WORST TSUNAMIS

| Year | Location | Fatalities |
|------|----------|-----------|
| 2004 | Sumatra–Andaman | 283,000 |
| 1755 | Lisbon, Portugal | 100,000 |
| 1908 | Italy | 70,000 |
| 1782 | China and Taiwan | 40,000 |
| 1883 | Krakatau, Indonesia | 36,000 |

# Extreme Earth

## TORNADOES AND HURRICANES

**PATH OF DESTRUCTION**
A tornado's funnel is like a giant vacuum cleaner that sucks up everything in its path. Buildings and trees in its direct path can be destroyed, but those just either side spared.

### FUJITA SCALE

This six-point scale was devised in 1971 to report tornadoes, based on the visible damage they cause.

| Scale | Speeds km/h (mph) | Damage |
|-------|-------------------|--------|
| F0 | 64–117 (40–73) | light |
| F1 | 118–180 (74–112) | moderate |
| F2 | 181–251 (113–157) | considerable |
| F3 | 252–330 (158–206) | terrible |
| F4 | 331–417 (207–260) | severe |
| F5 | more than 417 (260) | devastating |

### SAFFIR–SIMPSON SCALE

This scale was devised in 1955 by meteorologists at the U.S. Weather Bureau to report the strength of hurricane winds. The five-point scale also takes account of surface pressure and storm surges.

| Scale | Pressure hectopascals | Wind speed km/h (mph) | Storm surge m (ft) | Damage |
|-------|-----------------------|-----------------------|--------------------|--------|
| 1 | more than 980 | 118–152 (74–95) | 1.2–1.6 (4–5) | minimal |
| 2 | 965–980 | 153–176 (96–110) | 1.7–2.5 (6–8) | moderate |
| 3 | 945–964 | 177–208 (111–130) | 2.6–3.7 (9–12) | extensive |
| 4 | 920–944 | 209–248 (131–155) | 3.8–5.4 (13–18) | extreme |
| 5 | less than 920 | more than 248 (155) | more than 5.4 (18) | catastrophic |

**JOURNEY OF HURRICANE EMILY**
Emily developed off the coast of Brazil on July 12. By the 16th, winds were over 125 knots and gusting to 155 knots. After striking land on the 18th, Emily then headed back out to sea on the 19th to regain strength. On the 20th, she came ashore over Mexico as a Category 5 hurricane.

July 12, 2005

July 16, 2005

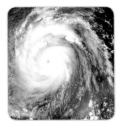
July 19, 2005

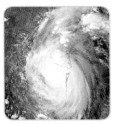
July 20, 2005

### EXTREME WEATHER FACTS

**WETTEST PLACE**
Cherrapunji, India 26,461 millimetres (1,042 in) of rain in 1860–61.

**DRIEST PLACE**
Arica in Chile's Atacama Desert Annual average rainfall is 0.5 millimetres (0.02 in).

**LOWEST TEMPERATURE**
Vostok Base, Antarctica Recorded a temperature of –89.2°C (–129°F) on July 21, 1983.

**HIGHEST NON-TORNADO WIND GUST**
Mount Washington, USA Recorded a wind gust of 372 km/h (231 mph) on April 12, 1934.

**HEAVIEST RECORDED HAILSTONES**
Gopalganj, Bangladesh  Recorded hailstones that weighed up to 1 kilogram (2 lb 3 oz) on April 14, 1986, killing 92 people.

**RAINIEST PLACE**
Mount Waialeale Crater, Kauai, Hawaii 350 days of rain each year.

**HIGHEST TEMPERATURE**
El Azizia, Libya Recorded a temperature of 57.3°C (136°F) on September 13, 1922.

**GREATEST TEMPERATURE RANGE**
Verhoyansk, Central Siberia Summer temperatures in this region can reach 37°C (98°F). Winter temperatures can go as low as –68°C (–90°F).

**HIGHEST RECORDED TORNADO WIND SPEED**
Oklahoma, USA In May 1999, winds gusted to 512 km/h (318 mph).

**HOTTEST REGION**
Sahara Desert belt Dallol, Ethiopia, averaged a daytime temperature of 34°C (94°F) between 1960 and 1966.

# Glossary

**abyssal plain** The smooth, almost level, deep ocean floor, located between the continental slope and the mid-ocean ridge.

**acid rain** An acidic form of rain that occurs when chemicals produced by the burning of fossil fuels mix with water vapour in the air.

**aftershock** A tremor that occurs hours, days or weeks after a major earthquake and starts near that quake's hypocentre.

**air mass** A large body of air, covering most of a continent or ocean, which has approximately the same temperature, humidity and density at every height.

**Antarctic Circle** The imaginary line, at 66.5°S, south of which there is at least one day each year when the sun does not rise above the horizon and one day when it does not sink below the horizon.

**Arctic Circle** The imaginary line, at 66.5°N, north of which there is at least one day each year when the sun does not rise above the horizon and one day when it does not sink below the horizon.

**arid** Having too little rainfall to be used for agriculture.

**ash** The mineral residue of a fire. Volcanic ash contains small pieces of rock and lava.

**atmosphere** A layer of gases surrounding a planet or moon, extending from the surface and held in place by gravity.

**atoll** A circular reef that encloses a lagoon. It is commonly formed on the crater rim of an extinct underwater volcano.

**biodiversity** Short for "biological diversity", the variety that exists among the living things in the world or in some part of the world.

**biome** A large area of distinctive plant and animal groups.

**caldera** The roughly circular crater at the top of a volcano, formed by the collapse of the roof of a magma chamber.

**canyon** A deep, steep-sided valley formed by river erosion.

**CFCs (chlorofluorocarbons)** Industrially produced chemicals used in aerosols, refrigerators and air conditioners.

**climate** A region's long-term pattern of weather conditions.

**cloud** A concentration of liquid water droplets or ice crystals in the atmosphere.

**condensation** The change from a gas to liquid, for example, water vapour changing to liquid water droplets.

**continent** A large area of continental crust with a surface that is above sea level. There are seven continents: Africa, Antarctica, Asia, Australia, Europe, North America and South America.

**continental drift** The slow movement of continental plates—the pieces of Earth's crust on which the continents are fixed. This is caused by convection currents circling in the mantle.

**continental rise** The ocean floor beyond the edge of the continental slope. It is covered with sediment and slopes gently downward away from the continent.

**continental shelf** The edge of a continent that lies below the ocean surface.

**continental slope** The steeply sloping area of ocean floor between the continental shelf and continental rise. Its surface is divided by deep canyons.

**convection** The upward movement of an air mass warmed by land or sea. As the warm air rises, condensation may occur, forming clouds.

**convection currents (mantle)** Movement within the mantle as hot rock rises and cooler rock sinks. This movement most likely causes the movement of Earth's tectonic plates.

**coral reef** A massive limestone structure built in clear tropical water from the skeletons (corallites) of small soft-bodied animals called polyps.

**core** The centremost part of Earth, which consists of a solid inner core surrounded by a liquid outer core, both made of iron.

**crater** A circular depression caused either by volcanic activity (volcanic crater) or by the impact of a meteorite (impact crater).

**crust** The outer layer of Earth, consisting of solid rock averaging 5 kilometres (3 mi) thick beneath the oceans and up to 64 kilometres (40 mi) beneath mountain ranges.

**crystal** A solid mineral with a definite geometric shape.

**current** There are two main kinds of water currents: an ocean current is a stream of water that moves through the water, like a river in the sea, and a surface current is driven by the wind.

**cyclone** An area of very low pressure, with often grey skies and steady rainfall. Air moves around a cyclone anticlockwise in the Northern Hemisphere and clockwise in the Southern. (See hurricane)

**deciduous** A plant or tree that drops its leaves in autumn, winter or dry season and grows new leaves in spring or wet season.

**delta** The mouth of a slow-moving river, which deposits a layer of sediment that extends beyond the coastline.

**desert** A region where the amount of rain each year is less than the amount of water that evaporates during the same period.

**down draught** A downward-moving air current.

**earthquake** A sudden, violent release of energy in Earth's crust, caused by the rocks cracking deep below the surface as they move to release the strain.

**ecosystem** A community of living things and the environment in which they live.

**El Niño** A periodic unusual warming of surface waters off the west coast of South America.

**epicentre** The point on Earth's surface that is directly above the hypocentre, or starting point, of an earthquake.

**equator** The imaginary line at 0° latitude that divides Earth into its North and South hemispheres.

**era** A division of time in Earth's history. Geologists divide eras into periods.

**erosion** The breaking down and removal of rock and soil by wind, water, ice and mass movements such as landslides.

**estuary** A partly enclosed area of coastal water that is open to the sea and into which a river flows.

**evaporation** The change of state from a liquid to a gas.

**fault** A crack in Earth's crust along which two sections of crust have moved in relation to each other.

**fjord** A long, narrow, steep-sided coastal inlet at the end of a glacial valley.

**floodplain** The part of a river valley that is covered with sediment deposited by a river that overflows its banks.

**fog** Cloud at ground level that reduces visibility to less than 1 kilometre (0.6 mi).

**fold** A bend in rock layers caused by movement in the crust.

**fossil** The remains, trace or impression of any living thing preserved in, or as, rock.

**fossil fuel** Material that comes from the remains of once-living plants or animals

that can be burnt to release energy. Peat, coal, oil and gas are fossil fuels.

**freezing** The change in state from liquid to solid, as from water to ice.

**front** A boundary between two air masses of different temperatures.

**geothermal energy** Heat that comes from an underground reservoir of rock or water that is much hotter than the surrounding rock. This energy can be used as power.

**geyser** An opening at Earth's surface, from which a fountain of hot water periodically spouts upward.

**glacier** A mass of ice formed by the buildup of compressed snow that moves slowly over the underlying surface.

**Gondwana** The former southern super-continent. It contained South America, Africa, Madagascar, India, Sri Lanka, Australia, New Zealand and Antarctica.

**greenhouse effect** The retention of heat in the atmosphere because certain gases, such as water vapour and carbon dioxide, absorb sunlight.

**groundwater** Water that moves through the spaces between rocks below ground.

**habitat** The area where a community of plants and animals lives.

**hardness** A measure of the ability of one mineral to scratch another.

**hemisphere** One half of a sphere, for example, Earth's Northern and Southern hemispheres.

**hot spot** A local area of high volcanic activity that does not occur at the edges of tectonic plates.

**humidity** The amount of water vapour present in the air.

**hurricane** The name for a tropical cyclone that develops in the Atlantic or Caribbean. (See cyclone)

**hypocentre** The place within Earth's crust where energy in strained rock is suddenly released as earthquake waves.

**ice sheet** The largest form of a glacier, sometimes called an ice cap.

**ice shelf** An area of floating ice, once part of a glacier, that is still attached to land.

**iceberg** A mass of ice that has detached (calved) from a glacier or ice shelf and floats in the sea.

**igneous rock** A rock that has formed from cooled, hardened magma. Earth's first rocks were igneous rock.

**intrusion** A body of rock that has formed within pre-existing rocks.

**invertebrate** An animal, such as a worm, mollusc, trilobite or insect that does not have a backbone.

**jet stream** A narrow, strong wind current 10–15 kilometres (6–9 mi) above Earth's surface.

**lagoon** A coastal area of shallow water that is almost completely enclosed, with only a small connection to the sea.

**Laurasia** The former northern supercontinent. It contained North America, Greenland, Europe and Asia (but not India).

**lava** Molten rock, or magma, that has erupted onto Earth's surface from a volcano.

**lightning** An electrical discharge between areas of positive and negative electric charge inside clouds and on the ground.

**lithosphere** The solid layer of Earth that comprises the crust and the brittle top part of the mantle.

**lustre** The ability of a mineral to absorb or reflect light.

**magma** Hot liquid rock and crystals found below Earth's surface. When magma erupts onto the surface, it is called lava.

**magma chamber** A pool of magma in Earth's lithosphere surface where magma is stored until it rises to the surface in a volcanic eruption.

**mantle** The part of the Earth between the underside of the crust and the outer core. It is semi-solid rock, about the consistency of modelling clay.

**margin** A boundary between two tectonic plates. These may be moving apart, pushing together, or slipping side by side.

**marsh** A permanently waterlogged area of land, in which grasses grow.

**meander** The winding course of a river as it flows slowly across almost level ground.

**Mercalli scale** A scale for measuring the intensity of an earthquake by direct observation of its effect, divided into 12 categories from "not felt" to "total devastation".

**mesosphere** The layer of the atmosphere above the stratosphere, from about 50 to 80 kilometres (30 to 50 mi) above sea level.

**metal** A material that is a good conductor of heat and electricity; most metals are solid and shiny at room temperature.

**metamorphic rock** Rock formed by the transformation of pre-existing rock as a result of extreme heat and/or pressure.

**meteor** A small extraterrestrial body that burns up as it travels through Earth's atmosphere, producing a "shooting star".

**meteorite** A small extraterrestrial body that has reached Earth's surface.

**mid-ocean ridge** The range of volcanic mountains that runs along the centre of an ocean floor. They occur where two tectonic plates are moving apart and mantle material is rising to fill the gap and form new oceanic crust.

**migration** A number of animals moving from one region to another, to breed or to find food during winter or summer.

**mineral** A naturally occurring substance with a characteristic chemical composition and crystal structure. Rocks are made of minerals.

**monsoon** A seasonal wind that produces heavy rain in tropical and subtropical zones, especially Southeast Asia.

**ocean** One of five great bodies of seawater: the Pacific, Atlantic, Indian Arctic and Southern. Together, oceans cover 71 per cent of Earth's surface.

**ore** A mineral or rock from which it is possible to extract other useful materials such as metal.

**ozone** A form of oxygen in which the molecule consists of three atoms ($O_3$) rather than the usual two ($O_2$).

**ozone layer** A region of the stratosphere 12–20 miles (20–32 km) above sea level where there is more ozone than anywhere else.

**Pangaea** The former supercontinent that contained all the present continents. It began to break up about 200 million years ago into Gondwana and Laurasia.

**period** A standard division of time in Earth's history that is shorter than an era.

**photosynthesis** The process by which plants produce their own nutrients, in the form of sugars, using daylight, water and carbon dioxide. Plants give off oxygen during photosynthesis.

**plate tectonics** The theory that Earth's crust consists of a number of rigid sections, called plates. These float on top of the mantle and move in relation to each other.

**polar regions** The areas around the North and South poles.

**precipitation** Water that falls from the sky, including fog, mist, drizzle, rain, hail, frost and snow.

**pyroclastic flow** A mass of ash, rock and gas that flows downhill from an erupting volcano.

**rainforest** A type of forest that develops in regions with high rainfall or frequent fog throughout the year.

**Richter scale** An open-ended scale that rates the magnitude of an earthquake based on the amount of energy released. Each number on the scale represents an increase 10 times greater than the number below it.

**rift** A break between two rocks that were formerly joined. Two or more parallel breaks may allow the section between them to sink, forming a rift valley.

**Ring of Fire** The region of high volcanic activity that surrounds the Pacific Ocean.

**scarp (escarpment)** A cliff or steep slope next to level or gently sloping ground.

**sedimentary rock** Rock formed by extreme compression from pieces of other rocks, often with plant and animal remains included.

**seismic waves** Energy waves transmitted through Earth that travel away from a seismic source, such as an earthquake.

**sheen** The reflection of light from structures within a mineral.

**soil** A mixture of mineral particles and decomposed organic material.

**stratosphere** The layer of the atmosphere that lies above the troposphere and below the mesosphere. The ozone layer is located in the stratosphere.

**streak** The mark of powdered mineral left when it is rubbed against unglazed white porcelain (a streak plate).

**subduction** The sinking of one tectonic plate beneath another. Usually oceanic plates sink below continental plates.

**swamp** An area covered by shallow water throughout the year, with plants or trees emerging above the water's surface.

**tectonic plates** The lithospheric plates that form the Earth's crust. There are two kinds of plates—continental and oceanic plates.

**temperate** Neither very hot nor very cold. Temperate areas have four distinct seasons.

**Tethys Sea** The sea that once separated the supercontinents of Laurasia and Gondwana.

**tide** The regular rise and fall of the sea due to the gravitational attraction of the Moon and, to a lesser extent, the Sun.

**tornado** Rapidly rotating air that is spiralling upward into a large storm cloud.

**trade winds** The winds that blow towards the equator from the northeast in the Northern Hemisphere and southeast in the Southern Hemisphere.

**trench** A deep depression in the ocean floor, often thousands of kilometres long.

**tropics** The zone between the Tropic of Cancer (23.5°N) and the Tropic of Capricorn (23.5°S) where there is at least one day each year when the noonday sun is directly overhead.

**troposphere** The lowest layer of the atmosphere. This is the layer in which we live and in which about 99 per cent of Earth's weather occurs.

**tsunami** A Japanese word for a sea wave that is caused by an earthquake, volcanic eruption or landslide. Tsunamis can reach significant heights in shallow water before crashing onto land.

**updraught** A rising air current.

**vent** A pipe inside a volcano through which lava and gas move from the magma chamber to erupt on the surface.

**vertebrate** An animal that has a backbone. Mammals, birds, reptiles, amphibians and fish are vertebrates.

**volcano** A landform created by the buildup of lava flows and ash. Volcanoes are typically cone-shaped.

**wave** A disturbance with a regular, repeating form that occurs in a solid, liquid or gas caused by the movement of energy.

**weathering** The breaking down of rocks and minerals as a result of the freezing and thawing of ice, the action of chemicals in rainwater or the force of extreme pressure and/or heat deep underground.

# Index

# Credits

## KEY

t=top; l=left; r=right; tl=top left; tcl=top centre left; tc=top centre; tcr=top centre right; tr=top right; cl=centre left; c=centre; cr=centre right; b=bottom; bl=bottom left; bcl=bottom centre left; bc=bottom centre; bcr=bottom centre right; br=bottom right

AAP = Australian Associated Press; ADL = Ad-Libitum; Alex Lavroff & Associates; AMNH = American Museum of Natural History; AUS = Auscape International; BCC = Bruce Coleman Collection; CBT = Corbis; COR = Corel Corp.; DS = Digital Stock; EGL = Encompass Graphics Ltd.; GI = Getty Images; iS = istockphoto.com; MP = Minden Pictures; N_EO = NASA/Earth Observatory; N_J = NASA/Jet Propulsion Laboratory; N_V = NASA/Visible Earth; NASA = National Aeronautics and Space Administration; NHM = Natural History Museum, London; NHPA = Natural History Photographic Agency; NMNH = National Museum of Natural History; PD = Photodisc; PE = PhotoEssentials; PI = Polar Images; PL = photolibrary.com; SH = Shutterstock; SOHO = Solar and Heliospheric Observaotry; SPL = Science Photo Library; TSA = Tom Stack & Associates; USGS = United States Geographical Survey; WF = Werner Forman Archive

**Front cover** Mick Posen/The Art Agency **Front flap** Mick Posen/The Art Agency **Spine** NASA **Back cover** b Chris Forsey t Mick Posen/The Art Agency **Endpapers** Juliana Titin

## PHOTOGRAPHS

**1**bc, br, tl COR bl DS tc, tr PE **2**c PL **3**c NASA **5**c SH **6**bcl, tcr PE bcr, br, tcl, tl COR bl DS **7**bc, tcl, tr COR bcl, bcr, bl, br, tl PE tcr DS **12**bcr NASA cl SPL **15**bcl, r SPL bcr, br, cr, l, r N_J cr NASA **16**c N_V **17**bcr, cl, cr, r iS **18**cr CBT **21**cr SOHO r SPL **23**bcr, tcr, tr NASA br PL **24**bcr, bl, br, tcl, tl USGS tr SH **25**b, tcl, tr SH tl USGS **27**r AUS tl CBT **29**cl CBT **30**bl CBT **32**bl CBT **34**bcl John Long l **36**bl CBT **43**bc SH br PL **44**l PL **45**br CBT r SPL **46**bl, br, tl SH tr USGS **47**bcl, br, tl, tr SH bl, cr USGS **48**c CBT **50**cr AUS tr SH **51**l SH tl GI **52**br CBT **54**br SH r iS **55**c PL **56**b, c, l, r Ad-Libitum **57**bc, br SH bc PL **58**bc, br SPL bl, br, c, cr Jim Frazier cl, t GI r Robert R Coenraads **59**bc NHM bl, l Robert R Coenraads c PL cl SPL tc CBT tl Jim Frazier **60**bcr Brian M. England bl, tr SPL c PL cl, cr Robert R Coenraads **61**bl GI c PL cl, tcr SPL tcl ADL tl CBT **62**bc, bcr SPL bcl CBT bcr, c, tcr PL c, cl Brian M. England r GI **63**c Ad-Libitum c NHM cl, tc PL l, r Brian M. England **64**b CBT bl AUS l SH **65**t CBT **67**r, tl iS **69**cr Ad-Libitum **70**bcl, r PL br NMNH c, r SPL c BCC cl CBT **71**bc GI bcl, c, l, r PL bcr Jim Frazier bl, l SPL c, l, tl Brian M. England cl SH **72**bcr tr Brian M. England, r AMNH r NHM r Jim Frazier **73**bcl, tcl PL l Jim Frazier l NHM **74**tr CBT **75**bl NHM br, r WF cl, l Brian M. England tr PE **76**tr SPL **78**bc, bl CBT bcr, tcr PL c NHM tr iS **79**bcl, c NHM bcr CBT bl SPL br, cl, tcl, tr PL cl, cr, tl SH **80**bc, bl, br, c CBT **81**b, c SH bcr AAP br WF tl AUS **82**b SH bl AUS **83**bcr SH bl Jan Tove Johansson/PEP tl GI **84**bcl, bl USGS br NASA tcl, tl, tr SH **85**bc, bl, br, c, tl SH tr NASA **89**bc iS bl SH **90**c GI **92**br PL tr CBT **93**bcl, bl, tc, tl CBT bcr, br GI tr AUS **94**tc GI **95**tc GI tl PL **96**bl l NHPA **97**br N_J **98**tr CBT **99**tcl AAP tl Gregory Smits **100**bl AUS **102**br, tr CBT **103**bc PL tcr, tl GI **104**c PL **105**tc, tl, tr PL **106**c CBT **108**c PL **110**c SH **113**bcr SH br AUS tcr iS tr PL **114**bcl USGS bl, br, tl, tr SH **115**bl, br, cr, tcl, tl, tr SH **118**bcl SH **119**bcr, r SH r iS **120**bcl SH bcr iS **121**b PL c iS cr NHPA cr SH **122**bl SH **123**bl, r iS l AUS **124**bl SH **125**bcr iS r AUS r SH tcr GI **126**bl SH **127**br, cr iS tcr PL tr AUS **130**c GI, **131**bl N_V bl, br N_EO **132**c CBT **134**bc, bcr, br SH **136**bc iS **137**bcr PL cr, r, tcr SH **138**l CBT **144**bcl GI, cl SH **146**bcl, tl USGS bl GI br CBT cr, tr NASA **147**bl NASA cr GI tl USGS **156**t iS **157**bcl, br, tc, tcr iS c CBT c AUS **158**tcr iS **159**tl, tr iS **164**c SH **168**bcl, bcr, bl, br, cr SH **170**br MP c SH **172**c SH cl PL **173**cl, tcl, tl SH **176**c iS **177**l CBT tr iS **178**bc, c, cl, tc, tr SH bl CBT **179**tl SH **180**br iS c, tr SH **181**bl, br USGS tr NASA **182**tr MP **183**tl AUS **184**c SH tr GI **186**b PL **187**tl NHPA tr iS **188**b PL **189**cr NASA r PL tr SH **190**b SH tr iS **191**bl PLbr SH **192**br GI cr PL tr iS **194**c iS **196**t SH **197**cr, tr SH **198**bcl, br, cr, tcl SH bl NASA t PD **199**bcl, bl, br, tcl, tl, tr SH **200**b, tr NASA **201**tl USGS tr NASA **202**bc iS br SH **203**bc, br SH bl iS **205**bc, bcl, bcr, br iS **207**tr PL **208**tr iS **209**br PL tr SH **210**c NASA/ EO **212**b CBT bc Pl c SH **213**b, t MP bc, c, tc CBT **214**tr CBT **217**br NASA **220**r GI **221**tr iS **222**cr iS **223**br, tr SH **227**bl SH br iS **228**bc Gerry Whitmont, tr SH **229**bcr MP bl SH cl PL l iS **230**bl, cl, tr SH br, tl NASA tcr iS **231**bcr, tcr, tr NASA bl, tl SH br USGS **234**tr iS **236**cl PL **238**b PL **240**b SH tl PD tr PL **245**bc, bcl, bl NASA **246**bc iS c MEPL **247**c, cr, l, r NASA

## ILLUSTRATIONS

**Susanna Addario** 152cl; **The Art Agency** 50b, 53b, 67r, 69bl tc, 70tcr, 210bc bl br, 211c, 216t, 217bcl bl cl tr, 218b; **Alistair Barnard** 42bl; **Julian Baum/The Art Agency** 23bcr cr; **Andrew Beckett/Illustration** 109c, 196b, 224l; **Richard Bonson/The Art Agency** 86c, 88c, 89bcr br, 129bl r tc; **Robin Bouttell/The Art Agency** 30l, 31br c, 78r; **Anne Bowman** 171r; **John Bull** 17c, 135bl, 137b, 138cr, 141c, 143r, 145c, 159bcr, 183bl r, 202bcl bl l, 212t, 214b, 220bl, 222bc bl br cl t, 223bl cl; **John Bull/Map Illustrations** 157t, 243c, 35br c, 37br c, 225t; **Peter Bull Art Studio** 89bcr; **Greg Campbell Design** 163c; **Brian Choo** 77tl; **Barry Croucher/The Art Agency** 195bc; **Andrew Davies/Creative Communication** 14t, 19c, 45r, 53t, 63c, 92c, 103c, 116bcl bcr, 131tl, 137tl, 161tc, 162tr, 168tr, 170tr, 176tr, 186tr, 188tr, 189t, 195t, 197tl, 232c cr, 233t, 234bc bl br cl; **Andrew Davies and Map illustrations** 9b, 134tc, 168tr, 172tr, 176tr, 246t; **Brin Edwards/The Art Agency** 34bl; **EGL** 177cr; **Simone End** 9br, 29bl, 137c; **Nick Farmer/Brihton Illustration** 221c, 247t; **Jesse Fisher** 75tl, 223tl; **Cecilia Fitzsimons/The Art Agency** 82bl br, 83bcr bl; **Giuliano Fornari** 206bl; **Chris Forsey** 55r, 57c, 65c, 87c, 94b, 99bcl bcr cr r, 111c, 208b, 216tr, 221bc bcl bcr bl br, 235tr, 237tl; **Mark A. Garlick/space-art.co.uk** 13c, 18bl br, 19bl, 20bcl, 21bcr, 22bcr, 23tcr, 51l, 204br, 205tr, 245br cr; **Jon Gittoes** 52bcl, 139c, 162bl br, 165tr, 179c; **Mike Gorman** 91bcr br r tcr tr, 131r, 156b, 187bcl, 189b l, 216b; **Ray Grinaway** 22b tr, 28bcr br, 68b bcl bl c cl l, 69bcr br r tcr tr, 98c, 99tcr, 151cr, 187tcl, 237bcr br r tc tcr tr; **David Hardy/The Art Agency** 14b, 20tcr, 23c, 133tl, 204bcl, 205cr; **Tim Hayward/Bernard Thorton Artists UK** 166b; **Steven Hobbs** 245bcr; **Phil Hood/The Art Agency** 83bcl; **Mark Iley/The Art Agency** 40bcl; **Ian Jackson/The Art Agency** 124r, 155r, 187bl, 167t; **Janet Jones** 74bl; **Suzanne Keating** 20l; **Steve Kirk/The Art Agency** 82bl, 83br; **David Kirshner** 40b, 82c, 83r, 107bc, 157bcl, 170bl, 174bcl bl, 175c, 187bc bcr br, 195cr; **Frank Knight** 76b, 83c, 15c cl cr r tcl, 17bc tl; **David Mackay** 28bl, 29tr; **Martin Macrae/FOLIO** 164b, 165c; **Map Illustrations** 72c, 90tc, 117c, 118cl, 120cl r, 122c l, 135cl r, 145tcl, 148c, 150t, 151cl, 152cl, 153c, 154l, 155cl, 165tcl, 167br, 168cl, 172bl, 193tl, 203t, 220cl, 229tl, 245c; **Shane Marsh/Linden Artists Ltd** 191t; **MBA Studios** 140cl, 98b; **Iain McKellar** 67c, 99tcr, 174cr tr; **James McKinnon** 39br c, 41br c; **Stuart McVicar** 38bcl bl, 232b; **Moonrunner Design Ltd.** 19bcr, 23br; **Colin Newman** 182bl; **Kevin O'Donnell** 100c cl cr; **Nicola Oram** 38l; **Mick Posen/The Art Agency** 12bl, 27tr, 32bcl bl, 49c, 52bl cl, 60bc r, 61bc br cr, 77c, 78cl, 87l t, 91c, 92bl, 95tc tl, 97bc, 105b, 107tc, 112bcl bcr bl, 113bcl l, 158c, 177bl br c l, 180bl, 181c. 244bcr tr; **Luis Rey/The Art Agency** 82br; **Oliver Rennert** 97c, 128b, 173b, 192bl, 195br, 204tr, 207br cr l tcr, 214bcl c tc tr, 215b, 219tc tl tr, 239c, 241br t; **John Richards** 44cr, 45t, 66c, 101c, 102bl, **Trevor Ruth** 139b, 142c, 153cr; **Claudia Saraceni** 187tc tcr; **Michael Saunders** 59bcr cr tcr, 61bcr cr tr, 63bcr cr r, 72bcl l, 167c cl, 171c, 236bcl, 171tr, 173tr; **Peter Schouten** 40cl, 42c l, 43t; **Peter Scott/The Art Agency** 26c, 40bcl bl l, 169c; **Steve Seymour** 235b; **Tom Stack/TSA** 238t; **Kevin Stead** 28b, 184bl br; **Steve Trevaskis** 160b, 246bl; **Guy Troughton** 195bl; **Erik van Ommen** 185c; **Glen Vause** 210tr; **Rod Westblade** 226tr; **Laurie Whiddon** 218tr; **Steve White/The Art Agency** 33br c, 113tcl; **Ann Winterbotham** 28t, 29tl